the complete
Potter

Swindon College

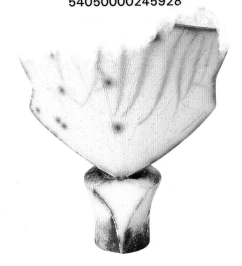

the complete
Potter

THE COMPLETE REFERENCE TO TOOLS, MATERIALS, AND TECHNIQUES FOR ALL POTTERS AND CERAMICISTS

STEVE MATTISON

APPLE

A QUARTO BOOK

First published in the United Kingdom
by Apple Press
Sheridan House
112–116a Western Road
Hove
East Sussex BN3 1DD
www.apple-press.com

Reprinted 2004

ISBN 1-84092-363-6

Conceived, designed, and produced by
Quarto Publishing plc
The Old Brewery
6 Blundell Street
London N7 9BH

QUAR: TCP

Senior editor Michelle Pickering
Senior art editor Sally Bond
Photographer Ian Howes
Designer James Lawrence
Illustrator John Woodcock
Indexer Dorothy Frame

Art director Moira Clinch
Publisher Piers Spence

Manufactured by Universal Graphics
Pte Ltd, Singapore
Printed by Star Standard Industries
(Pte) Ltd, Singapore

9 8 7 6 5 4 3 2

PUBLISHER'S NOTE

Pottery can be dangerous. Always follow the instructions
carefully, and exercise caution. Follow the safety procedures
mentioned. As far as the techniques and methods described
in this book are concerned, all statements, information, and
advice given are believed to be accurate. However, neither
the author, the copyright holder, nor the publisher can
accept any legal liability.

Contents

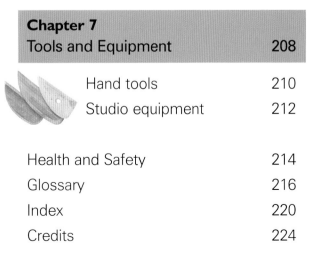

Introduction

Clay is an exciting material that can be used to create an infinite variety of objects, from everyday functional items to huge public sculptures. Techniques for shaping, decorating, and finishing ceramics have been passed down through history, and knowledge from past generations is continually being added to with fresh insights and technical developments.

HISTORY OF CERAMICS

The history of ceramics parallels the history of the human race and reflects the changing customs and rituals of civilizations. Since the earliest times, humans have made votive objects from clay to create a focus for worship. Functional pottery made its appearance at the same time as agriculture was developing around 10–8000 B.C., with early domestic vessels being used for storage, food containers, and funerary artifacts. They were made from coarse, groggy clays—often impressed, decorated with slip, and burnished—that were fired at low temperatures, making the pots fragile. This type of pottery, dating back to 6000 B.C., has been discovered in Azerbaijan and on the banks of the Danube in southern Hungary. Sumerian, the earliest known written language, was spoken in Mesopotamia (modern Iraq) and took the form of "word pictures." The earliest examples of the language date from around 3000 B.C. and consist of words drawn with a needle into small tablets of damp clay. These are all testaments to our ancestors' creativity. Many of these ancient works from the Middle East and the Mediterranean islands have still to be surpassed in their demonstration of technical skill and an assured aesthetic awareness.

In ancient China and Japan, potters began to fire stoneware to higher temperatures, bringing immortality to clay. Recently, ten pottery kilns dating back to the Yangshao period (about 5,000 years ago) were unearthed in China. Vitrified glazes appeared during the second millennium B.C., adding color and texture to the surface and exalting the inherent qualities in the clay. The whole range of possibilities for ceramic working was investigated—form was paramount, superfluous decoration dispensed with, and the effect of fire on raw clay cherished.

1 XXX

Dainis Pundurs *Latvian artist Dainis Pundurs creates large, often site-specific collections of thematic works. Here, an installation of thrown vessel forms haunts the vaulted space of a gothic church. The textural marks on the outside of these imposing pieces reflect the natural materials of the building, creating a space of peace and tranquillity.*

2 UMBILICAL CORD

Mikang Lim *With the vision of a sculptor or fine artist, Mikang Lim creates thought-provoking and often disturbing installations commenting on the human condition. She is happy to use a variety of media in her work, combining natural materials with the technology of video and digital imaging. The mother figure, made from coiled stoneware-fired clay, is joined by long strands of twisted thread to its child, depicted by video on the cold and clinical television monitor.*

2

3 TABLE JAR

Martin McWilliam This slab-built jar reflects traditional vessel forms but the similarity is only an illusion. The flattened sculptural piece hints at traditional pottery shapes but creates a strange, classical ambience, complemented by the cool white and brown surfaces of kaolin slips and wood-fired reduction.

CONTEMPORARY CERAMICS

Clay is a unique vehicle for personal expression and allows artists to create both functional and decorative work. Ceramicists are no longer limited by the local availability of raw materials and equipment. Today, materials are readily available and consistent in quality. Similarly, ideas flow from one civilization to another, no longer bound by geographical or cultural constraints.

UNIQUE ART FORM

Clay is unique in its ability to be molded by hand, with little or no use of tools, into objects of great beauty that can be turned to stone by exposure to great heat. Working with clay puts us in touch with the elements. Water and air provide the plasticity for working soft clay, while fire brings permanence to the earth we transform. Clay invites us to make our mark, squeezing the soft clay between our hands and giving form to our ideas. In this book, the potter's art is described in detail, from clay preparation and different forming techniques to various surface treatments and firing possibilities. As well as illustrating the techniques involved, a wealth of finished ceramics from well-known international makers is featured that will both captivate and inspire all those working in this wonderful medium.

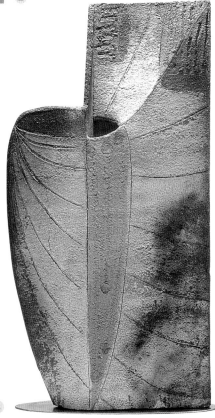

3

Chapter 1

CLAY AND POTTERY BODIES

All pottery is made from a very common and naturally occurring material—clay. It can be found in significant quantities virtually everywhere on the earth's crust. Clay becomes ceramic when it is exposed to extreme heat, which fuses the clay particles together and hardens the body to produce a stable material that is often more permanent than rock itself. It will not dissolve or combine with other materials, making it ideal for functional and domestic uses. It is also a wonderful material for the sculptor—it is soft and malleable and therefore easy to work with and form by hand, often without tools, and yet will fire to a permanent object.

CHOOSING CLAY

Whether you decide to prepare your own clay from local materials or to buy ready-made clay will depend mainly on how much work you are producing and any particular qualities you desire. Preparing raw, dug clay may be hard work but it can give some astonishing results. Commercially supplied clay will have greater consistency and arrives in clean, manageable packages. There is really only one factor you need to take into account when choosing the particular type of clay you use and that is the purpose to which the clay will be put. This could be an effect or quality you wish to achieve in the piece you are making or the clay's suitability for a certain technique.

PLASTIC CLAY

Clay is a highly malleable substance and its most important quality, plasticity, allows it to retain its shape when molded, leaving the surface smooth and unbroken. The clay's handling strength will depend on the amount of plasticity in the ware. It is only by handling the clay—seeing how it responds to bending, rolling, pulling, and pressing as well as its shrinkage rate, resistance to warping, its unfired strength, or its throwing ability—that you will be able to make an informed choice. In truth, there are few clays that will have all the qualities you wish and you may have to experiment with them before settling on your favorite body.

ASSESSING PLASTICITY

Assess clays for plasticity and their working qualities by rolling coils and bending them into tight loops or circles. Heavily grogged clays will split and open easily while the more plastic ones will bend without any visible sign of cracking.

Natural and Prepared Clay

There are two geological categories of clay—primary or residual clays, and secondary or sedimentary clays. Primary clays are those that have remained in their forming grounds, but these are comparatively few throughout the world. Secondary clays are those that have been eroded and carried away by water and earth movements to be deposited in sedimentary layers. Potters use five main types of clay: primary and secondary china clay (kaolin) and four secondary clays known as ball clay, fire clay, stoneware clay, and surface clay. Clay varies in color from white to reddish-brown, depending on the amount of iron and other impurities present.

NATURAL CLAY

Naturally plastic clays are those that can be used with only a minimum of cleaning. Primary china clay is very pure but is nonplastic due to its large particle structure. The weathering process undergone by secondary clays makes them more plastic because exposure to the elements has helped to break down the clay particles. However, it is rare for any natural clay to be used on its own, the addition of other raw materials being usual to achieve a workable balance of plasticity, shrinkage, firing temperature, and strength.

1 STONEWARE CLAY

Seldom found naturally, most stoneware clay is a mixture of ball clay and other minerals added to give particular qualities to the raw or fired state. Usually gray in color, it will fire from buff to white.

2 RED SURFACE CLAY

This is the most common natural clay. The iron oxide content gives it its characteristic color and also combines with the silica and alumina in the clay to help vitrification.

3 FIRE CLAY

A refractory clay—that is, a clay that can withstand high temperatures—usually found near coal seams, hence its name. It fires to a buff color and can be used on its own or added to other clays to form a workable body. Fire clay is also fired and ground into particles to form most types of grog.

4 CHINA CLAY

This high-firing primary clay is nonplastic on its own, but it is a common component in clay recipes and glazes. Molochite, the vitrified form of china clay, is used as a pure white, stable grog in many clay bodies.

5 BALL CLAY

A fine, highly plastic secondary clay, but too plastic to be used on its own. It fires white or off-white and is commonly used in glazes and as an ingredient in porcelain and stoneware bodies and decorating slips.

6 BENTONITE

A clay-like mineral added to clay bodies and bone china to increase plasticity. When used in small percentages in glaze mixtures, it helps suspension of the particles.

POWDERED CLAYS

These dry powdered clays can be used to mix your own clay. Some basic recipes are included in chapter two (see pages 18–33).

PREPARED CLAY

If you buy clay from a commercial supplier, it will be a combination of naturally occurring clays mixed according to a recipe. They will have been refined using either slip-house filter pressing or pan milling—either way, they will have been ground and cleaned with most impurities removed. The clays are then mixed together and combined with other materials to produce particular working qualities, colors, and textures. These prepared clays can vary over time when different areas of the clay mine, with their different impurities, are exposed, but efforts are made to maintain the consistency and quality as far as possible. Good suppliers offer a range of prepared clays, from earthenware and stoneware to high-temperature white porcelain, plus a few specialty clays such as T material.

MIXING YOUR OWN

Many studio potters prefer to mix their own clay to suit their particular way of working or to obtain a specific color or texture. The basis of the majority of pottery bodies is ball clay—a highly plastic, naturally occurring clay—with the addition of fluxes such as feldspar to achieve a good fired strength, and china clay and whiting to reduce plasticity. Coarse clays that are resistant to warping and thermal shock are achieved by adding grog or sand.

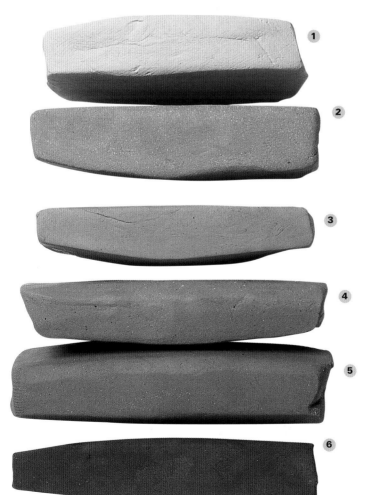

PREPARED CLAY BODIES

Manufacturers usually categorize clays according to their firing temperatures.

1 PORCELAIN

This has a fine particle size and is the whitest firing of all clays, becoming translucent where thin. Firing range: 2340–2460°F (1280–1350°C).

2 T MATERIAL

This highly plastic white-to-cream body is resistant to warping and thermal shock due to its high molochite content. It is excellent for large work, tiles, and raku. Firing range: 1830–2370°F (1000–1300°C).

3 STONEWARE

This smooth, plastic throwing clay is good for reduction firing. Firing range: 2190–2370°F (1200–1300°C).

4 GROGGED STONEWARE

The addition of grog or sand increases strength and resistance to warping. Firing range: 2190–2340°F (1200–1280°C).

5 RAKU BODY

This heavily grogged clay is ideal for handbuilding and raku firing. Firing range: 1830–2340°F (1000–1280°C).

6 EARTHENWARE

This low-firing clay can be red or white in color and needs glazing to be waterproof. Firing range: 1830–2160°F (1000–1180°C).

SEE ALSO
Clay additives, *page 15*
Common raw materials, *pages 174–175*

Refining and testing clay

Most potters buy their clay from commercial suppliers, enjoying the ease of working and the consistency of the product. However, even with these bought clays a potter can never know too much about the materials being used. While it can be hard work digging and refining natural clay for making pottery, it is an interesting experiment and an enlightening learning exercise. Whether clay is dug from the ground or mixed from purchased raw materials, the process of preparation and testing is the same. A specific clay body may be required to achieve a particular effect or working quality and will need the same thorough testing to get the right formulation. The main testing is done to ascertain four properties—plasticity, shrinkage, porosity, and firing temperature.

TOOLS
- Hammer or mallet
- Rolling pin
- Bowl
- Flat stick or rubber rib
- 80-mesh sieve
- Plaster bat

PLASTICITY

Rolling coils of clay and bending them into tight curves to see if they crack tests plasticity. If more plasticity is required, add highly plastic materials such as bentonite. Experiment with

PREPARING A SAMPLE

1 These chunks of clay were dug from the ground and contain many impurities, including stones, vegetable matter, and insect life. Allow the clay to dry thoroughly before breaking it up.

2 Mash the rock-like clay into smaller pieces with a hammer or mallet, then crush it using a heavy rolling pin. Place the crushed clay in a bowl and add water until the clay is just covered. If you are making clay from powdered raw materials, weigh out the ingredients, mix them together in a bowl, and cover with water.

3 Allow the clay to soak until it has become very soft. This will take less time with a grogged clay than it will with a more refined clay. Pour off any excess water and mix the clay into a thick paste.

SEE ALSO
Types of ware, *pages 18–33*
Glazes, *pages 178–187*
Kilns and firings, *pages 188–207*

1 & 2 TESTING SHRINKAGE

Roll out some sample pieces of clay into 6 in. (15 cm) long strips and scribe a 4 in. (10 cm) line down the center of each one. Measure the scored line after the clay has dried, after bisque firing, and after firing to its top temperature to assess the percentage of shrinkage in the clay. It is a good idea to score some small identification marks in the samples so that you can distinguish one from another.

the clay, bending, twisting, braiding, and stretching it to discover its capabilities (see page 9).

SHRINKAGE

Clay shrinks at three stages. First, when the clay dries out; second, when the clay is bisque fired; and third, when it is fired to its top temperature. The majority of shrinkage occurs at the bisque-firing stage. Accurately measured score lines on a test tile will indicate the amount of shrinking at these different stages.

POROSITY

The porosity of fired ceramic is extremely important because it dictates the amount of glaze that will be absorbed during decoration. Fire some samples to bisque temperature to see how much glaze is soaked into the body. The porosity of the clay will also affect how well the glaze adheres to the clay.

FIRING TEMPERATURE

Some clays melt when fired to higher temperatures, especially those dug from beach deposits because concentrations of iron oxide and salts from the seawater act as fluxes, lowering the melting temperature. Other clays can withstand temperatures up to 2550°F (1400°C) before maturing. When testing for firing temperature, make sure any clay samples are placed on scrap pieces of broken kiln shelf in case they melt and run onto other work or kiln furniture.

4 Add more water to make a creamy slip, then pass the slip through a small 80-mesh sieve. If necessary, use a flat stick or rubber rib to push any lumps through.

5 Pour the sieved slip onto a plaster bat and smooth it out. The slip will stiffen fairly quickly and will need frequent turning on the bat to stop it from hardening too much.

6 Peel the stiffened clay from the plaster bat, pressing the ball of clay down onto the slurry to pick up any residue. Wedge and knead the clay to homogenize any differences in consistency (see pages 40–41).

Reclaiming clay

All pottery processes create a certain amount of waste clay—the trimmings and scraps in the splash tray of the wheel, small coils that have become too stiff to be workable, or the offcuts from leather-hard slabs that have been put aside and allowed to dry out. Until it is fired, however, all clay can be reclaimed to a working condition. Contrary to expectations, clay improves with age, and if left in a soft condition, increases its plasticity.

It is a good habit to put the scraps from each type of clay you use into a separate bucket with a lid, which will stop any foreign matter from contaminating the clay. They can then be left to dry out, when they will be easier to slake down by adding water. It is possible to mix two types of clay at this stage by soaking the two clays together. The resulting mixture can then be stiffened again on plaster bats and wedged and kneaded for use. Reclaimed clay requires a greater amount of wedging and kneading because it usually contains lumps of drier clay. If you generate a great deal of waste clay, using a pugmill will speed up this process. The plaster bats should be at least 2 in. (5 cm) thick to absorb the water from the clay sludge. Allow the bats to dry after use, supporting them in a vertical position so that air can circulate underneath.

TOOLS
- Bucket
- Jug
- Plaster bat
- Wire

VARIOUS ADDITIVES

1 Dry porcelain crushed into chunks gives a heavy texture to the clay and produces softened lumps when fired.

2 Feldspar kneaded into stoneware clay will produce beautiful soft eruptions in the surface.

3 Grit and aggregate give a good, heavy texture for making sculpture. Some particles will melt while others will remain as rough-edged chunks.

4 Grog is fired and ground clay that is added to a clay body to increase strength and texture.

5 Coarse molochite is available in very large particles for coarse sculpture work.

6 Fine molochite is a good substitute for grog where retaining the whiteness of the clay is essential.

RECLAIMING CLAY

1 Pour clean water into the bucket of dried clay so that it is completely covered. Over a period of a few days the clay will disintegrate into particles and become a sludge, settling in the bucket. Scoop off any excess water by pushing a jug down into the sludge and allowing the water to flow in. Repeat this until only a small amount of water remains on the surface.

2 Lay out the softened clay on a plaster bat as evenly as possible so that it dries out equally. Turn the clay mass over regularly to ensure that it stiffens from both top and bottom.

3 When the clay has stiffened, peel it off the bat and wedge it thoroughly, wiring through the block many times (see page 40). Knead the clay to homogenize it before wrapping it in plastic to store until needed (see page 41). Work the clay softer than you would normally use so that it will not dry out too quickly and need reclaiming over again.

SEE ALSO
Common raw materials, *pages 174–175*

Clay additives

Many potters experiment with additives to improve the working properties of the clay or, more often, to enhance its surface textures or finishes. The most common additive is clay itself, which can be added in the form of grog. This is fired clay that has been ground down into various grades. It is mixed into plastic clay to improve the strength of the clay and increase its resistance to warping. Grogs range from fine powder to coarse grit, giving the clay a granular appearance. Red clay grog will produce spots and bursts of iron through the glazes, speckling the surface of stoneware pottery, especially if reduction fired. White grogs are available in the form of molochite, a calcined form of china clay that is a popular addition to white stoneware clays and porcelains because it does not affect the color. Feldspars and granite chips will melt at high temperatures to create softened, fatty eruptions on high-fired pottery surfaces. Large aggregates of refractory minerals can be added that fire into the clay but are inert and will not melt. These additions can reveal beautiful patterns when sanded smooth with grinders.

ADDING GROG

1 Weigh the quantity of grog required and place it in a bowl. A usual mix would be 2¼–3½ lb. (1–1.5 kg) of grog to 55 lb. (25 kg) of plastic clay. Dampen the grog to prevent its porosity from drying out the clay.

2 Use a wire to cut the lump of clay into slabs. Place handfuls of damp grog between the slabs, stacking the slabs one on top of another. Press down the clay and knead the grog thoroughly into the plastic clay in the normal way (see page 41).

3 Use a wire to cut the lump in half and run your finger across the cut surface to check that the grog is evenly dispersed throughout the body.

TOOLS
- *Scales*
- *Bowl*
- *Jug*
- *Wire*

Unglazed ceramics

For thousands of years potters have experimented with different types of clay, adding a variety of materials to alter the clay's properties and produce decorative effects. These examples reveal the beautiful clay surfaces that can be achieved without glazing.

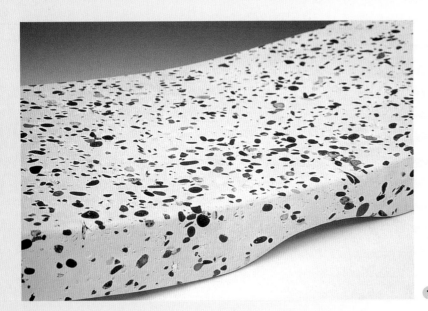

1 AGGREGATE FORM (DETAIL)

David Binns The artist's current work focuses on making simple, understated forms that have visual interest through the inclusion of a variety of aggregate materials in the clay body. Central to the work is a process of grinding and polishing the clay surface. The grinding reveals the aggregate in the body, a process seemingly more akin to stone sculpture than ceramics. The surfaces achieved are not dissimilar from those of polished beach pebbles.

2 STANDING FORM

David Binns Using large pieces of aggregate mixed into thick slip, Binns creates fascinating and beautifully minimal cast forms. The mixture was poured into a series of plaster molds and tamped down with a stick until the mold was filled. The solid piece was fired extremely slowly to stoneware temperature before grinding the surfaces to reveal the variety of colored particles integrated into the body of the work.

3 JUG

The Magopat Family This beautiful black-fired piece comes from a traditional pottery in northern Moldova where this style of pottery has been made virtually unchanged for a thousand years. The decoration was burnished into the red clay in sketchy lines, circles, and swirls. The firing took place in a large wood-fired kiln starved of oxygen for the entire firing, creating an intense smoked atmosphere that permeated the porous clay, blackening the body and causing the burnishing to shine.

4 RETURN TICKET

Graham Hay Conceptual ceramicist Graham Hay compares his making methods to those of the woodworker, especially the cabinet maker and boat builder. His techniques are not those of the traditional potter and many clay workers are surprised by his unconventional way of constructing his pieces. His most revolutionary method, a technique he calls "dip and stick," is demonstrated in this example. Totally dry slabs of clay were broken up into smaller pieces and literally stuck together with paper clay slip to create a form that the conventional potter would find difficult to achieve.

5 PÀRBAN (AS A COUPLE)

Gabriella Kuzsel *This piece was initially made from cut paper pieces, taped together until the desired form was created. The paper templates were used to cut slabs of grogged red clay that were joined together and then gently distorted from the inside by subtle and gentle hand pressure. The forms were burnished when leather-hard and fired to 1940°F (1060°C) in an electric kiln, giving a deep, rich, terra-cotta warmth. Selective applications of gold enhance the warmth of this sensuous piece.*

3

4

5

Chapter 2

TYPES OF WARE

All clay needs to be exposed to heat to become ceramic. Clay is usually fired to at least 1290°F (700°C) to become permanent—that is, the clay will not break down again when immersed in water and can no longer be reclaimed. The greater the heat, the denser, harder, and more durable the clay body becomes. When fired to a high enough temperature, the clay particles fuse and melt together, making the clay vitreous and impervious to water. It is essential to have a wide experience of all the types of clay available and an understanding of the fired properties of each, especially if you wish to make a range of different ceramic work.

CATEGORIES OF CLAY

Clay is usually classified into three main categories—earthenware, stoneware, and porcelain—depending on the fired density and strength of the ceramic ware. Many potters also use these categories to describe the color or working quality of the clay, but in truth the terms should refer to the qualities of the pottery after firing. Just to confuse the issue, it is possible to fire high-temperature clays at lower temperatures. For example, a grogged stoneware clay can be raku fired at 1830°F (1000°C) instead of a higher stoneware temperature of 2190–2370°F (1200–1300°C). However, the result can never really be called stoneware because the clay particles will not fuse and the fired strength is not the same as that of true stoneware.

FIRING TEMPERATURE

The fusing of the particles in any clay body is caused by fluxes present in the clay. Red earthenware clay or terra-cotta contains iron oxide, which acts as a strong flux. Most red clays therefore vitrify at lower temperatures of around 1940°F (1060°C). In stoneware and porcelain bodies, the proportion of flux is considerably smaller, and is often balanced by the addition of refractory materials such as grog, flint, or china clay to give a higher vitrification point.

ANGELS

Iva Ouhrabkova Making sculptures for outdoor use, usually 7–10 ft. (2–3 m) in height, Ouhrabkova employs the simple technique of pressing coils of clay together, leaving each successive coil visible. The gentle flattening of the coil creates a slightly undulating surface, reminiscent of soft, feathery wings. The two vertical sides are supported by an internal filigree of woven coils that create irregular shadows as light passes through them.

Earthenware

Earthenware pottery has been made since the earliest times. Storage vessels for the kitchen and dairy, dishes for cooking, platters for serving food, and jars and pitchers for wine and beer were all used on a daily basis. Handmade in vast quantities, these rich, simple vessels are often referred to as peasant pottery.

RED TERRA-COTTA CLAY

The warm, orange-red flowerpots that adorn gardens and houses are a familiar sight to most people. The red terra-cotta clay from which they are made is the most common form of earthenware clay and is used to make a wide range of products, including bricks, drainage pipes, and roof tiles. Terra-cotta is an Italian word meaning "fired earth," and when fired, terra-cotta clay is relatively soft and porous. The red color comes from the presence of iron oxide in the clay body, and the greater the percentage of oxide, the richer the color. The oxide content also contributes to the low firing temperature required to mature the clay.

1 COUNTRY SLIPWARE

Buckley and Ewenny Pottery *Traditional earthenware pottery was made in these famous Welsh potteries for hundreds of years, finally dying out in the 1940s and 1950s. Virtually every household in the country would have had some pieces.*

2 SLIP-TRAILED PLATTER

Clive Bowen *Many potters endeavor to continue the earthenware tradition, making robust, functional pottery with a fresh and contemporary approach. This magnificent platter has the vigorous, enthusiastic slip decoration typical of this master earthenware potter. It was raw glazed and fired in a large, down-draft, wood-fueled kiln to 1900–1940ºF (1040–1060ºC).*

Throughout history terra-cotta has been used to make domestic and cooking pottery because it has good resistance to thermal shock, especially over open fires. The porosity of the body also allows evaporation through the surface, keeping any liquid contents fresh and cool in hot climates. In colder regions, garden pots may be prone to frost damage and cracking when water absorbed into the clay freezes and expands.

WHITE EARTHENWARE

White earthenware clay is made primarily from a mixture of ball clays with the addition of other minerals. When fired it is a white or buff color, which is popular with potters who want a light ground color for bright decoration.

FIRING EARTHENWARE

Earthenware pottery is usually fired to 1830–1980°F (1000–1080°C). Adding sand or grog will allow the clay to be fired to higher temperatures, giving a more fused finish and decreasing the pot's porosity. Generally speaking, the higher you fire earthenware clay, the more resistant it will be to glaze crazing and the better suited it will be to domestic use.

DECORATING EARTHENWARE

Both red and white earthenware are ideal for slip decoration. Most traditional peasant pottery is decorated in this way, with motifs of painted slip or vigorous finger-wiped patterns. Traditional African pottery is earthenware and very low fired, usually only to 1470°F (800°C), and often has impressed decoration using dried maize husks.

3 NAGY FAZEK

Atilla Albert This large pitcher is a traditional shape from southern Hungary. The village of Magyarszombatfa still has 15 pottery families working there, producing wares for domestic use. Atilla Albert now fires his work in an electric kiln, the only one in the village, which gives him cleaner glaze finishes.

4 ROUND DISH WITH FEET

Michael and Victoria Eden Thrown with a soft, red earthenware clay, the form of this dish was altered when leather-hard by slapping the base on a board to cause the ends to turn upward and the shape to become oval. The lively feet and handles were created by pulling looped wire tools through slightly stiff clay. Colored transparent glazes give the dish a shiny, juicy surface.

SEE ALSO

Clay and pottery bodies, *pages 8–17*
Impressing, *page 129*
Slip decoration, *pages 134–143*
Common raw materials, *pages 174–175*
Kilns and firings, *pages 188–207*

Stoneware

Stoneware bodies are composed of mixtures of clays, minerals, and sand or grog. After a high firing, the density and weight of stoneware give it a stone-like feel—hence the name. Its durability, strength, and low water absorption rate make it ideal for domestic ware and pieces for outdoor use.

FINE AND COARSE STONEWARE

Fine stoneware clay is ideal for functional pottery such as pitchers, plates, and dishes because the particles of clay fuse at high temperatures, giving a hard, smooth finish. Although stoneware can have beautiful, natural colors, for domestic purposes it usually requires the application of a glaze for hygiene. Coarse stoneware clay has sand or grog added to increase its strength and is most suitable for large-scale sculptural work.

2 HELIX

Aigi Orav *This sculptural piece was formed from stoneware clay combined with thin surface layers of porcelain, which were stretched to form white striations and increase the dynamism of the spiral. Areas were highlighted with a blue pigment before firing to 2370°F (1300°C) in a wood-burning kiln with a soda glazing.*

3 GEOMETRIC DISH

Charles Spacey *A subtle range of ash glazes was used to create the geometric patterns on the interior surface of this stoneware dish. All Spacey's pieces are formed by draping the soft clay over cut wooden blocks.*

1 JAR

Ashley Howard *By altering the form of the pot while still fresh on the wheel, Howard has given this stoneware jar a fluid feeling that complements the soft quality of the glazing. A copper slip glaze was thickly applied to produce a deep mauve/purple color.*

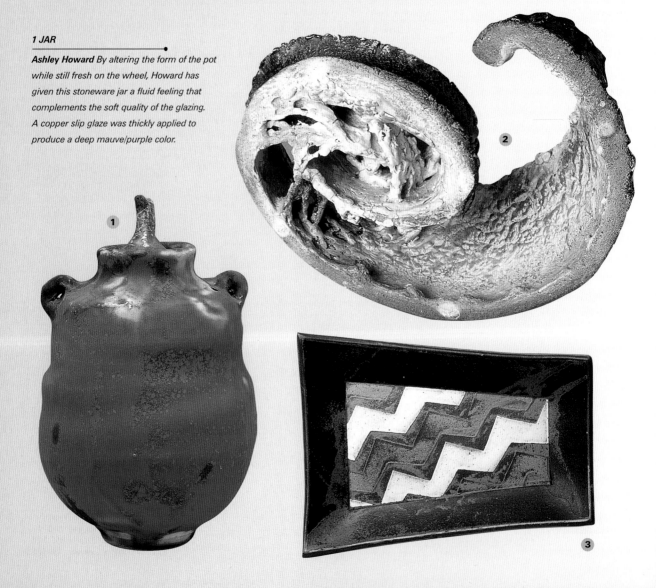

FIRING STONEWARE

Although stoneware clay matures at temperatures between 2190 and 2370°F (1200 and 1300°C), when it becomes fused and impervious to water, it is possible, and common, to fire it at lower temperatures. The main criterion for selecting a particular stoneware clay will be the type of firing you intend to use: oxidized or reduction firing. Oxidized firings ensure a clean and complete burning of the fuel by supplying adequate oxygen to the kiln atmosphere. With reduction firings, the flow of oxygen is restricted, and as a result, the fuel produces carbon monoxide instead of carbon dioxide, leading it to extract oxygen from the clay body in an attempt to burn efficiently. This produces changes in the color of the clay.

STONEWARE BODIES

A typical stoneware body can be composed of fire clay and ball clay, with the feldspar content varied to achieve different maturing temperatures. The more feldspar you add, the lower the temperature required. A low-temperature stoneware clay can be achieved by substituting a frit for the feldspar content. Replacing some of the fire clay with china clay and using a light-colored fire clay will produce a white-firing stoneware clay.

BASIC STONEWARE

Fire clay	60%
Ball clay	20%
Feldspar	10%
Silica	10%

LOW-TEMPERATURE STONEWARE

Fire clay	50%
Ball clay	20%
Frit	25%
Silica	5%

WHITE-FIRING STONEWARE

Fire clay	30%
Ball clay	20%
China clay	20%
Frit	25%
Silica	5%

4 FLAT VESSELS

Emily Myers These vessels were thrown without bases, then squeezed to flatten their shape and added to flat, thrown bases. Made from red stoneware clay, they were fired to 2230°F (1220°C). Myers' work conjures up many references to landscape and the natural world, not only in her choice of form but also in her mastery of dry barium-glazed surfaces.

5 DEEP PLATTER

Suzy Atkins This platter is made from stoneware clay with 15 percent fine grog added and is decorated with areas of slip superimposed on a base slip. Decorative areas were defined by a wax resist and the piece was then salt glazed, so that shinier parts were created by greater exposure to the salt vapors. Impressed marks in the clay are emphasized by gold luster.

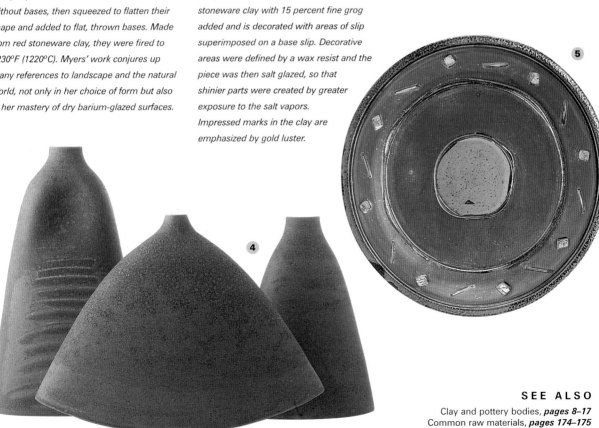

SEE ALSO
Clay and pottery bodies, *pages 8–17*
Common raw materials, *pages 174–175*
Kilns and firings, *pages 188–207*

Porcelain

Porcelain is usually white in color, fine in texture, and has a beautiful translucency when thin. A typical porcelain clay is fired at temperatures in excess of 2340°F (1280°C) to achieve the characteristic whiteness and density. Fired porcelain has incredible strength and is extremely durable. It is these qualities that give porcelain its industrial uses as insulators and acid-resistant containers.

WORKING WITH PORCELAIN

Porcelain clay bodies are the least plastic and the most difficult to throw and handbuild because the working time is critical, with a narrow margin between the clay being too soft and too dry. Porcelain pots must be handled with care before firing because they have very little strength. They also require careful preparation before firing or they can deform and crack easily. These difficulties mean that porcelain is rarely used for handmade domestic pottery but more usually for individual pieces or slip-cast production. However, even with all the apparent problems, many potters do use porcelain to great effect.

1 LIKE DOVES TO THE WINDOW

Michel Kuipers *This fine porcelain slab bears a Welsh proverb, finely lettered by hand using shellac directly on the leather-hard clay. The surface clay was washed away with a wet sponge, with the dry shellac resisting the erosive action of the water and leaving the letters raised above the etched surface.*

2 BOTTLES

Steve Mattison *This series of thrown porcelain bottles with blue celadon and barium glazes displays a calmness reminiscent of Morandi still-life paintings. The ragged tops, formed by throwing the clay thinner and thinner until it naturally tears, contrasts with the smooth lines of the bodies. The shaping of the bottles was completed during throwing, and once removed from the wheel, the bottles were allowed to dry without trimming.*

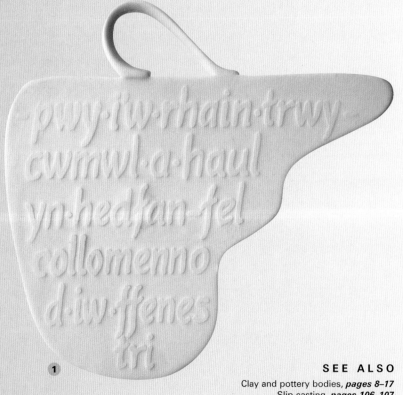

1

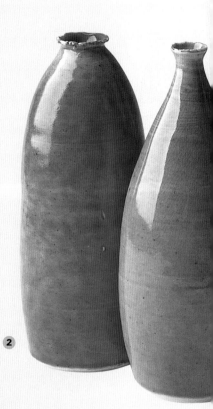

2

SEE ALSO
Clay and pottery bodies, *pages 8–17*
Slip casting, *pages 106–107*
Common raw materials, *pages 174–175*
Glazes, *pages 178–187*
Kilns and firings, *pages 188–207*

FIRING PORCELAIN

Although porcelain can be raw fired, it is usually given an initial low bisque firing to 1830°F (1000°C) to make it easier to handle while glazing and decorating, then fired again to full maturation. While the distinctive look and feel of porcelain can be reached at temperatures as low as 2160°F (1180°C), it only develops its clarity and translucency at high temperatures of 2340–2370°F (1280–1300°C). Porcelain shows its true qualities with transparent glazes and can develop beautiful densities of color—celadon glazes pooling in surface marks can be stunning, for example. As the glaze and porcelain body mature, they combine fully and the defining layer between the glaze surface and the clay body is no longer visible.

PORCELAIN BODIES

Prepared porcelain clay, in both plastic and powdered forms, is available from commercial suppliers but many potters prefer to mix their own to suit their individual ways of working. A typical high-firing porcelain body is composed of varying quantities of clay and feldspar. If the feldspar is replaced with a material that melts at a lower temperature, such as frit, you can develop a translucent porcelaneous body firing as low as 1940°F (1060°C).

BASIC PORCELAIN	
China clay	25%
Ball clay	25%
Feldspar	25%
Silica	25%

LOW-FIRING PORCELAIN	
China clay	25%
Ball clay	25%
Frit	40%
Silica	10%

3 CELADON GINGER JAR

Margaret Frith This finely thrown ginger jar was carved with a floral decoration when leather-hard using a sharp bamboo tool. The light blue celadon glaze pools in the carved lines, giving darker hues and enhancing the design. Care must be taken when handling unfired porcelain because it has little strength and is easily broken.

3

Raku Clay

The raku process involves the rapid firing and cooling of the ware, with the pots being removed red hot from the kiln. Clays subjected to this extreme of expansion and contraction must have a coarse, open texture in order to survive the thermal shocks. High percentages of grog should therefore be wedged into the body. This grog content means that the clay is also resistant to warping, making it ideal for large tiles, slab pottery, and large-scale sculptural work. Commercial suppliers produce many different clays specially formulated for this type of work, although you can make your own. The addition of talc to the body will help it to withstand thermal shock during raku and sawdust firing.

BASIC RAKU CLAY	
Fire clay	50%
China clay	15%
Ball clay	15%
Grog (80s to dust)	15%
Talc	5%

1 BOTTLE

Martin Everson-Davis *This thickly thrown bottle is made from a clay body with a high percentage of molochite—a white, china clay grog—giving good resistance to thermal shock. The alkaline-based frit glaze produced good open crazing while cooling, enhanced by the smoking of post-firing reduction.*

2 ADAM AND EVE

Steve Mattison *The interaction of fire on the ceramic surface is of prime importance in this piece, which was fired in a live-flame kiln. The figures were raku fired with a copper matte glaze to give earthy colors reminiscent of archeological finds.*

SEE ALSO
Clay and pottery bodies, ***pages 8–17***
Common raw materials, ***pages 174–175***
Raku firing, ***pages 200–201***

1

2

Sculpting Clay

Clay that has a heavy grog content, both in terms of the percentage added and the large particle size, is referred to as sculpting clay or sculptor's marl. This coarse clay has a good resistance to shrinkage and warping and is excellent for large-scale sculptural work. It is usually made from stoneware clay, into which coarse grog is kneaded in order to open up the clay body and increase strength and texture (see page 15). This openness causes the clay to dry fairly rapidly, allowing large work to be built more quickly because the drying lower parts can support more weight. Sculpting clay is less plastic than many other clays and easily breaks apart when bent. It is difficult to handle the clay for any length of time because it dries quickly from the warmth of the hands. The openness of the clay makes it suitable for raku work because the grog gives it good resistance to thermal shock.

SEE ALSO
Clay and pottery bodies, *pages 8–17*
Raku firing, *pages 200–201*

1 SOMETIMES IT'S NICE TO BE DIFFERENT

Meri Wells The artist enjoys working with heavily grogged clays, which give strength and durability. All her work is coiled and scraped to create rich, textural surfaces, which are enhanced by layers of colored slips and oxides before soda firing with wood. Here, the particles of white grog can be seen prior to the application of color.

2 BOUNCER

Meri Wells This life-sized sculpture was coiled using a heavily grogged, white-firing stoneware clay. It was built in two parts that were joined together after firing to 2550°F (1400°C) in a gas kiln. The combination of strong clay and high-temperature firing makes the clay virtually like stone and therefore suitable for outdoor locations.

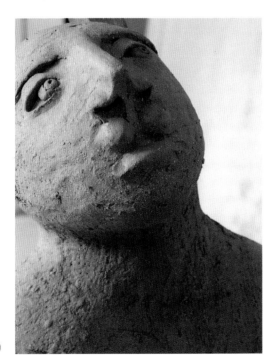

Casting Clay

SEE ALSO
Clay and pottery bodies, *pages 8–17*
Slip casting, *pages 106–107*

Casting clay, or casting slip, is essentially a clay body in liquid form, enabling it to be poured into molds so that repeat shapes can be made. Casting slip contains 40–45 percent water, while the slip used for decorating contains 60 percent. Although many potters buy ready-made casting slip from commercial suppliers, it can easily be made in a home studio for virtually any clay body and any firing temperature.

DEFLOCCULENTS

Casting slip requires the addition of chemical deflocculents to ensure a free-flowing slip in which the clay particles remain in suspension without settling in the mold. Ideally, the slip should not shrink too much when it dries and it should have a good dry strength for handling. Deflocculents increase the fluidity of the slip by dispersing the clay particles more efficiently, and as a result, less water is needed, thereby reducing the shrinkage rate.

MIXING THE SLIP

Small amounts of casting slip can be mixed in a bucket using a metal mixing blade attached to an electric drill. Commercial blungers are available for mixing large quantities. If you are making slip from plastic clay, boil about 2 pints (1 liter) of water and add the required amount of deflocculent. When it has dissolved, pour it into a bucket with the rest of the water in the recipe. Add the clay in small pieces so that it breaks down more easily. Mix thoroughly, then allow the slip to stand for a while to check the thickness. If it is too thick, add a little Dispex. Be careful how much deflocculent you add because one drop can make a big difference. If you are making slip from powdered clay, add the required amount to the water in one go. Powdered clay is often easier to use than plastic clay but not all clays are available in powdered form.

LEFTOVER SLIP

Store leftover casting clay in an airtight container such as a bucket with a tight-fitting lid. Dried scraps of slip can be recycled by adding them to a new batch of casting clay as long as no more than 20 percent scraps are used. Using more than this is likely to upset the ratio of clay and deflocculent.

COMMON DEFLOCCULENTS

Sodium silicate

This is available as a thick liquid in two strengths, depending on the ratio of silica to sodium. The strengths are indicated in degrees twaddle (°TW) and three grades are usually available: 70, 100, and 140°TW. The higher the TW, the thicker the liquid.

Soda ash and sodium carbonate
These two deflocculents are commonly used together.

Dispex
This is a commercially manufactured combination of soda ash and sodium silicate and is used for adjusting the thickness of casting slip after mixing.

WHITE EARTHENWARE CASTING SLIP

1830–2100°F (1000–1150°C)

White earthenware plastic clay	55 lb. (25 kg)
Sodium silicate 100°TW	1/16 oz. (2.5 g)
Soda ash	3/8 oz. (11 g)
Water	3¾ pints (2.1 liters)

SEMI-PORCELAIN CASTING SLIP

Semi-porcelain plastic clay	55 lb. (25 kg)
Sodium silicate 140°TW	3/16 oz. (5 g)
Soda ash	7/16 oz. (12.5 g)
Water	4½ pints (2.5 liters)

STONEWARE CASTING SLIP

2120–2340°F (1160–1280°C)

Stoneware plastic clay	55 lb. (25 kg)
Sodium silicate 140°TW	2 oz. (56 g)
Soda ash	7/16 oz. (12.5 g)
Water	7 pints (4 liters)

VASE AND BOWL

Sasha Wardell Bone china produces an incredibly fine, translucent body, especially when thinly slip cast. Consecutive layers of white and blue casting slips were poured into the molds for this vase and bowl, allowing small blue marks to be revealed when the surface was incised.

Low-shrink Clay

Special pottery bodies can be formulated that have virtually no shrinkage. They are made from a high percentage of talc mixed with a low percentage of standard clay. Although the result is not strictly clay, it will behave like plastic clay to a certain extent and can be worked in much the same way. Talc is magnesium silicate, and when mixed with water, has many of the properties of clay but with little or no shrinkage. It is also highly resistant to thermal shock and can therefore be fired in minutes instead of the usual hours.

SEE ALSO

Clay and pottery bodies, *pages 8–17*
Tiles and murals, *pages 116–117*
Kilns and firings, *pages 188–207*

WORKING PROPERTIES

When mixing a low-shrink body, you can use up to 90 percent talc. If you use any more than this, the body will lose its workability and firing strength. With the addition of 10 percent standard clay, the necessary chemistry for firing is retained. Low-shrink clay should only be used at low temperatures because talc loses its density at 2110°F (1100°C) and will collapse dramatically. When fired to a temperature of around 1900°F (1040°C), the body will fuse and be almost as dense as porcelain. When used in low quantities in clay bodies, talc acts as a refractory ingredient, giving good resistance to heat and thermal shock and making it an ideal addition to ovenware pottery bodies.

TILE MANUFACTURE

Talc clay bodies are mainly used for commercial tile manufacture because the bodies can easily be rolled or pressed, will shrink little or not at all, and will not warp when drying or firing. Talc is also far cheaper than clay and its low expansion makes for a good, craze-free glaze fit.

Paper Clay

Of all the clays that have recently been developed, paper clay has to be the most versatile. Quite simply, paper clay has the ability to stick to itself in any state—wet or dry, thick or thin, with additions being attached using paper clay slip as glue. It really is a magnificent material.

USES OF PAPER CLAY

Paper clay can be left to stiffen on plaster bats without warping, lifted off when leather-hard or even bone dry, and cut into sheets for assembling. Alternately, it can be scraped from the bat while still wet and kneaded to form a plastic clay for coiling or modeling. You can even throw with it. While still a slip, it can be poured or spread into molds and allowed to dry. Your work does not even have to be made hollow for firing. Using paper clay, you can make large-scale work that is extremely strong in both green and fired states and a fraction of the weight of regular clay. The small hollow fibers of cellulose found in paper pulp provide capillaries for wet clay to soak into and adhere firmly. When fired, the paper burns away, leaving a honeycomb of holes through the clay body, thereby reducing its weight.

1

1 VORTEX

Graham Hay This garden sculpture is one of Hay's assembled series. Accustomed to breaking and joining dry and wet paper clay elements, it was a natural progression for Hay to create works that are assembled after firing. The twisting spines were made by rolling plastic paper clay into long coils. After firing, they were placed through holes in the central tube, allowing the viewer the opportunity of rearranging them.

MAKING PAPER CLAY

1 Mix up a thick slip from powdered clay. Here, water is added to a bucket of porcelain and stirred with a stick. You should wear a mask because adding water to the dry powdered clay may cause dust to rise.

2 Use a metal mixing blade attached to an electric drill to blend the dry powder into the water. The finished consistency should be like thick cream.

3 Put the dry paper fiber into a bowl and soak it with water. This commercially supplied fiber can give off a fine, dry dust, so make sure you wear a mask until it is all soaked.

MAKING PAPER CLAY

You can make your own paper pulp by shredding and soaking tissue paper or newspaper, passing it through a domestic liquidizer, and then adding it to a clay slip. You can also buy dry paper fiber from most ceramic suppliers to add to clay slip. You can use any clay slip or make your own from powdered clay.

2 RUN AGROUND

Graham Hay *The framework of this boat sculpture was assembled from dry paper clay "planks," cut from slabs with a sharp knife when leather-hard. Liquid paper clay in a squeeze bottle was used to glue the remaining planks to the framework. The finished sculpture was fired to earthenware temperature.*

3 DYFODOL YR IAITH

Steve Mattison and Meri Wells *Part of a larger sculptural installation, these tiles use the natural paper-like qualities of handmade paper clay to good effect. The text, in the minority Welsh language, contains words for growth, nurture, care, and for language itself. The tiles were installed on the pathways of the National Botanical Gardens of Wales, where plants are preserved for the future. Visitors walked over the installation, slowly destroying it and treading the pieces into the ground, contrasting the optimistic text with the fragility of the tiles, the environment, and the language.*

TOOLS

- Bucket
- Jug
- Stick
- Electric drill and metal mixing blade
- Bowl
- Plaster bat
- Rib or similar tool
- Rolling pin

4 Mix the water into the pulp until every fiber is saturated. The color will darken—a good indicator of whether it is thoroughly soaked. The quantity of pulp you will need depends on the results you wish to achieve, but usually 30–50 percent pulp can safely be added to the clay slip.

5 Squeeze the water from the paper pulp and add it to the slip. Thoroughly mix the paper fibers into the slip using the mixing blade. The thick slip will become runnier as the water from the fibers is absorbed.

6 Pour the paper clay slip onto a plaster bat and use a rib or similar tool to smooth it out into a sheet. If you allow the surface to dry, it will have the quality of handmade paper with deckle edging. Alternately, you could use a rolling pin to smooth it when the paper clay is leather-hard.

Colored Clay

Staining the body clay a different color gives an infinite variety of decorative possibilities. Strong colors can be achieved for creating bold and striking pieces, or you may prefer subtle variations in tone. With the wide availability of commercial colorants, an extensive palette of hues is at your disposal. White-firing clays are best for producing bright colors. Test the intensity of commercial colorants by mixing sample batches of colored clay using quantities of 5 percent colorant upward. At bisque temperature the colors will appear dull and muted but they will intensify at higher temperatures. If you are using oxides to stain your clay, bear in mind that if you use a large quantity, it will act as a flux in the body and lower the maturing temperature of the clay. Calculating the quantity of colorant by weight is always a more accurate method and will give greater control when you need repeat batches of the same color. Mix the stain with powdered clay, as shown below, or add a little water to the stain to make a paste and knead it into plastic clay in the same way that you would add grog (see page 15). Alternately, you can use commercially bought decorating slips and pour them onto plaster bats to remove some of the moisture, before peeling them off and kneading them for use.

TOOLS

- *Scales*
- *Bowl*
- *Stick*
- *Slip trailer*
- *Plaster bat*

SEE ALSO

Clay and pottery bodies, *pages 8–17*
Pigments and stains, *pages 176–177*

COLORING CLAY

1 In this example, 10 percent blue body stain is added to powdered white porcelain clay. Mix the two powders together roughly while dry. Make sure you wear a mask because the dust is a hazard.

2 Slowly add some water to the dry powder, stirring to mix the constituents evenly. Add the water gradually or the clay can easily become too runny. A slip trailer has been used here to give greater control over the flow of water being added.

3 Mix the clay and stain thoroughly into a stiff paste. Try not to make the mix too wet or too dry—it should have the consistency of soft, plastic clay. Scoop the clay from the bowl and knead it on a plaster bat until the color is evenly dispersed throughout and the clay is in a workable condition (see page 41).

Bone China

BASIC BONE CHINA
Calcined bone ash 50%
China clay   25%
Feldspar   25%

Bone china is renowned for its whiteness, translucency, and extreme fired strength. It enables potters to make work that is exceptionally thin, almost becoming transparent. Bone china clay was developed for use in the ceramics industry, producing wares with porcelain qualities but at a lower cost. It is still used mainly in slip form for casting, when incredibly thin walls can be achieved. The whiteness and purity of the body make it ideal for enamel or transfer decoration.

BONE CHINA BODIES

Bone china clay contains a high percentage of calcined bone ash, which acts as a strong flux in the body, making the clay fuse at temperatures in excess of 2260°F (1240°C). The low clay content means that unfired pots have little strength and must be handled carefully to avoid breakages. Bone china has a limited firing range and is easily overfired, when the fluxes will cause the pottery to sag, distort, or even collapse. As a precaution, bone china is usually fired to its maturing temperature at the bisque stage, with subsequent glaze and enamel decoration firings at lower temperatures.

1 BONE CHINA VASES

Dainis Pundurs Bisque clay roulettes were used to impress rippled textures in the surfaces of the thrown pots. Molds were taken from the thrown work and used to produce a series of cast bone china vases. The slip was tinted with oxides and stains to give subtle variations of pastel colors, hardly noticeable when the pieces are viewed individually.

2 BONE CHINA HEART

Urmas Puhkan This assemblage of slip-cast bone china domestic items alludes to the importance of the kitchen as the heart of the home. The separate cast pieces and handbuilt elements were joined with china slip and fired to 2300°F (1260°C) with a transparent glaze. Pieces of natural amber were applied with silicone adhesive after firing.

SEE ALSO
Clay and pottery bodies, *pages 8–17*
Slip casting, *pages 106–107*
Enamels and lusters, *page 147*
Printed transfers, *page 165*
Common raw materials, *pages 174–175*
Kilns and firings, *pages 188–207*

Chapter **3**

FORMING TECHNIQUES

The three basic techniques for making clay objects are handbuilding, throwing, and mold making. The method you choose will depend on several factors: the size and shape of the piece you wish to make; the use of the object; the number of repetitive forms it requires; and your level of experience. You will need to take the possibilities and limitations of each forming technique into consideration when designing and developing any project. In the hands of a skillful potter, armed with knowledge gained from a personal journey of experiments, the different techniques can be combined to create surprising and original works.

HANDBUILDING

Handbuilding, the most ancient and versatile technique, includes pinching out shapes from soft clay, coiling ropes of clay, and building forms from flat slabs of clay. Handbuilding gives the clay artist the most scope for free expression and encourages an intuitive feel for this most tactile of materials.

THROWING

Throwing pots on a wheel is rhythmic and sensuous and requires practice to master. Although throwing always produces essentially round forms, there is plenty of scope for personal expression by altering or faceting the forms on the wheelhead, or by paddling or cutting afterwards.

MOLD MAKING

Molds are used to reproduce a series of identical objects from a prototype model. These can be cast from poured slip to produce ceramics in small- or large-scale production runs—fine in quality and finish, but often without the human touch of the potter. Alternately, pressing sheets of clay into or over molds produces more original items.

A WORD ABOUT WATER

Contrary to popular belief, the less water you use while making your work, the better. Inexperienced students often use copious amounts of water to smooth the surface of pots, but in fact they are only washing away the clay and exposing any grog content, which makes the surface rough like sandpaper. Water also makes the clay flabby and unable to retain its shape, especially when throwing, where you should only use small amounts of water to prevent the spinning clay from sticking to your hands.

PADDLING TOOLS

Most of these wooden tools can be bought from a kitchenware store. Although they are not designed specifically for ceramic use, they make ideal implements for paddling clay in order to shape or texture it.

JOINING PIECES WITH SLIP

Once the clay has started to stiffen, you will usually need to score and slip any edges that are to be joined in order to create a firm seal. To make the slip, put a few chunks of clay in a bowl, add some water, and mix into a paste. Alternately, press your thumb into a ball of clay, then rub a wet brush inside the indentation to form a slip. Use a comb or similar tool to score the edges that are to be joined, then brush some slip onto them. Firmly press the edges together.

Design and Inspiration

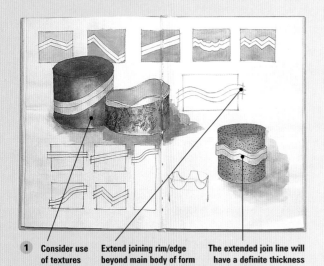

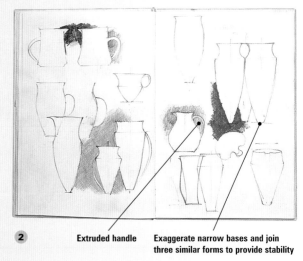

1   **Consider use of textures**   **Extend joining rim/edge beyond main body of form**   **The extended join line will have a definite thickness**

2   **Extruded handle**   **Exaggerate narrow bases and join three similar forms to provide stability**

The beauty of clay as a working material is that it can be manipulated into an immense variety of shapes using an equally wide choice of techniques. A good sense of shape and form is essential for any ceramic work. Creating a successful design also requires imagination, and you can find sources of inspiration all around you.

FORM AND FUNCTION

From the earliest times, the form of a pot was dictated by its function, with the most suitable forms evolving gradually. Similar shapes of pottery can be found across continents and cultures, and have become timeless, classical pieces that still appear fresh today, even when placed alongside contemporary ceramics. Many modern ceramic artists and potters continue to use these aesthetically pleasing basic forms, making subtle changes in shape, volume, and scale to express their own vision.

APPEARANCE AND PRACTICALITY

The way you approach the design of a piece will depend on whether the finished item is going to be put to practical use or whether its visual appearance is more important. If the latter, your design choices will mainly be concerned with aesthetic

Extreme cut at back

Exaggerate undulation

Carry on linear elements beneath undulating rim to imply undulating sides

3

1 DESIGNS FOR LIDDED POTS

Steve Mattison *These sketches show the design process for a series of handbuilt slab boxes. The shape and proportion have been investigated through a number of outline sketches, as well as alternatives for the joint between base and lid. Should it be flat, angular, or curvilinear? This sketching process circumvents many hours of work to discover the best option. The three-dimensional drawings give potential clients a better feel for the object.*

2 SKETCHES FOR URNS

Steve Mattison *This is one of a series of sketchbook pages investigating classical shape and form. Simple outline drawings, occasionally silhouetted with color to emphasize particular areas, show a range of shapes in different proportions. This is an ideal way to free up the mind and focus on the aesthetics of the form.*

3 SKETCHES FOR RAKU POTTERY

Steve Mattison *These sketches analyze the relationship of a cut rim with dark linear decoration. Many pages of quick sketches like these soon open up a wealth of possibilities and alternatives.*

considerations. If the former, both practical and aesthetic elements will have to be considered. The balance of a teapot in the hand, how a pitcher pours, the security of a lid, and the comfort of picking up a filled cup with a well-pulled handle—all these sensations should be pleasant and need careful thought when designing pieces for practical use.

SKETCHING A DESIGN

All ceramics, whether functional, decorative, or sculptural, rely on a balance of shape and form for their success. In industry, the process of design and manufacture are often separated, with different people doing each task. The studio potter is in the unique position of controlling every stage of the process—an often daunting prospect for the beginner. Few potters have a natural feeling for shape and form, and perseverance and practice will be required to develop it. Drawing sketches is an excellent way to start developing a design. It allows you to investigate a range of possibilities and rule out the forms that are unsatisfactory before making them. The sketches can be simple outlines concentrating on the silhouette of the form, or beautiful artistic renderings of three-dimensional objects. Use whichever type of sketch you feel most comfortable with so that the process is enjoyable. Advanced drawing skills are not necessary—making sketches is only a means to an end.

4 SKETCH FOR EASTERN GATEWAY

Alan Sidney *Creating this complex slab-built, pinched, and modeled sculpture involves careful planning so that the multiple parts can be cut and bent accurately, ready to be assembled when leather-hard. Drawings are essential to Sidney's working process, with detailed plans being sketched out prior to making each piece.*

5 EASTERN GATEWAY

Alan Sidney *This wonderful creation invites us into a world of imagination and humor. It was made from red clay and built from a combination of pinch pots, press-molded pieces, and slabs, onto which the artist applied modeled details. After bisque firing to 1760°F (960°C), a series of slips and oxides were applied, washed off, and reapplied, before the piece was given a second firing to fix the slips. It was then given a coating of off-white matte glaze. Rich interactions occurred between the glaze and the multiple slip and oxide layers during firing.*

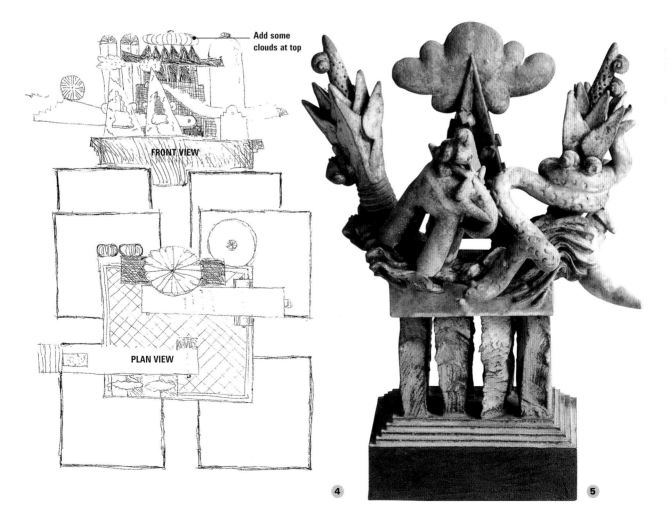

Add some clouds at top

FRONT VIEW

PLAN VIEW

4

5

DESIGN AND INSPIRATION

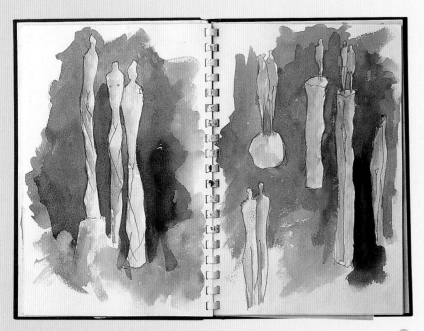

FINDING INSPIRATION

Good sources of inspiration are museums and exhibitions where historical and contemporary pots can be viewed. These will always provide rich and unexpected experiences. Try to handle as many pots as you can. Not only will you see how other artists have resolved design issues, but you will also feel it. Experienced potters have experimented and achieved a multiplicity of design solutions over the years, adding to a pool of knowledge from which everyone can learn.

EXPERIENCE

You can develop an instinct or awareness for form and design in the same way that you refine your pottery-making skills over the years. With time, you will find that the mental process of making decisions about form, shape, function, and appearance becomes second nature. Forms thrown directly on the wheel with ease and confidence often have years of experimentation and experience behind them. Similarly, the clay sculptor's apparent ability to assemble a variety of elements into often complex structures disguises a deep knowledge of the materials and a clear image of the end result.

1 SKETCHES FOR FIGURATIVE SCULPTURE

Steve Mattison These sketchbook pages show investigations in shape, form, scale, and proportion for the artist's current series of figurative sculptures. The simple line drawings are enhanced and given a three-dimensional quality by shading with watercolor washes.

2 MAQUETTES

Steve Mattison From the initial drawings, a series of small, quickly made clay maquettes help the artist to confirm and elaborate his ideas. Many small figures are made, taking the ideas in many directions, before the selected pieces are worked up to larger sizes, some over 7 ft. (2 m) in height.

3 VENUS

Steve Mattison A lone female stands delicately on the peak of a rock, her legs slightly twisting. With inspiration drawn from early Mediterranean and African sculpture, the artist has used the image of Venus rising from the waters in a contemporary way, but still classical in its roots. Made from a grogged white stoneware clay, this piece was raku fired to 1830°F (1000°C) with a matte copper glaze.

DESIGNING WITH COMPUTERS

In recent years, computers have become firmly established as a tool for the ceramic designer and artist. Many ceramicists use painting or drawing programs to sketch their ideas. The use of computers allows color changes and textures to be applied at the touch of a key, bringing new and endless possibilities. Many ceramicists are also experimenting with CAD (computer-aided design) and three-dimensional modeling software, producing radical and exciting "virtual pottery." Dutch ceramicist Jeroen Bechtold has been a pioneer of CAD and 3D modeling work, creating often seemingly impossible designs on computer. From initial experiments with ceramic objects freely floating in virtual space, the work has taken on new significance by his collaboration with teapot factories in Yixing, China. The skills of these master makers are transforming Bechtold's imagination into reality by producing these amazing objects commercially. At whatever level you use computers, they can be a valuable tool for the ceramicist, allowing three-dimensional objects to be created on the screen with a vast array of manipulation tools for altering the form, shape, color, and texture.

5 DESIGNS FOR COMPACT LIVING

Jeroen Bechtold These teacups and saucers are part of a series of designs that were intended as a comment on a future where everyone would always be logged onto a computer, living in a virtual world. "If we live in a virtual world, we should at least make it look like home," says Bechtold.

4 DOUBLE TEAPOT

Jeroen Bechtold This fantastic teapot was never intended for production, but while visiting a teapot conference in Yixing, China, Bechtold demonstrated his virtual pottery and a master maker from Purple Sands Factory #5 actually made it before his eyes. Bechtold now designs futuristic teapots for the factory, which produces the wares commercially.

4

5

Preparing the Clay

Before any clay can be shaped successfully, it must be thoroughly mixed in order to expel any pockets of air and distribute the particles in the clay to achieve an even consistency. Production potters often use a pugmill to do this, since it is faster and produces large quantities of workable clay. Most potters, however, mix clay by hand using wedging and kneading techniques. If you are not going to use the prepared clay immediately, wrap it in airtight plastic bags or containers until required. The clay will improve over time.

WEDGING

Wedging distributes the clay particles and additives such as grog evenly throughout the clay mass. Wedging is easier if the clay is slightly softer than needed for working (you can stiffen it afterward by kneading it on a plaster bat). If the clay is too hard, cut it into slabs and sandwich softer clay between the layers. Alternately, soak the hard clay slabs in a bowl of water for a few hours to soften them. If the clay is groggy, it will soften in water more quickly.

①

BASIC WEDGING

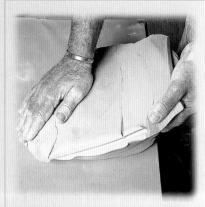

1 Place the clay on a strong, firm surface. This should be absorbent so that the clay does not stick to it. A table covered with stretched canvas, as shown here, makes an ideal wedging bench. It should also be of a comfortable working height to help avoid back strain.

2 Allowing the clay to overhang the edge of the table slightly, pull a wire through from side to side.

3 Pick up the cut piece of clay, rotate it 90° so that the cut edge is facing you, and slam it down on top of the clay on the bench. Try not to trap air between the layers. Repeat this sequence until the clay is mixed thoroughly. Throw the chunk of clay onto the table repeatedly, always keeping it in a wedge shape and never allowing it to flatten out.

KNEADING

All clay bodies must be kneaded in order to homogenize the clay. If the clay is too stiff at this stage, poke fingertip holes into the mass of clay and fill them with water. After a short while you can begin kneading. A method known as spiral kneading (sometimes referred to as spiral wedging or Japanese wedging) is demonstrated here. It requires some practice to become proficient, but it is the best method for expelling air and ensuring uniformity. It can also replace the previous wedging technique if the clay is already of even consistency and only requires air bubbles to be removed. Trapped air, especially in thrown pottery, can create bulges when the air expands during firing. In extreme cases, they can explode off, leaving large craters in the surface of the pot, or actually break the pot.

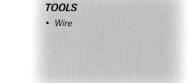

TOOLS
• *Wire*

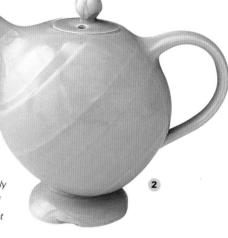

1 LANDSCAPE BOWL

Billy Adams *The jagged, textured surfaces of this bowl show Adams' deep affinity with his native Irish landscape. Constructed from layered clays, the bowl was given multiple glaze firings in reducing temperatures of 2340, 2050, and 1980°F (1280, 1120, and 1080°C), with a final luster firing at 1460°F (795°C). When working with such uneven thickness of clay, attention has to be paid to adequate preparation of the clay.*

2 XING TEAPOT

Joanna Howells *Porcelain, above all other clays, must be prepared well prior to throwing. The classic blue celadon glaze gives a juiciness to this finely thrown and trimmed teapot. The shape of the knob complements the body of the pot and adds a delicate detail to the lid. The thrown-on foot lifts the pot, emphasizing the spherical form.*

2

SEE ALSO
Clay and pottery bodies, *pages 8–17*
Types of ware, *pages 18–33*

SPIRAL KNEADING

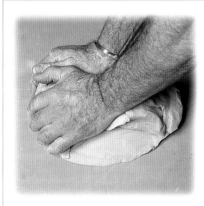

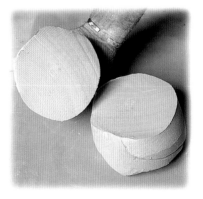

1 Working on an absorbent surface, push down firmly on the lump of soft clay with the heel of your hands. Keeping one hand pushing down on the clay, use the fingers of your other hand to lift the clay up and pivot it a quarter turn.

2 Repeat this process at least ten times in quick succession. By using more downward pressure with the heel of one hand and lifting with the fingers of the other, the clay will form into a compacted spiral.

3 If you have kneaded the clay with an even rhythm in a continuous motion, any air will have been pushed to the surface. To make sure the clay is sufficiently homogenized, cut it in half and check to see if there are any irregularities or air bubbles. Continue kneading if necessary.

PREPARING THE CLAY

MIXING DIFFERENT CLAYS

Potters sometimes mix different clays together, either to change the working quality of the clay or to alter its color. By this method it is possible to make clays more pliable, increase the clay's strength by mixing in a proportion of grogged clay, or produce clay of a different or marbled color. Start by cutting the different clays into slices, then layer the slices and knead them together to mix them thoroughly. The marbled clay illustrated here is achieved by insufficient mixing, leaving the different colored clays clearly visible for an interesting decorative finish.

MARBLED VASE

Reg Moon *This unglazed porcelain vase illustrates the subtlety of color that can be achieved by throwing with marbled clay. When thrown on the wheel, the particles in the clay become aligned in a spiral formation. As a result, the colors appear in different densities according to the way they have been arranged during the throwing process, producing beautiful swirls of color.*

TOOLS
• Wire

MARBLING

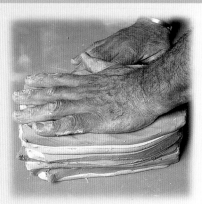

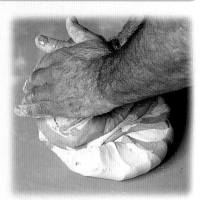

1 Use a wire to slice two lumps of different colored clays into layers. Stack the slices of clay one on top of another in alternating layers.

2 When enough layers have been built up, press down firmly with your hand to flatten them.

3 Knead the clay until the required level of mixture is achieved (see page 41). The more kneading you do, the more subtle the marbling effect will be in the finished pot.

Handbuilding

Handbuilding is without doubt the oldest method of forming clay objects and includes techniques such as pinching, coiling, and slab building. The use of handbuilding methods to squeeze and press clay into a particular shape will help you develop the sensitivity needed for all clay work. Making a pinch pot will help you learn what size of piece can be made from a given weight of clay. Coiling and slab building will teach you how to control the clay on a larger scale. With practice, you will soon develop a rhythm to your working, and many potters find handbuilding techniques calming and contemplative.

COMBINING TECHNIQUES

It is easy to think of handbuilding techniques in isolation, with each technique producing its own series of shapes. However, all of these methods can be combined to create an entirely new range of possibilities—the only constraint is your imagination. Handbuilt elements can also be combined with thrown or even molded pieces. However, care should be taken when attaching different clays together because of differences in shrinkage rates, although most types can be joined successfully.

3 HANDBUILT TEAPOT

Yang Qinfang *This master teapot maker from Yixing, China, makes his handbuilt teapots from thin slabs, paddled with a wooden mallet on a sturdy table. This paddling not only expands the clay thinly and evenly but also compacts and strengthens it. These beautifully constructed pots are made on a curved wooden block, used as a turntable, and can be so rounded as to seem wheel-thrown. The fine purple zisha clay fires to a slightly porous, stained finish without glaze.*

1 RED FIN

Meri Wells *Cave paintings, crustaceans, encrusted undersea detritus, ancient burial sites, and the fossilized remains of prehistoric life forms provide the inspiration for this archaic ceramic form. The thinly coiled vessel was refined using metal scrapers. After bisque firing, it was glazed through stencils and raku fired to 1830ºF (1000ºC).*

2 RAZOR WAVE

Beverley Bell-Hughes *Working in a tactile and intuitive way, Bell-Hughes coils and pinches her landscape-inspired forms. Crushed, dry chunks of porcelain were kneaded into the grogged clay to give heavily textured elements that were softened by applications of glaze. The piece was reduction fired in a gas kiln to 2370ºF (1300ºC).*

HANDBUILDING

Pinching

Making a pinch pot is often a student's first experience of working with clay. Any type of clay can be used successfully with this technique. Grogged stoneware clays will hold their shape well, while fine porcelain allows you to work thinly and will become translucent when fired. Whichever type of clay you use, pinching will introduce you to its individual characteristics and help you discover the best way to handle it. Always have a clear idea of the shape you want to create before you begin working, because it is very easy for the clay to take on a direction of its own. Clay dries out more quickly in the warmth of your hands, so the longer you work on a piece, the drier it will become and soon the rim may begin to crack.

1

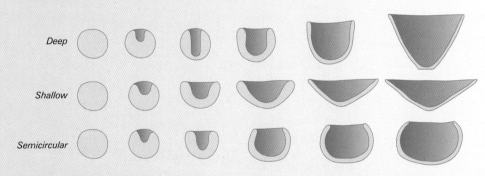

Deep

Shallow

Semicircular

PINCH POT SHAPES

These illustrations show, in cross-section, the stages of making for three different shapes of pinch pot: deep, shallow, and semicircular.

SEMICIRCULAR PINCH POT

1 Hold the ball of clay in the hand you write with and press the thumb of your weaker hand into it. Judge the thickness of the base between your thumb and forefinger. Slowly begin to squeeze the base between your thumb and the flat of your fingers on the outside of the clay.

2 Slowly rotate the ball, squeezing with your thumb every ½ in. (1 cm) or so. This rotation should even out any indentations made by your fingers. When the clay reaches the thickness you require at that point, move farther up the wall of the pot and continue the process.

3 Continue squeezing the walls and finally the rim to the desired thickness. The pot shown here is semicircular, but virtually any shape can be made.

1 BURNISHED EGG FORMS

Gerhild Taschler-Nagy *These two finely burnished egg forms were made by joining two pinch pots together and paddling them into shape. The pieces were wrapped in straw among chunks of wood, small packets of salt and copper oxide were placed around the pots, and they were then wood fired. Salt volatizes during firing, flashing incidental colors across the surface.*

2 DANCING FIGURE

Jolanta Kvasyte *By pinching small pieces of clay between her fingers into small, flat disks, Kvasyte allows her sculptures to grow organically. This figure, made from porcelain with glaze and on-glaze enamel decoration, retains the indentations of the construction in the surface, adding to its liveliness.*

3 PODS

Catrin Mostyn Jones *Pinch pots are the starting point for most of Mostyn Jones' work. Handbuilt using buff earthenware clay, the form was modified by modeling and sculpting. Earthenware glazes were sprayed in multiple layers over wax resist patterning. These vivid vessel forms reflect the artist's interest in undersea life and the unexpected vibrant colors found there.*

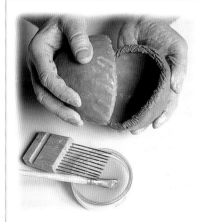

TOOLS
- *Comb or similar tool*
- *Brush*
- *Paddling tool such as a piece of wood*

SEE ALSO
Preparing the clay, **pages 40–42**

PINCHED SPHERE

1 Two pinch pots can be joined together to form the starting point for hollow pieces such as boxes and bottles. Here, two semicircular pinch pots are joined to create a hollow sphere. Score the rims of both pots with a comb or similar tool and use a small brush to apply some slip to improve adhesion (see page 35).

2 Firmly seal the two edges together with your fingertips. The strength of this seal is crucial in order to retain the air inside the sphere. The air pressure will act as a support while you do any additional work on the surface of the piece.

3 Refine the sphere's shape and surface by lightly tapping it with a tool such as a piece of wood—this is known as paddling. This secures the joint and smooths the surface of the clay. You could paddle the sphere into a cube shape if you wish.

HANDBUILDING

Coiling

This handbuilding technique involves making forms from coils, or ropes, of clay. The coils can be rolled by hand one at a time as you use them, or you can make several at once, wrapping them in plastic to keep them damp until you need them. For speed, some potters extrude coils using a machine with a shaped die plate at one end; different die plates can be used to produce different coil profiles. Clay used for coiling should be fairly plastic to prevent it from cracking as you work. It should also have 20–30 percent grog or sand content to increase its strength.

WORKING WITH COILS

The coils should be slightly larger in diameter than the required thickness of the wall of the pot, because the coils will be thinned slightly when they are joined together. Always make sure you have a clear idea of the shape you wish to achieve before you begin because any changes of direction need to be built in as you work. If your shape is to taper inward, each successive coil should be smaller in diameter; they should be larger if your shape is to grow outward. The joints between coils must be firmly sealed on the inside of the pot to prevent horizontal cracks from appearing, but

TOOLS
- Rolling pin
- Turntable or banding wheel
- Knife
- Wooden smoothing tool
- Metal scraper or rubber rib

1

BASIC COILED POT

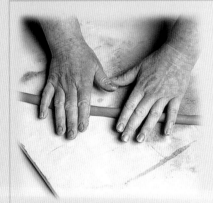

1 Use the palms of your hands to roll out even coils of clay on an absorbent surface such as a canvas-covered table so they will not stick. Rotate the coils several times to keep them round; short, forward movements will make the coils oval in section. Move your hands gently outward, stretching and lengthening each coil as you roll.

2 For the base of your piece, flatten out a pad of clay with the palm of your hand or use a rolling pin. Place the base on a turntable or banding wheel and cut a circle of the required diameter. You can cut around a circular object as a template if you wish.

3 Place the first coil on top of the base, wrapping it around the circular shape. If the clay is soft enough, the coil will adhere without water. Some coil builders only apply one coil circle at a time, but you can use the entire length of the coil if you wish, as illustrated here.

can be left visible on the outside to give a decorative finish. You will need to allow your pot to stiffen occasionally as it grows so that it does not collapse under the weight of the clay. You can use a gas torch or hair dryer to dry off the clay more quickly. If the top coil dries too much, score and slip the edge so that the next coil will adhere (see page 35).

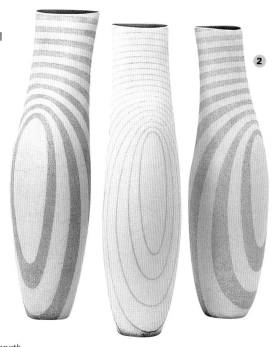

2

1 COILED POTS

Nigeria and Kenya *These large coiled pots were made without the use of a turntable or banding wheel. Starting with a small piece of clay supported in a concave shard of fired clay, roughly squeezed coils were added and refined. Moving around the work, the potters blend the coils and quickly smooth the vessel with a damp cloth or piece of leather. Fired at low temperatures in open bonfires, the pots are still porous, which helps to keep the liquid contents fresh.*

2 BOTTLE FORMS

David Roberts *These statuesque bottle forms demonstrate Roberts' mastery of coiling. The gradual growth of form, the subtle changes in direction, and the smooth, polished, pebble-like finish give his work a quiet strength. The concentric patterns on the surface enhance the figurative qualities of these raku-fired pieces.*

SEE ALSO
Clay additives, *page 15*
Preparing the clay, *pages 40–42*

4 Firmly join the coil circles together on the inside of the pot by smoothing them in a vertical direction using your fingers or a wooden tool. Support the outside of the pot with your other hand while you do this. Repeat this process on the outside of the coils if you want a smooth outer surface.

5 When you have secured the first few rows, add the next series of coils and smooth together once again. Many people add around four rows at a time before smoothing the joints. Position the joints at the ends of coils in a different place on each row to prevent any vertical weaknesses from developing.

6 Use a metal scraper or rubber rib to refine the shape of the pot and produce a smooth surface for decoration (unless you want the coils to show). Even if you intend to decorate using texture, starting from a smooth surface will enhance your mark making.

HANDBUILDING

ADAPTING COILED POTS

Many potters find the coiling technique a naturally expressive way of working. Being able to change direction in all three dimensions is a rare quality and ideally suited to soft, organic forms and figurative sculpture. If you use thick, roughly squeezed ropes of groggy clays such as a raku body, you can build shapes quickly, whereas clays such as porcelain are slower to use but will produce fine-walled structures. Slow drying is essential because stresses can occur between thick and thinner sections, causing pieces to crack. Try to keep pieces wrapped in airtight plastic when you are not working on them to prevent them from drying out too much. If they do dry out a little, soften the uppermost coil with water and crosshatch with a knife or comb to equalize the consistency with the coils to be attached.

1 CREATURE FROM THE PROCESSION

Meri Wells *Working intuitively and spontaneously, Wells uses combinations of coiled, slabbed, pinched, and modeled clay pieces to create zoomorphic figures. Starting with cut and joined coiled sections, the freely modeled details breathe life into this creature.*

1

COILED SCULPTURE

1 In this example, a basic organically shaped coiled pot is used as the starting point for a sculpture of a rabbit (see pages 46–47). Use a wire to cut the soft clay of the pot vertically into two pieces. Carefully separate the two halves to form the basis for two separate figurative works.

2 Roll out a slab of clay and join it to the cut coiled section (see pages 50–53). Make sure you score and slip the joints so that they adhere securely (see page 35). Use an appropriately shaped tool to paddle the body of the sculpture into the required shape.

3 Add more coils to the top of the shaped piece to continue building the body as far as the shoulders. Smooth and refine the shape with a metal scraper. Pieces of clay have also been added to the base to form feet and a tail; this will obviously depend on your design.

2 ROUND FORM

Külli Kõiv *This piece was constructed from ribbons of flattened clay joined together in an asymmetric spiral to convey the impression of whirlpools. Incised hollows allowed the glaze to pool and break across the surface. The turquoise barium glaze was fired to 2300°F (1260°C) in an electric kiln.*

3 CA HOUSE

Itsue Ito *This sculptural building was created from paddled and refined coils of clay. Reflecting the peeling paintwork of Californian houses, the surface treatment and coloring denote the life within. Painted low-fire glazes, successively fired, create layers of texture that signify the passage of time.*

4 MEMORY OF HOUSE

Yasuo Hayashi *The cube forms the basis of Hayashi's art. Extruded coils were hand-squeezed together to form volumes that were then shaped into curvilinear forms. The sides create an optical illusion, drawing you into the implied deep spaces, while the white incised lines create simple bends across the dark, landscape surfaces.*

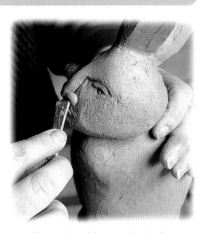

4 Form a head from a pinched out ball of clay (see pages 44–45) and model the details onto the face. Any other elements, such as arms, ears, or wings, can be made from coils or slabs of clay. Remember to score and slip any edges that are to be joined so that they adhere securely.

5 VESSEL AND PEDESTAL

David Roberts *This coil-built vessel has an overwhelming feeling of simplicity but is deceptively complex. The piece was burnished and then covered with a refractory slip, which cracked and peeled away after firing to leave shadows of crazing on the smoked surface. Rhythms of undulating patterns punctuated by random intersecting smoke lines resonate with the landscape that inspired the artist.*

TOOLS

- Wire
- Rolling pin
- Comb
- Brush
- Paddling tool
- Metal scraper
- Modeling tools

SEE ALSO
Types of ware, *pages 18–33*

HANDBUILDING

Slab building

Slab building allows the clay artist to construct both angular, sharp pieces and softer, organic forms, depending on the stiffness of the clay when assembling. Forms can be designed and constructed from pieces of thin cardboard, which can then be dismantled and used as templates for cutting out the required shapes from the clay. You can then build up the clay shapes into the required design. Using wooden templates will allow you to make numerous identical pieces. Softer work may need support during building. Crumpled newspaper can be placed inside, temporary or permanent clay stretchers can be inserted, or wooden supports can be used until the clay stiffens sufficiently to be self-supporting. Pieces of clay can be squeezed into different shapes and used to support projections until they are dry enough to stay in position.

MAKING THE SLABS

The first thing you need to do is flatten and roll out the clay into slabs of the appropriate width, length, and thickness. This can be done roughly by hand, using pushing, beating, or throwing actions, and then the flattened pieces can be rolled smooth using a rolling pin; smaller pieces of clay can usually be rolled out straight away. Alternately, cut slabs from a block of clay using a wire.

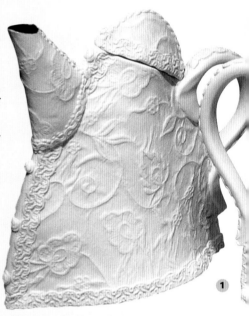

1

PUSHING OUT	BEATING	"THROWING"

  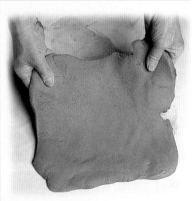

PUSHING OUT
A quick way of producing basic slabs is to push out the ball of clay with the heel of your hand. The surface of the slabs can then be smoothed using a rolling pin. A clean, canvas-covered table makes a good absorbent work surface.

BEATING
Beat large lumps of clay flat with the side of your fist, a wooden mallet, or a smooth piece of wood. Smooth the flattened surface with a rolling pin.

"THROWING"
For large slabs, "throw" the clay outward while gripping the edge nearest you, and slap it down onto the absorbent surface. Repeat this process until the required size is reached, then smooth the surface with a rolling pin.

1 PORCELAIN TEAPOTS

Gwen Bainbridge Inspired by Elizabethan costume, Bainbridge's slab-built teapots feature molded details created by taking plaster casts of textiles with appliqué designs. Sheets of rolled porcelain were then pressed into the plaster molds to give a relief surface pattern prior to building the slabs into pots.

2 COLOMBIN

Eduardo Andaluz These architectural sculptures are made from slab-built sections of heavily grogged clay, pierced with slab cylinders to give an indication of interior space and volume. Here, Andaluz is stacking the pieces into monolithic forms after firing.

2

ROLLING OUT

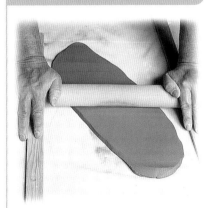

Use a rolling pin to roll out lumps of clay between two wooden guides of the same thickness to produce even slabs. Begin in the center, rolling both toward and away from yourself. Lift the slab from the table and turn it 90° after every roll. Do not force the clay or you will weaken it.

CUTTING

Cut the slabs using an adjustable wire harp. Use firm pressure to keep both sides of the harp evenly on the table surface to prevent the wire from rising as it cuts through the clay.

TOOLS

- Rolling pin
- Wooden mallet or smooth piece of wood
- Two lengths of wood of the same thickness
- Wire harp

SEE ALSO
Preparing the clay, *pages 40–42*
Supporting structures, *pages 56–59*

HANDBUILDING

FORMING THE SLABS

Every potter will have his or her own variation on how to build forms from slabs of clay, but some basic points should be adhered to. The stresses on the clay cannot be underestimated and therefore edges must be securely joined to prevent cracks from opening up. Thickness is important in the clay walls—it can be thick as long as it is even. If the cross-section varies too much from thick to thin, the clay will shrink unevenly, which is the reason most pots warp or crack during drying and firing.

1 DEPENDENT

Graham Hay *Paper clay brings new dimensions to ceramic work, both in construction and texture. Cut slabs were shaped and allowed to dry out completely before being assembled using paper clay slip as glue. The joints firm up almost immediately and the work can be fired within the hour.*

1

SLAB BOX

1 Allow the slabs to firm up a little so they are still slightly flexible but stiff enough to be self-supporting. This condition is known as leather-hard. Cutting the slabs at this stage means your cuts will be clean, not dragging soft, sticky clay. Here, cardboard templates are being used as guides for cutting the slabs.

2 Use a comb to score the edges that are to be joined and brush on some slip (see page 35). This must be done sufficiently because leather-hard clay is not sticky enough to adhere on its own. If the clay is still slightly soft, however, simply wet the edges with a sponge and firmly rub them together; this creates its own slip.

3 Firmly press the two edges together. You will see the slip spread out from the joint. Apply a slight sliding movement to help the pieces join. You will be able to feel the two pieces stick together.

2 SLABBED FORM

Jacqui Atkin The smooth, burnished surfaces of this slab-built pot form the perfect base for the dark, intricate decoration. The patterns were created with narrow lines of masking tape, then a refractory slip was applied and the piece was smoke fired in newspaper. The slip was chipped off after smoking to reveal the carbonized areas in the body.

3 RAKU BOX

Tim Proud A variety of textured slabs form the body of this small box. Constructed initially as a cube, the lid was cut off and small strips of clay added inside the box to hold the lid firmly. The piece was raku fired using transparent and copper-bearing glazes to about 1830°F (1000°C).

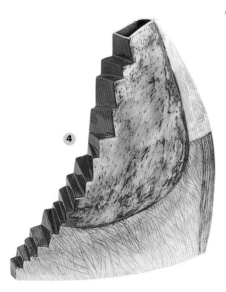

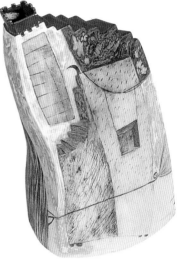

4 TALLIN

Kärt Seppel Drawn from the artist's personal experience of the narrow, twisting streets and wooden buildings of medieval Tallin in Estonia, Seppel's slab-built forms have painterly, graphic surfaces. Incised lines and scratched marks lend detail to the oxide-washed and glazed areas. The pieces were fired in an electric kiln to 2300°F (1260°C).

4 Roll out a thin coil of the same clay (see page 46) and press it down along the internal joint of the slabs. This reinforces the joint and also distributes any stresses out through the sides away from the seam. You can use a wooden tool if you find it easier.

5 Add the base and continue to construct the box, reinforcing each joint with a coil of clay as you go along. When completed, you can refine and smooth the outside of the piece with a metal scraper or add texture with various tools or stamps.

TOOLS

- Knife
- Comb
- Brush
- Sponge
- Wooden smoothing tool
- Metal scraper, texturing tools, or stamps

SEE ALSO
Slab building, *pages 50–51*

HANDBUILDING

BUILDING CURVED SHAPES

Slab techniques can be used for shapes other than angular. To build curved forms, do not allow the slabs to become leather-hard. While the clay is still soft and pliable, it can be molded into organic, curved shapes, cylinders, and even gathered into soft, textile-like folds. Use this technique to make round boxes, cups, vases, or bases for sculpture.

1 WHITE POT

Elizabeth Raeburn *The deceptively simple freedom of this piece belies an innate awareness of classical form. There is a sense of natural growth, reflecting a flower head emerging from its bud. Raeburn works exclusively in the raku technique. A copper/turquoise glaze was applied to the interior of the vessel and a resist slip on the outside produced areas of soft smoked crazing.*

2 MUSES

Steve Mattison *Made from a soft, rolled slab of clay, the cylindrical column forms the base for a sculpture. The surface was altered and distressed by paddling with smooth timber battens when the clay was leather-hard. The freely modeled figures still retain the softness of the making after firing.*

①

②

SLAB CYLINDER

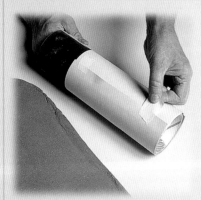

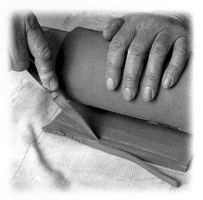

1 Use a cardboard tube, glass bottle, or other cylindrical object as a mold. Wrap and tape layers of paper around the mold so that the clay can be removed easily when you have finished.

2 Gently roll the clay around the mold. Overlap the excess length of clay, then use a knife to cut through both layers at an angle of 45°. Remove both offcuts. Score and slip both edges and smooth them together to form a tight seal (see page 35).

3 Alternately, cut one edge of the slab straight and then roll the slab around the tube. Gently press the cut edge onto the overlapping clay, then peel back. A line will be impressed into the overlapping clay. Use a knife to cut through the clay, leaving a small excess. Roll the slab around the tube again and firmly press the two edges together.

4 TWO BEAKERS

Petra Reynolds *All of Reynolds' functional domestic pottery is handbuilt and fired in a soda-vapor atmosphere in a wood-burning kiln. Made from delicate slabs of soft, folded clay, the beakers retain a sensuality that invites their use.*

3 FIGURA

Vladimir Tsivin *Concerned with the human figure, Tsivin draws inspiration from ancient Greek and Egyptian sculpture. Each piece was made from a single sheet of clay rolled between layers of fine textiles. These impressed details were augmented with mark making to create the drapery, while the figures were given form by gently pushing the clay from inside.*

TOOLS

- Cardboard tube or glass bottle
- Paper
- Sticky tape
- Knife
- Comb
- Brush
- Wooden smoothing tool

SEE ALSO
Slab building, *pages 50–51*

4 If you wish, you can leave the overlapping clay in place as a decorative feature. Simply wrap all of the clay around the mold, note where the clay overlaps, then open out the clay and score and slip the areas that overlap. Wrap the clay around the tube once again.

5 Brush some slip around the edges to ensure a clean, secure joint. Carefully slide the clay off the mold before the clay dries out. If you do not, the clay will shrink as it dries and trap the mold in place.

6 Stick the cylinder onto a flat slab of clay to form a base; remember to score and slip the edges. Trim to the required shape, smooth the joint with your finger or a wooden tool, and brush with slip. When firmly joined, attach another slab to the top of the cylinder if required.

HANDBUILDING

Supporting structures

Working with soft clay can be problematic, especially when producing large pieces where the weight of the growing form can cause the clay to squash down, distorting the shapes or even collapsing the work. There are three main ways in which clay can be supported during building to alleviate such problems. Slabs can be stiffened over preformed shapes or molds until they are sufficiently stable to be relatively self-supporting; soft clay can be worked using temporary supports of wood or clay; or clay structures can be built into the piece to support it during drying and firing. The method you choose will depend on the type of work you are making and the size of the pieces.

FIGURATIVE WORK

Many artists have developed their own techniques to suit their particular way of working. Figurative work is often the most problematic, especially where arms or legs are fine and protrude from the body. With mass-produced figurines, arms are usually to be found against the body or

1

BAMBOO SKEWERS

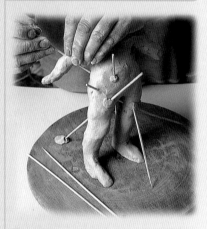

Figurative work often requires support while drying, especially if arms are outstretched or legs are thin. Here, bamboo skewers are pierced through the clay to support the object in many directions. When stable enough to be freestanding, the skewers can be removed and the holes filled with clay.

CLAY AND STICKS

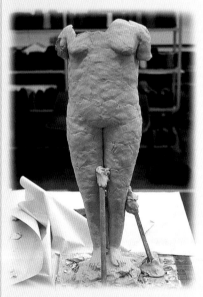

Lumps of clay are used to hold thin sticks against the surface of this pinched porcelain figure. As the figure dries and shrinks, the lumps of clay will also shrink to prevent the rigid wooden supports from distorting the body.

WOODEN DOWEL

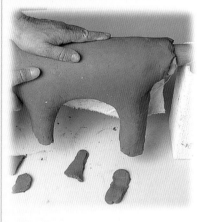

A thick wooden dowel is suspended between a pair of bricks to provide support for the slabbed body of this animal sculpture. The legs and belly of the piece can still be worked on until it is firm enough to stand by itself. The support can then be slid out and the neck and rear closed.

touching in several places for strength. More expressive ways of working require more inventive methods of support. Small sticks and skewers can be used to hold delicate pieces while drying or, with larger work, internal supports and large pieces of timber may be needed. These wooden pieces should be removed before firing and any holes in the clay repaired.

1 VESSEL

Jim Robison This slabbed vessel form was made from several pieces of clay pressed together in curved molds. The central section was made from small pieces of clay decorated with slip using textile stencils. The two sides were then joined together and added to the base. Robison's love of the countryside and rock formations are evident in this highly textural piece.

TOOLS
- Bamboo skewers
- Thin wooden sticks
- Thick wooden dowel
- Pair of bricks
- Wooden boards
- Metal frames
- Lengths of timber
- Molds, newspaper, or cardboard supports

2 ELEMENTAL CONCERNS

Jim Robison This large sculpture, designed for the entrance to a hospital, consists of three tall columns, each made from three slab-built sections formed in concave wooden molds. Here, the artist is checking that the sections fit together accurately after firing.

INTEGRAL SUPPORTS

These large coiled figures have integral clay supports coiled into the interior of the pieces as they are being built. The supports add strength to the figures and prevent the bodies from distorting and the heads from sagging at high firing temperatures.

BOARDS AND FRAMES

These 7 ft. (2 m) high minotaur figures are made in sections. The legs are standing on the floor and the top section of the bodies are supported above the legs on wooden boards lying across metal frames, allowing the sculptor to see the whole form of the figures as they are constructed. Without the boards, the weight of the upper body would collapse the legs. Lengths of timber stop the heads from sagging until dry.

MOLDS

Large slabs are laid into curved molds, made from masonite and timber, until the clay stiffens and becomes leather-hard prior to assembling the slabs into structures. For smaller slabs, pieces of newspaper or rolled cardboard supports could hold up the walls temporarily while drying.

HANDBUILDING

HIGH-RELIEF WORK

High-relief panels can require considerable support from inside during construction for a number of reasons. First, working on panels can be an ongoing process over a period of time and the clay needs to be kept reasonably soft to join pieces together. As a result, it is not always possible to dry areas so that they are self-supporting and therefore supports are needed to keep the soft clay in the required shape. Another important reason is that large panels are often constructed in sections for easy transportation and installation, with the edges of the various pieces often being considerably raised from the base. These require supporting walls to keep them at the correct height and ensure that the pieces can be butted against each other accurately when they are eventually assembled. Networks of ribs can be used to support the top surface of the panel, providing depth without adding excessive weight.

CAREFUL PLANNING

You need to have a clear idea of the shape, relief areas, and separate sections that will be needed before you start work. It is important to try to calculate the best places for the supporting network of slabs before you start because it can be difficult to adjust later. Start by making full-size color drawings of the piece, then draw smaller sketches indicating the divisions

TOOLS
- Knife
- Comb
- Brush
- Newspaper
- Needle
- Wire mesh

SEE ALSO
Slab building, *pages 50–51*

SUPPORTING A HIGH-RELIEF PANEL

1 These sketches show how a high-relief panel of a table setting will be divided into sections for ease of making and fitting into the kiln. They also indicate which areas will be raised from the base clay. The initial color drawing is the actual size of the panel. From this life-size sketch, templates can be cut for the slabs of clay.

2 Construct a network of slabs to support the raised areas of the panel. Although they will not be seen on completion, joints must still be neat and firmly secured so that the panel will not crack or distort during drying and firing (see page 35). Use coils of clay to secure the joints, smoothing them down with your finger.

3 Cut pre-stiffened slabs of flat clay and attach them to the supporting network of walls, scoring and slipping the edges to give a firm joint. Cut the edges of the slab where needed to give a clean fit.

MURAL (DETAIL)

Sandor Kecskeméti *This mural is made from many interlocking parts of relief-built clay, underpinned with a structure of supporting clay walls. Each of the surfaces was formed by molding the soft clay slabs over parts of the artist's body—his knees, elbows, shoulders, and arms—to create these gently undulating shapes. Dry ash glazes and smoked areas give the impression of a natural landscape.*

of the panel and the areas that are to be constructed in high relief. This process identifies the areas that will need support while making, drying, and firing to ensure that the pieces do not bend or sag and, with distortion, no longer fit the other sections of the panel. Crumpled newspaper can be used to support small areas while drying; they will burn out during firing to leave the work hollow. Make sure the kiln is well-ventilated when firing paper-supported clay to ensure adequate dispersal of smoke.

4 Use crumpled pieces of newspaper to support small slabs of soft clay. Here, newspaper is used to support the leaves of the plant in the still-life panel. Make a small pinhole in the slabs so that the air can escape when the newspaper burns out during firing.

5 To support the slabs for the folds of cloth on this panel, pieces of fine wire mesh have been squashed into undulating shapes. The wire can be bent to form a variety of shapes to support the clay while it dries. Put a thin sheet of paper on the wire before draping the clay onto it to make it easier to release the metal later.

6 Once the folded clay has stiffened, carefully remove it from the wire support. It will now be easier to handle as you cut and join it to the panel. Trim the underlying clay supports to the required heights to fit the folds.

Handbuilt ceramics

Handbuilding techniques can be used individually or in combination with other methods to produce highly original ceramic pieces. The tactile nature of handbuilding gives the clay artist the widest scope for free expression.

4 STILL LIFE WITH DOGS

Karen Koblitz Made from low-fire clay, the thrown vase and bowl and coiled and pinched fruits sit on a slab base impressed with linoleum block prints. Designs were carved into the surfaces and decorated with underglaze colors before bisque firing. A transparent glaze was then applied and the piece was fired in an electric kiln.

5 ORANGE GROVE ON A BLUE NIGHT

Philip Cornelius The artist has pioneered his own technique, known as "thin ware." This intricate vessel form was constructed from sheets of wire-cut, almost paper thin, porcelain. Such thin sheets dry out quickly, so Cornelius has to work with speed to assemble them while still plastic enough to bend into shape.

1 UNTITLED TRIPTYCH

Vaclav Serák Large slabs of clay provide the canvas for modeled, slabbed, and thrown additional elements. The dynamism of this wall piece comes from the immediacy of the artist's mark making—pressing, pushing, scratching, and slashing at the soft clay. The painterly applications of stains, commercial colors, and glazes enhance the impression of the movement of light across the surface.

2 SHELL III

Edita Rydhag Using white-firing stoneware clay, Rydhag has emphasized the form of this handbuilt shell by dramatically increasing its scale.

3 CURRACH VESSEL ON STAND

Billy Adams This geological piece reflects the fractured rocks of harsh coastlines. Multiple firings give depth of color to the surfaces and mimic the processes of the earth's formation.

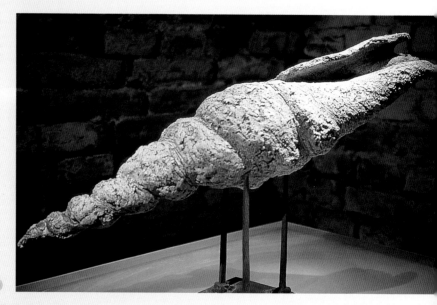

3

4

5

6 THE VIEW WITH UTUWA

Shinji Otani *Thrown tea bowls placed on a paddled slab shelf maintain a tension between the functional and the sculptural, the traditional and the experimental. Carved squares on the surface are filled with commercially manufactured porcelain mosaic tiles. The underside of the 3 ft. (1 m) wide, 1 in. (2.5 cm) thick shelf is grooved to prevent warping and supported on clay feet that were paddled into random shapes.*

6

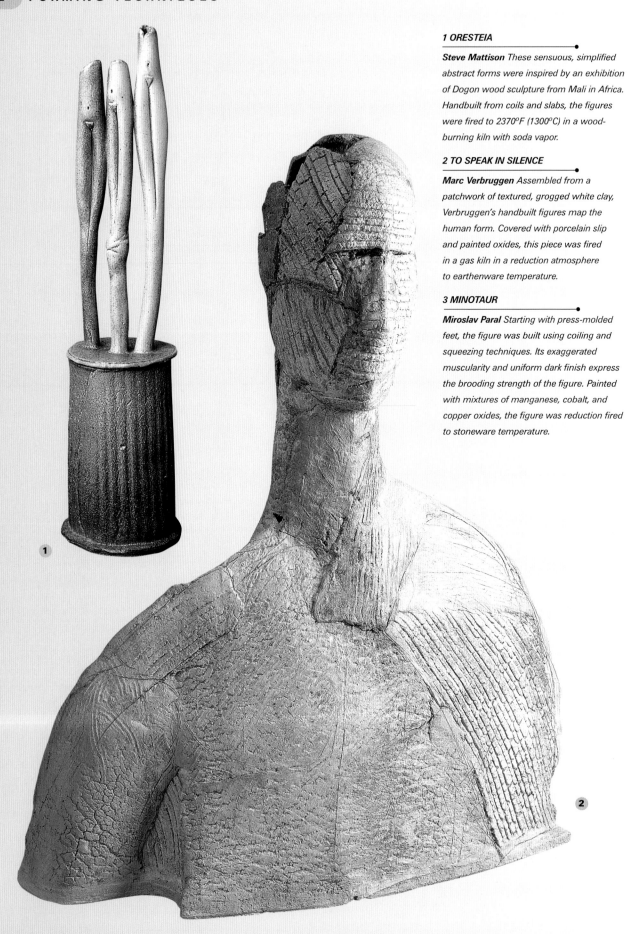

1 ORESTEIA

Steve Mattison These sensuous, simplified abstract forms were inspired by an exhibition of Dogon wood sculpture from Mali in Africa. Handbuilt from coils and slabs, the figures were fired to 2370°F (1300°C) in a wood-burning kiln with soda vapor.

2 TO SPEAK IN SILENCE

Marc Verbruggen Assembled from a patchwork of textured, grogged white clay, Verbruggen's handbuilt figures map the human form. Covered with porcelain slip and painted oxides, this piece was fired in a gas kiln in a reduction atmosphere to earthenware temperature.

3 MINOTAUR

Miroslav Paral Starting with press-molded feet, the figure was built using coiling and squeezing techniques. Its exaggerated muscularity and uniform dark finish express the brooding strength of the figure. Painted with mixtures of manganese, cobalt, and copper oxides, the figure was reduction fired to stoneware temperature.

4 MINOTAURUS

Imre Schrammel This figure is formed with such sensitivity that it loses nothing of the softness of raw clay. Fired in raku and smoked in mixtures of straw and sand to control subtle areas of reduction, this vulnerable, godlike creature is both human and monumental in scale.

5 THE KISS

Jolanta Kvasyte These complicated structures were built using pellets of porcelain pressed flat between the artist's fingers. Using historic and religious iconography, the narrative of the composition develops fully with the exquisite on-glaze enamel and luster painting.

6 COME UP AND SEE ME SOMETIME

Ian Gregory Sitting on top of a hollow block of clay, this burlesque figure was squeezed and freely modeled from grogged clay.

Throwing

Throwing on the potter's wheel requires practice, patience, and concentration. Watching professional potters throw piece after piece can make this technique seem deceptively easy, but the control and sensitivity required to use this quick-forming method take time to acquire.

EARLY WHEELS

The potter's wheel first appeared about 5,000 years ago in Egypt, the Middle East, and Asia. The heavy wheelheads were usually made of stone or wood and were spun by inserting a stick in a hole at the top of the wheel and turning it. In certain areas of the Mediterranean, assistants turned the wheels with ropes or, lying on their backs on the ground, with their feet. The potter's wheel evolved over the years into a more comfortable and easy-to-operate system, with the wheelhead raised so that the potter could sit instead of squat. A long shaft joined the wheelhead to a heavy flywheel at ground level. A small stick placed in a hole, again on the wheelhead, allowed the wheel to be rotated.

MODERN WHEELS

Today, the potter's wheel is a highly controllable, sophisticated electronic device, allowing much larger pots to be made by one person, who can accelerate or decelerate the wheel by the touch of a foot pedal or lever. However, many potters still prefer to use a momentum or kick wheel

BASIC TOOL KIT

Pottery suppliers sell a vast array of tools, and although it is tempting to buy a whole range, you will probably find that you never use some of them. Many potters make their own tools or adapt manufactured ones to suit their particular needs. A good basic tool kit for throwers includes:

*1 **Throwing ribs**, usually made of wood or plastic, to help pull up the walls of large pots and compact the centers of plates.*

*2 **Sponges** for mopping up water and for applying water to the rims of pots during throwing. A sponge on a stick is useful for soaking up water from inside the bottom of tall pots.*

*3 **Metal scrapers and rubber ribs** for cleaning slurry off the surfaces of pots before lifting them off the wheel and for scraping pots when trimming.*

*4 **Wires** held between wooden toggles for cutting pots from the wheelhead and for faceting. Several strands twisted together are best. Use strands of thick wire wound together to create deep decorative marks.*

*5 **Calipers** for measuring diameters when making multiple-part pots and to ensure that lids fit.*

*6 **A potter's needle** for testing the thickness of bases during throwing, for cutting the rim of the pot to make it even, and for popping any air bubbles that wedging and kneading have failed to remove.*

*7 **Metal trimming tools** for use during any finishing process. These can be looped wire tools or bent metal ones with a honed edge.*

because it gives a more individual, spontaneous quality to the work. The major difference in operation is that with momentum wheels the creation of the spin is a separate action to the throwing. The kicking propels the wheel, followed by the throwing. The throwing is therefore done as the wheel decelerates, and the pressure of the hands on the clay makes the wheel slow even more. With an electric wheel, the speed of the wheel can increase even if the pressure of the potter's hands becomes greater, or if working with a heavier weight of clay.

CLAY PREPARATION

The consistency and softness of the clay you use for throwing is more important than with any other making method. The clay should be wedged and kneaded sufficiently to homogenize all the particles and differences in hardness and to remove any air bubbles (see pages 40–41). If the clay is too soft, it can be centered more easily on the wheelhead but it will lose its strength as you pull it up to form the walls of your pot. If the clay is too hard, you will need to apply greater pressure to shape the clay and this can strain the walls of the pot, leading to twisting, warping, and cracking. It is advisable to start with softer clay until you are more confident and have mastered the initial centering technique, progressing to stiffer clay for taller pieces. During throwing, the clay should slide easily through your fingers and not stick or drag, so you need to use water or slip for lubrication. However, try to keep it to a minimum because clay becomes soft and flabby if overwatered.

HAND SHAPING

The hands are the potter's most significant tools for throwing. They control and center the clay, support it against the centrifugal forces, and most importantly, shape the pottery. Almost every part of the hands is used during the throwing process, each hand position producing different results.

1 The heel of the hand is used mainly during centering. Apply direct downward and inward pressure to control the spinning clay and to push it into the center of the wheel.

2 Knuckles are used to lift the walls of the pot from the lump of clay at the base. Known as "knuckling up," this technique involves pressing the clay inward with the knuckle of the forefinger of a clenched fist and lifting a weight of clay, thereby thinning and raising the pot. When compacting and flattening the bases of plates and platters, downward pressure with the knuckles is also used.

3 Fingertips are incredibly sensitive and are used for secondary thinning of the pot after knuckling up. Firm but gentle pressure with the fingertips is used to shape and refine the form of the pot.

4 The thumb joint is used to keep the top of pots even and level by crooking it over the rim and exerting a slight downward pressure.

5 Thumbs are used for opening up the spinning clay to begin forming the pot. The end of the thumb can also be used to form the rims and flanges of many pots.

6 The palm of the hand is used for applying an even downward pressure when centering clay on the wheel. The palm is also used when flattening the bases of plates.

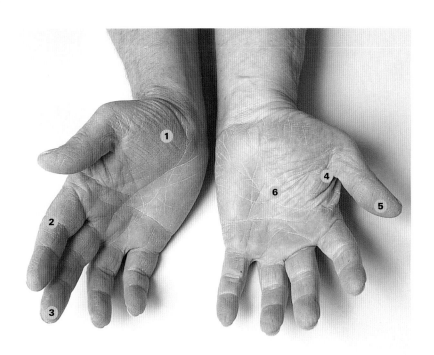

THROWING

Centering

Centering is the process used to ensure that the ball of clay is positioned in the exact center of the wheelhead. This technique must be mastered if you are to throw pots successfully. There are many ways of centering the clay, but the most common involves putting pressure on the clay from one side against the centrifugal force of the spinning wheel. Whatever method you use, the principle of pressure is the same—position your hands so that the centering pressure is leaning into the direction of the wheel. If your wheel turns counterclockwise (the most usual), your hands should be at about the 8 o'clock position to push downward. The method illustrated here will always center your clay, no matter how much you are using.

BODY POSITION

The position of your body is very important. Your back, shoulders, and neck should be rigid and your upper arms firm and tucked against your sides (this will support your forearms so they are not doing all the work). The clay should be level with your lap and your body should be at a height over the wheel to give stability. At times when more pressure is needed, lock your hands together to provide extra support. You will soon learn how to judge the amount of pressure needed for successful centering.

1

CENTERING

1 The wheelhead needs to be damp to help the clay adhere, so wipe it with a damp sponge if it is dry. Take care not to wet the wheel too much or the clay will slide off as the wheel gathers speed.

2 Firmly slam the ball of clay down onto the wheelhead, using both hands to prevent the clay from splaying outward too much. Apply a slight backward and forward movement with your hands to see if the clay is sticking sufficiently. If it is too slippy, the wheel is too wet, so wipe off some of the moisture.

3 Set the wheel spinning. When it reaches its fastest speed, place the palms of your hands on opposite sides of the clay. Hold your hands steady for a few turns, then begin to squeeze inward slightly and lift your hands upward. The clay will rise into a cone shape.

TIME AND SPEED

Do not spend too long centering the clay or you will overwork it, making it tired and unable to expand well. Good centering not only means the clay is circular on the wheel but also that the clay particles have been aligned throughout the lump for easier throwing. During the initial centering process, the wheel needs to be spinning at speed, slowing down as you open up the clay and begin to lift the walls of the pot.

1 JUG AND BAGUETTE POT

Martin Everson-Davis *Accurate centering and speed control is essential to successful throwing, especially when undertaking large pieces such as these terra-cotta pots. Both pieces have a transparent glaze on the inside, and a copper slip was applied over the rim of the jug before bisque firing to color the glaze.*

2 TALL LEAF VASE

Cathi Jefferson *The throwing rings on the surface of this porcelain vase add texture and are emphasized by the effects of the soda glazing. Working thinly with fine porcelain, the clay needs to be well centered.*

2

TOOLS
- Wheel
- Sponge

SEE ALSO
Preparing the clay, *pages 40–42*
Throwing, *pages 64–65*

4 When the cone is completed, start to press down on the clay with your thumb. As the mound of clay becomes wider, move your whole hand over the top of it and press down. Use your other hand to give extra support to both the clay and the hand that is pressing down. Lean in to give added pressure.

5 As the cone compacts, push down with the side of one hand while your other hand pushes inward. The combination of both hands squeezing in these two directions will push the clay into the center of the wheel.

6 Run your fingers lightly across the top of the clay; you will easily feel the center point. Supporting the clay with one hand on the outside, begin to press downward with the fingers of your other hand to open up the clay. Lock your hands together for greater stability.

THROWING

Throwing a cylinder

The starting point for all tall pots is the cylinder; most other shapes are variations of it. If you intend to adapt the cylinder into another shape, try to leave the clay thicker in those areas that will be stretched or pulled. As with any pottery-making technique, there are no set rules and, with experience, you will find methods and variations that you prefer. As you open up the clay and lift the pot, the wheel should be turning more slowly than when you centered the clay. The effects of centrifugal force increase as pots get taller and thinner, so keep reducing the speed or the clay will be flung outward and off the wheel. In the final stages of shaping, the wheel should be only just turning.

1 LIDDED JARS

Chris Keenan *These refined cylindrical vessels were thrown using a fine porcelain body. They were reduction fired in a propane gas kiln to 2300°F (1260°C). A fine line of contrasting tenmoku glaze meanders around the forms.*

BASIC CYLINDER

1 Push the fingers of one hand down into the centered mass of clay and slowly pull outward. Support the wall of clay with your other hand and lock your hands together for stability. Take care not to push down too far. Until you become more experienced at gauging the thickness, insert a needle to measure the depth of the clay base.

2 Lift the roll of clay between your fingers and thumb to start raising the walls of the cylinder. Use the palm of your other hand to help push up the clay and support the walls so that they do not expand outward too far.

3 With your supporting hand wrapped around the clay, the cylinder will become narrower as it grows upward. This collaring action helps to counteract the centrifugal force of the wheel. Apply downward pressure with the crook of your other thumb to keep the top of the pot level.

2 OVAL VASES

Joanna Howells *This series of celadon-glazed porcelain cylinders have a restrained quality that encourages contemplation. Thrown on the wheel, they were gently pushed into oval forms. A slight blush of reduction gives the pieces additional interest.*

TOOLS
- Wheel
- Needle
- Wire

SEE ALSO
Preparing the clay, *pages 40–42*
Throwing, *pages 64–65*
Centering, *pages 66–67*

4 With the fingertips of one hand on the inside of the pot and the knuckle of the forefinger of your other hand on the outside, begin to lift the clay. Position your knuckle slightly lower than the fingers inside the pot and press it inward along the wheelhead to gather up a roll of clay.

5 Lift the roll of clay upward in a smooth motion, keeping the pressure even. Pulling up too fast will stretch the clay and cause it to tear. The clay will thin as the pot increases in height. If you squeeze too hard, you will thin the wall too much and the pot will twist or collapse.

6 Repeat the lifting process to thin the walls again and pull the pot taller. Use the final lift to refine the shape and rim, making sure that the clay is of an even thickness. It is always best to lift and shape your pots gradually. When finished, use a wire to cut the pot from the wheelhead.

THROWING

Throwing a pitcher

The pitcher presents the potter with a number of design decisions, all of which affect the practicality of the vessel. Should the body be wider at the base like strong medieval pitchers, or tall and elegant like the ancient pouring vessels from the Middle East? Where will the handle be attached: high up for comfort and stability, or elsewhere for aesthetic reasons? Will the spout have a throat running down the side of the pot or will it begin high up at the rim?

FUNCTIONAL CONSIDERATIONS

We all use pitchers but rarely stop to think about how they function. Handles are usually placed directly opposite the lip, but in certain countries the handle is positioned at 90° to the lip and the pitcher's contents are poured using a twisting movement of the wrist. Handles can be pulled for comfort or added as a cut slab or a rolled coil (see pages 84–85). The function of the object and its comfort for the user must be major considerations when making a pitcher.

1

TALL PITCHER

1 Start by making a basic cylinder shape (see pages 68–69). Narrow the cylinder slightly toward the neck by exerting inward pressure with your supporting hand. After each lift, use your fingers to compress the rim inward and downward at the same time to keep it level.

2 Lift the clay once again to thin the walls of the pitcher and increase its height. The wheel should be turning slowly at this point or it will be difficult to form the neck.

3 Leave the rim slightly thicker than the rest of the walls to give the pitcher a visually bold edge and also to have clay from which to pull the lip.

1 FACETED JUG

David Frith This tall pitcher has been faceted using a cheese wire; the walls of the cylinder were thrown slightly thicker than required for the finished pot to allow for the depth of the cut. A final throwing with pressure only from the inside gave the pot its finished shape. This robust piece has all the strength and style of early European pitchers and is glazed on the inside with a green celadon glaze, the flashing from wood firing decorating the outside.

2 SALT-GLAZED JUG

Michael Casson The neck of this pitcher was thrown separately and added when the wide belly was firm enough to support the weight. The sudden change of direction in the clay is highlighted by a series of incised circles. The lip was pulled and a bold handle applied. Handles should always be thicker than you imagine in order to support the weight of both the pot and its contents. The decoration was created with a finger wiped through wet slip and the finished jug was salt glazed in a wood-fired kiln.

TOOLS
- Wheel
- Wire

SEE ALSO
Preparing the clay, *pages 40–42*
Throwing, *pages 64–65*
Centering, *pages 66–67*

4 Give the rim area a final shaping by collaring. Collaring is achieved by using three points of pressure on the rotating clay. Use your fingers to hold the clay in place at two points at the front of the cylinder. Use your thumbs, held together, to provide the third point of contact. Squeeze gently to narrow the opening.

5 Pinch the beginning of the lip using a gentle pressure between the knuckle of your forefinger on the outside and your thumb on the inside. Try not to thin the clay too much.

6 Lift the edges of the lip upward with two fingers of one hand. Meanwhile, push the forefinger of your other hand gently downward in the center of the lip to make it rounded and give it a slight throat. The aim is to achieve a smooth channel down which the liquid will flow freely. Use a wire to cut the finished pitcher from the wheelhead.

Throwing a bowl

The bowl is a universal pottery form and every culture has its own variation on shape and function. Whichever shape you wish to make, it is always a good idea to visualize the finished form, either by keeping a clear image of it in your head while you throw or sketching your ideas on paper. Throwing the bowl on a bat makes removing the pot from the wheelhead much easier (see page 74). This is especially important when you are throwing fine porcelain bowls.

①

SHAPING TECHNIQUES

Unlike pulling up the walls of a tall pot, the walls of a bowl are progressively increased in width and height simultaneously. As you begin to widen out your bowl, it will become increasingly difficult to control the clay because gravity will push it down onto the wheelhead. It is easier to widen a shape from a taller form than to close a form once it has been widened too much. Keep the final shaping of the profile until the end of your throwing and pay more attention to the inside than the outside, because the latter can be trimmed afterwards.

1 FOOTED PORCELAIN BOWL

Margaret Frith Throwing porcelain is more difficult than most clays. This wood-fired pedestal bowl shows an accomplished integration of form and decoration. The height and width of the foot relate well to the form of the bowl, while the swirling decoration of glazes, brushwork, and wood ash create movement across the surface.

SHALLOW BOWL

1 Center the clay and open it out to the desired width. Run your fingers back and forth across the base to compact the clay and prevent the base from cracking as it dries. Begin to lift the walls in the same way as a cylinder (see pages 68–69), but do it with a gentle outward rather than vertical movement.

2 Take your time and make sure the inside shape is a smooth, concave hollow. Finish the inside curve, then pull up the walls to a taller shape, tapering toward the rim. Do not open the bowl too wide at this stage—it is always better to work gradually.

3 Widen the bowl to its final diameter and refine the rim to a suitable thickness. The rim should not be too thin and your movements must be smooth because the slightest jerk will be magnified on the pot. The walls should be thicker near the base to give support to the rim.

TOOLS

- Wheel
- Throwing bat
- Rubber rib
- Wire
- Comb
- Brush

2 WHITE RAKU BOWL

Steve Mattison *This large bowl was thrown from a white-firing clay with 30 percent molochite added to increase its strength. This helps the clay to withstand the stresses of the rapid raku firing technique and sudden cooling. Narrow masking tape was used to create the decorative lines. The post-firing reduction in sawdust blackened these resist lines and smoked the crazing in the glaze.*

3 MIXING BOWLS

Joe Finch *These two thrown mixing bowls show strength and simplicity of form, making them superbly functional pots, each having a pulled lip for easy pouring. They were raw glazed on the inside and fired in a wood kiln to 2390ºF (1310ºC) for 12 hours.*

4 Use a rubber rib to smooth and compact the inside and outside of the bowl. This will also remove any residual slurry, which is important because any water left in the pot would cause cracks to appear at the base.

5 When leather-hard, use a wire to cut the bowl from its bat and invert it on the wheel to trim a footring (see pages 90–93). Alternately, trim the base of the bowl smooth and attach a separate ring, as shown here. The thrown ring should be attached as near the center as possible, scoring and slipping it into place (see page 35).

6 Raise and thin the walls of the ring to the required height in the same way as you would raise the walls of a cylinder. When the ring is stiff enough to support the weight of the bowl, turn the bowl right way up and allow to dry.

SEE ALSO

Preparing the clay, *pages 40–42*
Throwing, *pages 64–65*
Centering, *pages 66–67*

THROWING

Throwing a plate

While most pottery can be thrown directly on the wheelhead, it is best to throw plates on a removable bat. If you throw directly on the wheel, you may distort the plate when removing it, whereas it can be set aside on the bat and allowed to harden until it is stiff enough to handle. A bat can be secured to the wheelhead temporarily with a pad of soft clay, but usually the metal wheelhead is drilled and spigots bolted through it into holes in the bat. This means bats can be removed and replaced in exactly the same place, and always in center.

SHAPING TECHNIQUES

Plates must to be thrown with wide bases that are thick enough for any trimming that is needed on the underside when the clay has stiffened. Most of the shaping involves making the base wide enough and creating a shallow curved face from the center of the plate to the rim. After trimming, the base should be about the same thickness as the rim of the plate. If it is too thick, it may crack.

1 RIM-CUT PLATE

David Frith *This large plate was altered after throwing. The edge was cut in four places and the soft clay overlapped and rejoined to form a petal-like rim. Brushed wax decoration over a celadon glaze, overglazed with khaki, gives a deep richness to this robust piece.*

2 PLATE

John Glick *Lavish use of multiple glazes, resists, and glaze painting gives this plate a strong sense of movement and vibrancy, while at the same time echoing the peaceful atmosphere of Chinese and Japanese landscapes. The plate was reduction fired to stoneware temperatures.*

ATTACHING A BAT

1 Flatten a pad of soft clay on the wheelhead and use your fingers to groove it with concentric circles to help create suction when the bat is applied. Throwing bats can be made of bisque-fired disks of clay, commercial wall tiles, but more commonly thin plywood. They are usually round but may also be other shapes.

2 Dampen the underside of the bat and place it onto the clay pad. Center the bat and use your fist to stick it to the clay, keeping the bat flat on the wheelhead. Alternately, screw the bat in place through holes in the wheelhead.

BASIC PLATE

1 With the side of your hand, press down on a centered lump of clay so that the clay splays out wider across the bat. Keep widening evenly until the desired size is reached.

SEE ALSO
Preparing the clay, *pages 40–42*
Throwing, *pages 64–65*
Centering, *pages 66–67*

1

2

TOOLS
- *Wheel*
- *Throwing bat*
- *Throwing rib*
- *Needle*
- *Knife or wooden tool*
- *Wire*

2 Refine and flatten the interior curve with your fingertips or a throwing rib. This also compacts the base to stop cracks from forming. You can gauge the thickness of the base with a needle if you are in doubt. Make sure you have enough clay left to form the walls, using your fingertips on the inside and outside.

3 Throw the rim using the excess clay at the edge of the plate. Refine the change from the base of the plate to the rim by gently pressing a fingertip inside the plate at this point. Hold the rim between the thumb and forefinger of your other hand to refine and round its shape.

4 Use a throwing rib to refine the shape of the plate and clean off any slurry. Use a knife or wooden tool to clean the underside and lift the bat from the wheel. When the clay has stiffened, use a wire to remove the plate from the bat and invert it onto the wheel ready for trimming the footring (see pages 90–93).

THROWING

Throwing a platter

Beautifully made tableware can be visually exciting objects in their own right as well as have practical uses in domestic situations. Nothing enhances a dining table more than serving food from handmade platters, especially when the decoration complements the colors of the food. When throwing large platters, the process is basically the same as for plates but you need to use a greater quantity of clay and wider bats. In the example shown here, a faceted rim is created for added interest.

TOOLS

- *Wheel*
- *Throwing bat*
- *Throwing rib*
- *Needle*
- *Wire*
- *Knife or wooden tool*

COUNTRY POTTERY

Atilla Albert *In this photograph, the edge of a thrown platter is being decorated by thumb-pressed marks to produce a "pie crust" rim. Albert makes traditional functional pottery in Magyarszombatfa, a small pottery village in southwestern Hungary. Using locally dug clays and a contrasting slip decoration, his pots are all suitable for baking.*

FACETED PLATTER

1 Throw and open out a wider and thicker version of a plate, leaving the rim considerably thicker (see pages 74–75). With a taut wire, cut equal facets from the rim in an upward motion, taking care not to cut through the side completely. Start by cutting opposite sides to make sure they are evenly spaced.

2 Once the cuts have been made, continue throwing the rim of the platter. Use the fingers of one hand inside the rim to ease it outward, while your other hand supports the rim on the outside.

3 Continue throwing the rim until it reaches the desired width. The edge will still retain the cut facets but will become softer as the rim opens out to its full extent. Finish the platter in the same way as a plate.

SEE ALSO
Preparing the clay, *pages 40–42*
Throwing, *pages 64–65*
Centering, *pages 66–67*

Throwing off the hump

Throwing a series of pots from a large lump of clay is known as throwing off the hump or stack throwing. This is a valuable technique for production batches of small items, but it does require practice. Cups, small dishes, and tea bowls are usually thrown in this way because it would be too time-consuming to center a small lump of clay for each pot. The principle is that a large lump of clay is roughly centered and then each pot is thrown from the top of it, accurately centering the top section quickly for each pot.

THROWN TEA BOWLS

1 Cathi Jefferson Paddled porcelain tea bowl, salt glazed and wood fired.

2 Mike Dodd Faceted tea bowl, ash glazed and wood fired.

3 Patrick Sargent Stoneware tea bowl, fired in an anagama kiln.

4 Frederick Olsen Random-faceted porcelain tea bowl, salt fired.

5 John Maltby Tea bowl with on-glaze enamel decoration.

6 Steve Mattison White clay tea bowl, raku fired.

7 John Pollex Squared earthenware tea bowl, slip decorated.

TOOLS
- *Wheel*
- *Rib or wooden tool*
- *Wire*

TEA BOWL

1 Center a large piece of clay and form it into a tall cone. Slightly pull up and center a large knob of clay at the top of the cone.

2 Supporting the underside of the knob with one hand, press the thumb of your other hand down into the clay. Lift and thin out the knob of clay into the required shape—here, a tea bowl shape. Refine it with a rib or wooden tool.

3 Use a wire to cut the bowl from the hump of clay and set it aside until it is leather-hard and ready for trimming (see pages 90–93). Recenter the top of the hump and throw the next bowl until the clay is used up.

SEE ALSO
Preparing the clay, *pages 40–42*
Throwing, *pages 64–65*
Centering, *pages 66–67*

THROWING

Making a teapot

The teapot is the greatest challenge to the potter because it involves lots of different techniques to make the various elements—pots, lids, spouts, handles, flanges, and footrings. All of the components should be completed during the same session so that they dry together. This reduces the danger of cracking at the joints. A potter working in series would perhaps throw half a dozen teapot bodies, then throw the lids and spouts. Handles are usually made later because they are applied slightly softer for easier working.

DESIGN AND FUNCTION

Making a teapot gives the potter a number of design challenges. Where should the handle be placed? How big will it be? What shape should the spout be? Will all the elements be thrown or should the teapot have a slab-built lid or a bamboo handle? All of these aesthetic factors must be considered. Teapots must also possess certain attributes in order to be functional. The pot must be thick enough to retain the heat of the water and to withstand sudden changes in temperature. It must have an integrated strainer to catch tea leaves at the spout, and the handle should be comfortable to use.

1 TEAPOT

Terry Bell-Hughes This is an elegant and generously sized thrown teapot. The handle was made by pulling a twisted loop of wire through a lump of clay. Sgraffito lines incised through brushmarked slips enrich the surface.

2 TWO TEAPOTS

Morgen Hall These pots are made from smooth red earthenware clay with cobalt slip decoration. After being bisque fired to 1830°F (1000°C), a light rutile stain was sponged over a white tin glaze and fired to 2050°F (1120°C). The rutile gives a mottled depth to the surface that contrasts well with the precise stenciled shapes. Trailed spots of cobalt slip decorate the spouts and handles.

MAKING THE ELEMENTS

1 Pull up a slightly narrowing cylinder from a centered ball of clay (see pages 68–69). Using the crook of your thumb, press down gently on the rim to keep it level, supporting the clay with your other hand.

2 Establish the flange on which the lid will sit by splitting the rim and pushing it slightly down with your fingertips. Doing this now ensures that you will always have enough clay to form a suitably sized flange.

3 Begin to "belly out" the teapot body by putting one hand inside and applying pressure with your fingers from the inside. Meanwhile, lift the clay on the outside with the knuckle of your other forefinger.

SEE ALSO
Preparing the clay, *pages 40–42*
Throwing, *pages 64–65*
Centering, *pages 66–67*

TOOLS
- Wheel
- Sponge
- Wire
- Calipers
- Knife
- Surform
- Awl
- Comb
- Brush

4 When the body is the shape you require, refine the flange and clean off any slurry with a sponge. Cut the teapot from the wheel with a wire and allow it to stiffen slightly.

5 Measure the diameter of the opening with a pair of calipers. Make sure that you measure the full opening, including the flange on which the lid will sit. This is important so that you can make the lid accurately.

6 Center a lump of clay and throw the lid and knob (see pages 83 and 85). The external diameter of the lid should be measured with the other end of the calipers. Throw a spout (see page 82). Allow all the components to stiffen until they are leather-hard.

THROWING

ASSEMBLING THE TEAPOT

1 Cut the base of the leather-hard spout at the desired angle. Try various angles for aesthetic appeal, but the tip of the spout must always be above the level of the liquid. As a guide, try to keep the tip of the spout level with the rim of the body.

2 Place the spout on the body of the teapot and use the tip of your knife to draw around it so that you know the exact area to work for the next stage.

3 Shave the marked area flat using a surform or other suitable tool. Be careful not to cut too deep and go through the side of the pot.

4 Use an awl or similar tool to punch a series of holes into the flattened area to strain the tea leaves. Do not make the holes too big or leaves will escape—it is better to have a series of narrow holes than a few large ones. Make sure you support the wall on the inside while you do this or it could give way.

5 Secure the spout to the body by scoring and slipping the clay around the edge of the spout and the appropriate area on the pot (see page 35). Press it into position. Clean around the joint and use your fingertip to blend the overlapping clay together.

6 Pull a handle and firmly attach the wider end to the teapot body (see pages 84–85). Try to position it as high up and tucked into the rim overhang as possible. Smooth the body and handle together well and reinforce with small coils around the joint.

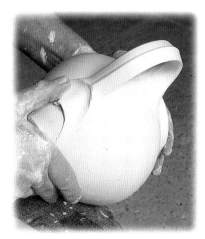

7 Pull the handle thinner and bend it around to form a sweeping curve. The inside space between the handle and body is important, not only for comfort but also for the look of the finished teapot. Cut the handle to size and join securely, making sure the base and top of the handle are aligned.

8 Score and slip the joint at the bottom of the handle and smooth firmly into place. Reinforce the inside joint by smoothing in a small coil. Decide how to finish the handle. Here, two sweeps with the thumb make an interesting detail at the base of the handle.

9 Clay has a "memory," especially porcelain, so the spout will naturally want to twist during drying and firing. Shave the beak of the spout at a slight angle to compensate for this. Allow all the parts of the teapot to dry together, with the lid in place on the rim to prevent any possible warping.

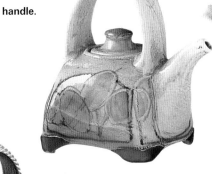

1 YIXING TEAPOTS

Cathi Jefferson These finely thrown teapots show different handle positions and added clay feet. The spouts have wide throats that complement the squared-off shape of the teapot bodies. Influenced by the Yixing teapots of China, they are made from a porcelaneous stoneware body, which was salt and soda fired.

2 TWO SALT-GLAZED TEAPOTS

Jane Hamlyn These pots demonstrate control and precision in their throwing and assembly. After the bodies were thrown, the bases were cut at an angle and then the pots were joined to new flat bases. These were finished with a stepped detail, giving the pots a wonderful animated character. Rolled and impressed handles contrast with the smooth refinement of the body surface. They were salt glazed in an oil-fired kiln to 2340°F (1280°C).

THROWING

Spouts

A well-made spout should funnel the liquid with sufficient pressure for a continuous flow and have a sharp enough lip to cut off any drips. Always throw spouts longer than you need so that you can trim some away to achieve an accurate fit to the body of your teapot. It is a useful exercise to sketch out the style of spout that will look best on your teapot. You can also experiment with different angles, and as long as the tip of the spout is above the level of the liquid, you can play with its shape. Always throw a couple of spare spouts in case you make a mistake. Throwing is just one way of making a spout; you could also slab-build, cast, or roll a spout around a narrow wooden dowel.

TOOLS
- *Wheel*
- *Metal scraper or rubber rib*
- *Wire*

TEAPOT

Walter Keeler *This white earthenware teapot has echoes of early Staffordshire "faux arcadian" creamware, yet is distinctively Keeler's style. Rich, juicy glazes run down the surface carrying pools of color. The handle repeats the form of the teapot, creating a satisfying negative space. The branch-like spout, growing from the body, counters the backward tilt of the piece.*

SEE ALSO
Preparing the clay, *pages 40–42*
Throwing, *pages 64–65*
Centering, *pages 66–67*

THROWING A SPOUT

1 Pull up a conical-shaped cylinder from a centered lump of clay (see pages 68–69). With your hands positioned around the top of the cone, begin to narrow it in.

2 Keep narrowing until you reach the required diameter. Notice how wide the spout is at the base.

3 Clean up the spout with a metal scraper or rubber rib and undercut the spout so that you have a guide to wire through. Cut the spout from the lump of clay and allow it to stiffen before attaching it to your pot (see page 80).

Lids

There are several points to consider when making lids for your pots. They must have a good fit to the body of the pot, they must be easy to grasp and lift on and off, and they should also be aesthetically pleasing and relate to the form of the pot. It is rarely possible to make a thrown lid entirely in one go on the wheel. They will always require some form of trimming at the leather-hard stage (see pages 90–93).

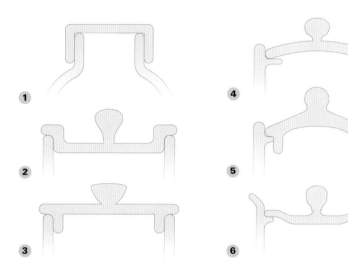

BASIC LID SHAPES

In some instances the clay is left thick on part of the lid so that a knob can be trimmed from it (diagrams 3, 4, and 5). In many cases (diagrams 2 and 6), it is easier to throw the knob at the same time as the lid (see page 85), while it is also possible to throw a knob onto the lid separately at a later stage.

1 *A ginger jar lid* that fits over the neck of the opening.

2 *A sunken lid* that rests on the neck of the pot and locates itself inside the rim.

3 *This flat lid* rests on the rim and has a flange inside the neck for a secure fit.

4 *A domed lid* that rests on an internal flange.

5 *This domed lid* has a deep flange and rests on an internal flange in the pot.

6 *A concave lid* with a slightly curved edge for a secure fit over the flange.

TOOLS
- *Wheel*
- *Calipers*
- *Wire*
- *Trimming tool*

THROWING A LID

1 A pair of calipers is an important tool to acquire for throwing lids. The most useful type allow you to measure the outside diameter of an opening at one end of the calipers, automatically transferring the information to the other end to give the internal measurement.

2 This ginger jar lid (see diagram 1) is thrown using the "off the hump" technique (see page 77). Use the appropriate end of the calipers to measure the diameter of the lid.

3 Cut the lid from the hump of clay and allow it to set leather-hard. Return it to the wheel and trim the outside of the lid to the desired profile.

SEE ALSO
Preparing the clay, *pages 40–42*
Throwing, *pages 64–65*
Centering, *pages 66–67*

THROWING

Handles and knobs

For any thrown pottery, it is always more appealing to "pull" your handles, although they can also be coiled, extruded, cut from slabs, and rolled. Knobs are often thrown on the lid, although other methods can also be used, including modeling, press molding, pulling, twisting, and rolling the clay.

HANDLES

Handles can be made separately, bent into the required shape, and then attached to the pot when both pieces are leather-hard. However, the most common handles for thrown work are pulled on the pot. This involves attaching an elongated lump of soft clay to the leather-hard pot and pulling it between the fingers and thumb into the most appropriate shape. Pulled handles tend to be stronger, being stretched in the same way as the body of the pot. Handles that are to be attached to the side of a pot should be positioned with the top of the handle just below the rim. This is important, because if the handle is too low, the vessel can be top heavy when it has the added weight of liquid. Perhaps the most important factor, the aesthetic one, is often understated—the handle must suit the form as well as be comfortable to use.

TOOLS
- *Knife*
- *Comb*
- *Brush*
- *Smoothing tools*
- *Texturing tools*

SEE ALSO
Preparing the clay, *pages 40–42*
Coiling, *pages 46–47*
Slab building, *pages 50–51*

PULLING OFF THE POT

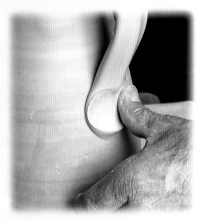

1 Grip an oval lump of clay in one hand and draw the clay down from the lump in between your thumb and fingers. You can make the handle round or oval, depending on how you shape your hand. Pull the handle longer than needed, lay it down on a table surface, and cut the pulled handle from the lump with a knife or by simply pressing down across the clay with your thumb.

2 Allow the handle to stiffen a little, then attach the thicker end firmly to the top of the leather-hard pot. Score and slip the edges to create a secure joint (see page 35). Bend the shape of the handle to suit the profile of the pot.

3 Securely attach the bottom of the handle by scoring and slipping the joint. Smooth the outside with your thumb. Many potters press a stamp into the soft clay at this point to give a decorative detail.

KNOBS

Knobs can be thrown at the same time as you throw the lid, or you can attach a lump of clay to the leather-hard lid and throw it into a knob later. You can also throw a knob separately and attach it when both lid and knob are leather-hard. Alternately, leave a thick area of clay on the lid so that it can be trimmed later to form a knob.

JUG

David Miller *A pulled handle was added at a quirky angle to this thrown jug with a wire-cut rim. The exuberant slips over the red clay body give a depth reminiscent of watercolor painting. Black slip-trailed lines define the edges and add exciting detail.*

THROWING A KNOB

Gather a small lump of clay between your fingertips and thumb to form a knob at the same time as you throw the lid. The shaping of the knob also establishes the curve for the top of the lid. Complete the lid in the usual way (see page 83).

PULLING ON THE POT

Attach an oval lump of clay to the body of the pot at the correct position for the top of the handle, scoring and slipping for a secure joint. Pull the clay gently but firmly downward between your thumb and fingers. Use enough water so the clay slides easily; if it drags, you could pull the lump off the pot. Curve the handle into shape and attach the base securely to the pot.

SLAB HANDLE

Handles can be cut from slabs of clay in a variety of different profiles. Here, angular shapes are cut from a thick slab of clay, then attached to the body by scoring and slipping. The handles can then be smoothed and refined.

COIL HANDLE

Textured coils can yield sensuous handles, soft in feel and comfortable to use. Try rolling the coils over rubber mats, found textures, or carved plaster slabs, or impress them with linear marks. Once the coils are twisted and bent into shape, the marks can become even more interesting.

THROWING

Throwing in sections

TOOLS
- Wheel
- Throwing bat
- Calipers
- Wooden throwing rib
- Wire harp

Some pots may be too large to throw in one piece. The weight of clay may be too much to center, your wheel not strong enough, or the pot too tall to be stable when pulling up in one piece. Since ancient times potters have evolved methods to surmount this problem. One popular technique is throwing on coils, where the pot is thrown to a manageable height, then a thick rope of clay is added to the rim and throwing continues. Each completed section must be stiffened up with a gas torch or hot-air gun before adding the next coil and continuing. The most common technique, however, is to throw two sections and join them together, then throw another section and add it on again, each time securing the edges and refining the shape. It is a good idea to work on several pots at the same time, allowing each to set while you work on the next and returning to it when it is firm enough.

1 STORAGE JAR

David Frith This large jar was thrown in three separate sections, each part being joined to the previous one and the shape refined by throwing them together. The jar was decorated with impressed rope marks and small porcelain sprigs before being ash glazed and fired in a wood kiln.

SEE ALSO

Preparing the clay, *pages 40–42*
Throwing, *pages 64–65*
Centering, *pages 66–67*

LARGE URN

1 It is essential to use a bat with this technique (see page 74). Throw a wide cylinder on the bat to form the first section of the urn (see pages 68–69). The clay should be thick enough to support the weight of the rest of the pot. Use a finger and thumb to finish off the rim with a sharp, pointed edge. This will help you to locate and join the next section.

2 Use calipers to measure the diameter of the rim. Remove the first section from the wheel on its bat and put it to one side to dry a little while you continue working.

3 Throw the next section on another bat. This section does not need a base because it is only continuing the wall of the pot. Check that the diameter is the same as the previous section, then use a wooden throwing rib to cut a V-shaped groove around the rim. This will fit over the pointed edge of the first section. Remove the bat from the wheel.

2

2 OVOID FORMS

Dainis Pundurs These large ovoid forms were thrown in sections and refined using bisque-fired ceramic roulettes to give texture at the same time as shaping the clay. The fractured surface gives a sense of tension and movement to the pieces.

3 RAKU VESSEL

Martin Mindermann This large vessel form is 3 ft. (1 m) in diameter and was created by adding coils and throwing them on. After bisque firing to 1830°F (1000°C), the pot was subjected to rapid firing by the raku technique. The clay must be strong and heavily grogged to withstand the stresses.

3

4 Replace the first section onto the wheelhead. Invert and position the second section on top of the first, locating the pointed and V-shaped grooves together. Cut the bat off the top piece using a wire harp held firmly against the bat.

5 With the bat removed from the top of the pot, you can now work on the inside as well as the outside of the piece. Use a throwing rib to secure the joint between the two sections on both the inside and outside. If you need the pot to begin to belly out, start refining the form at this stage.

6 Continue adding sections to the pot until you have reached the desired height and shape, joining each section as in the previous stages. Continue developing the shape. Here, a slight belly has been made by pushing out the walls from the inside while supporting the outside of the pot. Allow the pot to stiffen before cutting it from the bat.

THROWING

Altering a thrown form

While all pottery made on the wheel will inevitably be round, the shape of your work can be altered both during and after throwing. The effects will be very different, depending on when you do the altering. Facets can be cut directly into the wet clay on the wheel, giving soft angles to the work, or cut at the leather-hard stage to give a crisper finish. Using twisted or braided wires to cut the clay will produce bold, irregular patterns. Try experimenting with different tensions and twists for a variety of surfaces. Bellying out the faceted pot from the inside while still on the wheel will soften the look of the marks. Pots can also be squared off from the inside with the fingers or wooden tools, creating soft, rounded corners, or they can be paddled from the outside when firmer for a sharper feel. Thrown cylinders can be cut at angles when leather-hard and attached to new bases. Sides can be sliced and distorted, pressed and squashed, cut and rejoined. The best thing to do is give your imagination free reign and experiment.

1

SOFT SQUARING

Freshly thrown pots can be squared off while still soft on the wheel. Start by pulling yours fingers up the inside wall of the pot to distort the pot into a rough square shape. Then pull a piece of wooden dowel or a similar tool up the inside wall to form the corners. This will square off the sides and rim of the pot.

LEATHER-HARD SQUARING

1 Alter the shape of a thrown pot at the leather-hard stage by pressing it between your hands. This thrown ginger jar is being squared off by gently tapping it on a hard surface while applying hand pressure on either side.

2 Tap the walls with a wooden paddle to refine and complete the squaring of the edges.

1 CUT AND FACETED POTS

Japan These wire-cut cups and saki bottles show several different variations that can be achieved by faceting. The cut decoration was completed before removing the pots from the wheel. When leather-hard, a coating of contrasting white slip was poured over each piece to emphasize the cut ridges when fired.

2 TEAPOT

Walter Keeler Inspired by metal watering cans and olive oil pourers, the clean lines and precise throwing demonstrated in this classic Keeler teapot reflect early English industrial wares. This piece was finely trimmed, altered, and assembled after throwing. Applied slips give various textures to the salt-glazed finish.

2

TOOLS

- Wooden dowel
- Wooden paddle
- Cheese wire
- Knife
- Comb
- Brush
- Wooden smoothing tool

FACETING

1 Cut the walls of a freshly thrown thick cylinder into facets with a cheese wire. Work on opposite sides of the pot to ensure the facets are evenly spaced.

2 Continue the throwing process, placing one hand inside the pot and applying gentle pressure to belly out the form. The facets will stretch and soften.

OVAL DISH

Throw a round dish and allow it to stiffen until it is leather-hard. Use a knife to cut a petal-shaped piece from the base of the dish, then apply gentle but firm pressure equally from both sides to close the gap. Score and slip the edges (see page 35), then press a small coil of clay over the joint and smooth it with a wooden tool to create a firm seal.

THROWING

Trimming

This is the process of trimming off excess clay from the base of thrown forms. It is sometimes referred to as turning because it involves removing excess clay while the pot is rotating. Pots are usually trimmed at the leather-hard stage, when cutting is more precise and the risk of damaging your pots while handling is reduced. You will soon learn the best state of dryness for trimming—too dry and the clay will come off in flakes, too soft and it can distort. The ideal is where the trimmings peel off the surface evenly and cleanly.

FOOTRINGS

The main reason for trimming is to cut footrings into the base of pots that could not be achieved or would be difficult to accomplish during throwing. A footring gives definition to pottery. Trimming can also be used to refine and narrow bases, giving a pot "lift." All potters have their own variations on trimming techniques and tools. You can use hand-carved bamboo tools, commercially made metal tools and scrapers, or make your own cutters and scrapers from the metal strip around the edges of packing cases.

BASIC FOOTRING SHAPES

A footring is used to give greater definition to the shape of the pot and reduce the area in contact with the table surface. These diagrams show different footring profiles for different shapes of pot. The crosshatched areas show the clay that is removed during the trimming process.

1 Straight-sided deep dish incorporating footring.

2 Standard footring on a rounded pot.

3 Bold internal footring.

4 Shallow dish with single footring.

5 Flat, wide plate with two footrings.

6 DEEP BOWL

Rupert Spira *This thinly thrown, 20 in. (50 cm) diameter bowl was finely trimmed down to a narrow base, giving the form lift and visual lightness. It was decorated with lines incised through black pigment over a white glaze and then reduction fired.*

TEA BOWL FOOTRING

1 Dampen the wheelhead with a sponge. Centering your work is all-important. A simple method is to support the pot with one finger and gently tap the pot to the center of the wheel with your other hand at an 8 o'clock position (if your wheel turns clockwise instead of the usual counterclockwise, use a 4 o'clock position). You will easily feel when the pot is on center.

2 Once centered, press the pot down onto the damp wheel to stick it firmly. Begin to trim any surplus clay from around the base; a commercially bought metal trimming tool is used here. This defines the outside profile of the footring.

3 Using the same tool, carve into the base of the pot, trimming the footring to the desired depth. Take care not to cut through the base of the pot completely. After every few cuts, press the base gently with your fingertips to check the remaining thickness.

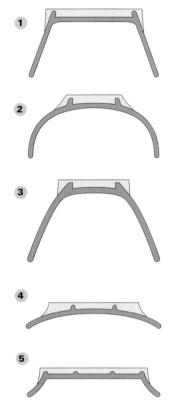

7 TRIMMED POTS DRYING

Japan These pots were thrown using a grogged stoneware body on a traditional oriental momentum wheel. The center of the tea bowl was scraped with a rough tool before bellying out from the inside, allowing the outer clay surface to begin to tear. All the pots have freely trimmed footrings, giving them strong bases—good for support and for handling when glazing. The teapot was paddled into its shape when leather-hard.

TOOLS

- Wheel
- Sponge
- Trimming tool

SEE ALSO

Throwing a plate, *pages 74–75*
Throwing off the hump, *page 77*

PLATE FOOTRING

2 This cross-section shows a thrown plate before trimming. You can see the thickness and the excess of clay where the base joins the walls.

1 Secure the plate in the center of the dampened wheelhead and trim a footring in the same way as a tea bowl (see page 90). If the base of the plate is very wide, you may need two concentric footrings or, at the very least, a small nipple of clay left in the center to support the base and prevent it from sagging during firing.

3 This cross-section shows the profile of the footring. It has been trimmed as wide as possible while still leaving the thickness of clay at the bottom of the wall to support the rim of the plate during firing and prevent warping. The small nipple of clay in the center supports the base of the plate.

THROWING

STABILIZING POTS FOR TRIMMING

Until fired, all pots are vulnerable and must be handled carefully, and it is essential that you stabilize any upturned pot when trimming it. Various methods can be used to adhere the piece to the wheelhead. The wheel can be dampened so that the clay pot sticks to it naturally (as shown in the examples of footrings on pages 90–91) or the pot can be attached to a dampened bat. Pots with narrow or enclosed necks, or items such as lids with knobs, can be inverted into a soft or leather-hard clay chuck. If a pot has an uneven rim, such as a pitcher with a pulled lip, it can be secured with a thick coil around the rim of the pot.

KEEPING IT TO A MINIMUM

Trimming is a lengthy process and should only be used when needed. Beginners often throw pots quite crudely and rely on trimming to improve their weight, look, and shape. However, in the time taken to trim a pot, several more could have been thrown, improving your throwing skill. Another good reason to keep trimming to a minimum is because the surface of a trimmed pot is very different from that of a thrown one. Changes in texture on the outside of a piece can spoil the finish, so try to blend in any trimmed marks. You could lightly trim the entire surface to mask any differences, but this can result in a very mechanical-looking pot.

①

1 TEA BOWL

Phil Rogers This tea bowl was freely thrown on the wheel and then slightly squared off with hand pressure applied from the inside. Rogers trimmed as much as possible from the outside of the piece while it was still soft, then allowed it to dry leather-hard, returned the pot to the wheelhead, inverted it, and secured it on a soft clay chuck for trimming the footring. Painted areas of cobalt give variations to the surface color, enhanced by the flashes of salt glaze during a 2340°F (1280°C) reduction firing in an oil-fired kiln.

USING A BAT	USING A HARD CHUCK

You can trim items on a throwing bat instead of directly on the wheelhead (see page 74). Dampen the bat with a sponge and attach the pot to its center (see page 90). Keeping the base of the pot flat, trim around the edge to give a clean, crisp finish.

1 You can support items such as lids on the rim of a leather-hard chuck. A chuck is simply a cone of clay. Using a chuck made from the same clay as the item you are trimming will prevent any contamination. This is especially important with a pure white body such as porcelain. Dampen the rim of the chuck and secure the lid to it.

2 Trim the underside of the lid using an appropriate trimming tool. Remember to keep measuring the diameter of the lid with a pair of calipers to check that you do not remove too much clay.

2 TEA CABARET SET

Morgen Hall *Although meticulously thrown, this tea set still retains a lively theatricality. When leather-hard, the pots were trimmed to create the precision Hall demands; she often spends hours working on a single piece, refining the shape and adding detail. The combination of red clay, tin glaze, and cobalt and rutile decoration gives richness and warmth to the surfaces. The precise decoration was achieved by the use of computers and plotter-cut stencils to provide resists for the pigment.*

USING A SOFT CHUCK

Pots can also be supported in a soft clay chuck when trimming. This cone of thickly thrown clay is covered with plastic wrap to stop the clay from sticking while still allowing the chuck to change its shape to grip the pot.

USING COILS OF CLAY

Thick coils of clay are a good way of securing pots to a wheel, bat, or leather-hard chuck. This can work well for pots with a lip, where a good seal cannot be achieved otherwise.

TOOLS
- *Wheel*
- *Throwing bat*
- *Sponge*
- *Trimming tool*
- *Calipers*
- *Plastic wrap*

SEE ALSO
Lids, *page 83*
Throwing a pitcher, *pages 70–71*

Thrown ceramics

Almost all beginners to ceramics regard throwing as the technique that most represents the potter's skill. Thrown pots can be precise and mechanical in their appearance or free and lively, revealing the distinctive character of the potter who made them.

1 OPEN BOWL

Rupert Spira This wide, elegant bowl reflects Spira's precise throwing technique. The fine trimming at the foot has given the pot lift and provided a smooth surface for the decoration of incised lines through a black pigment applied over white glaze.

2 TEA SET

Kang Hyo Lee This traditional thrown Korean tea set features a large open bowl with a spout for mixing green tea with hot water before pouring it into small tea cups. The coarse, open clay allows the heat of the liquid to permeate the cups and warm the hands. The pieces were decorated with a white semi-matte glaze, a band of oxide around the rims, and a simple splash of color on the sides before being wood fired to 2340°F (1280°C).

1

2

3 BOTTLE AND BOWL

Chris Keenan Thrown using fine porcelain, these two vessels exude the characteristic quietness of oriental pottery. The dark tenmoku glaze, with its highlighted spots of contrasting celadon glaze, has a highly reflective quality, emphasizing the smoothness of the surfaces. The pieces were gas fired in a reduction atmosphere to 2300°F (1260°C).

4 HEART JUGS

Jane Hamlyn Working almost entirely within the functional pottery genre, Hamlyn is one of the leading salt-glaze potters. These lively pitchers were thrown on the wheel without bases and altered into heart shapes while still soft. When leather-hard, the bottom of the pitchers were cut at an angle and joined to flat thrown bases, and curled handles added. The variety of finishes and colors were created by the controlled use of slips, which reacted with or resisted the effects of the volatizing salt during firing in an oil-fueled kiln.

5 ALTERED VESSEL

Rachel Ferguson *This vessel was thrown very freely from stoneware clay. Ferguson exerts greater pressure at the neck to produce her characteristic torn rims, which add to the freely thrown quality of her pieces. Glazed with vanadium pentoxide slip and barium carbonate glazes, the vessel was fired in an electric kiln to 2230°F (1220°C).*

6 FACETED BOTTLES

Emily Myers *The walls of these statuesque bottles were thrown considerably thicker than usual to allow for the depth of cutting into the sides. The strong spiraling facets give a dynamic movement to the forms that is enhanced by the coating of dry barium glazes, which produce beautiful mottled purple and blue hues.*

Mold Making

Plaster, or gypsum, is a versatile substance for the potter. It can be cast into slabs and used as a surface for drying and processing wet clay, for making wheelheads and bats, and most commonly, for making molds for pressing clay into shapes and for mass production of pottery by slip casting. The use of molds allows potters to create pieces that cannot be built by hand or throwing as well as reproduce specific shapes more quickly and accurately.

TYPES OF PLASTER

There are many kinds of plaster available, and depending on the supplier you use, they will be called different names. Always be sure to read the supplier's catalog thoroughly. Plaster falls into two main groups for ceramic application. The first is used to make molds for slip casting and jobs that require a certain amount of water to be absorbed. This plaster needs to be dried out after use, and because it is softer, it may need replacing at regular intervals. Molds made from this plaster are usually called "working molds." The second sort of plaster is much harder and is used for making press

TOOLS
• Bucket
• Scoop
• Stick or similar tool
• Paper towels

MIXING PLASTER

1 Lightly sprinkle the plaster powder into a bucket of water. The water should be equal to the amount needed to cover the model from which you are casting the mold. Add the plaster gradually and evenly until the absorbed plaster breaks the surface of the water. Gently shake the bucket to slake down all the plaster and allow to stand for a few minutes, until the plaster has absorbed the water.

2 Use a stick or similar tool to stir the mixture gently, making sure that there are no lumps (approximately 2–3 minutes). Every so often, wiggle your fingers at the bottom of the bucket to make any air bubbles rise to the surface and remove them by tapping them with your hand or paper towels. Keep testing the viscosity of the mixture, and when it no longer runs off your fingers, it is ready to pour.

1

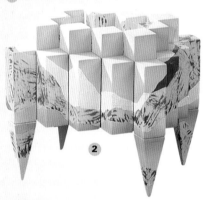

2

1 BOWL

Sasha Wardell This finely slip-cast bone china bowl was decorated with a "water erosion" technique. When the bowl was leather-hard, patterns were painted on the outside with shellac, which acts as a resist. When dry, water was sponged over the surface, etching away exposed areas. The variations of depth in the wall are revealed by light.

2 SAN GEKI

Itsue Ito This complex form was constructed from a number of slip-cast modules to create a sculpture reminiscent of ritual artifacts. Glazed with multiple low-fire commercial glazes, the casket-like structure perches on four narrow, pointed legs, adding to the feeling of preciousness.

molds and hump molds. This harder plaster is often called "casing plaster," because it is also used to make a positive copy of the working mold, known as a case mold. The case mold is then used to make new working molds (see pages 104–105).

WORKING WITH PLASTER

You can use different mixes of plaster in pottery, depending on the hardness you require and the porosity. Once dry, the plaster will absorb moisture from wet clay and from casting slip, making it a useful material in the studio. Be sure never to contaminate your clay with bits of plaster because they will cause damage to your pots when firing in the kiln. Most potters keep separate areas in their studios for plaster work. Any excess plaster can be used to make a flat bat or poured onto newspaper to set before disposal. Never pour leftover plaster down your sink because it will set in the waste pipes, causing severe blockages.

MIXING PLASTER

Plaster begins to set by chemical reaction as soon as it comes into contact with water, and once this process has started, it cannot be reversed. The speed of setting will depend on the type of plaster, the quantity you use, and the temperature of the water. Warm water will make the plaster set more rapidly. When mixing plaster it is important that you have enough to cover the model for your mold completely. If you do not cover it in one go, any consecutive pours of plaster will leave a visible line on any pieces you cast. If in doubt, over-estimate.

Plaster should always be added to the water, never the other way around. Sprinkle the plaster onto the water and allow it to sink in. Keep adding plaster until the dry material is level with the surface of the water. An alternative method is to measure the amount of plaster needed for the amount of water you are using before you start. This will give a consistency to your mixing, which is especially useful when making multi-part molds. The mixed plaster should have the consistency of thin cream. It is difficult to add more plaster once you have started mixing, so it is better to make it a little too thick and add more water if needed.

**ORDINARY
PLASTER MIX**

1½ lb. (675 g) plaster

1 pint (575 ml) water

Gives a good, strong mix for most pottery uses.

HARD PLASTER MIX

1¾ lb. (800 g) plaster

1 pint (575 ml) water

Produces a hard mix suitable for multi-part molds that will be used repeatedly.

3 PIERCED FORM

David Binns Allowing this cut and pierced slab to stiffen in a shallow plaster mold created the simple curved shape of this large piece. The regularity of the square penetrations and the scored torn edges reflect Binns' interest in industrial archeology and manufactured equipment.

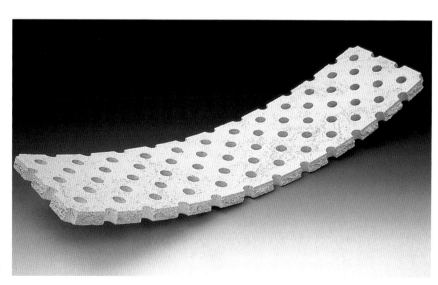

3

MOLD MAKING

One-piece press molds

Although these are the simplest type of mold to make, they can be used to create sophisticated and beautiful forms. Generally these are shallow objects, such as bowls and dishes, but it is possible to make tall vessels as well, although the weight of the mold could be a restriction. Press molds are an easy way of producing simple repetitive forms. Usually a clay model is made of the shape that is to be molded, although plaster and wooden models or even actual objects can also be used. In industry, original models are always made from plaster for durability and accuracy. The most important thing is that there are no undercuts on the model because this will make it impossible to remove the plaster mold from it. Your first couple of pressings from the mold will usually be contaminated with plaster dust and should be thrown away. One-piece molds can also be used for slip casting (see pages 106–107).

TOOLS
- Wooden bat
- Length of rubber, wooden boards, string, clothespins, or similar items
- Bucket
- Metal scraper
- Surform
- Wooden potter's knife
- Sponge
- Rolling pin
- Cloth
- Rubber rib

Clay model

Plaster mold

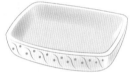

Finished dish

MAKING THE MOLD

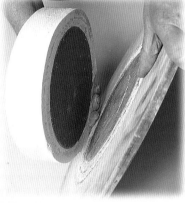

1 A small upside-down dish trimmed from a solid lump of clay is the model in this example. Place it on a wooden bat and build up a wall around it, leaving a 1 in. (2.5 cm) gap all around. You could use a length of rubber, wooden boards, or slabs of clay. Seal the walls to the bat with a coil of clay so that no plaster will run out. Mix some plaster (see pages 96–97).

2 Pour the plaster over the model slowly and evenly. Once you have covered it, gently tap the bat with the side of your hand to bring any air bubbles to the surface. Burst them by tapping the surface with your palm. As it sets, the chemical reaction will cause the plaster to become warm. To check it has set hard, tap the mold with your knuckle. It will now be possible to remove the wall.

3 Smooth the base of the mold with a metal scraper and use a surform to round off any sharp edges that might chip off during use. When the mold has dried further, pull it from the bat. Carefully remove the model from inside using your fingers or a wooden potter's knife. Use the scraper to clean up the top edges and around the outer rim. Wipe away any excess clay with a soft, damp sponge.

PRESSING A SINGLE SLAB

1 If the mold is shallow, a single slab of clay can be pressed into it. Roll out a large slab of clay on a piece of soft, clean cloth. Make sure you take the depth of the mold into account when calculating the size of slab you will need. Using the cloth to support the slab, place it onto the mold.

2 Remove the cloth and gently ease the slab of clay right into the mold. You can use a dampened sponge and rubber rib to finalize the shaping and smoothing of the inside surface. Remove the excess clay from the rim of the mold using a wooden potter's knife; this will not cut into the mold as a metal knife would, causing damage to the rim. Remove the pot as described in step 4 (see right).

PRESSING MULTIPLE SLABS

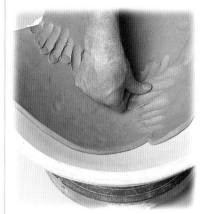

1 If you are using a large or deep mold, such as this bowl mold, you may need to use smaller slabs of clay. Join the overlapping edges securely with pressure from your thumb. Keep adding slabs of clay until the mold is filled.

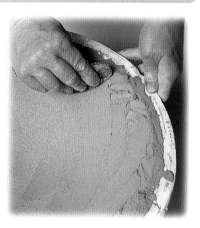

2 Cut the rim with a wooden potter's knife and add soft clay to repair any tears. Make sure the edges are filled to an equal thickness because this is what the eye will see. Small irregularities farther down in the mold will not be visible.

3 Use a metal scraper to even the clay and finally a rubber rib to smooth the surface. If there are any bumps, scrape them flat or fill and smooth them. You can leave the irregular edge around the rim of the bowl as a decorative feature if you wish or cut it clean.

4 As the plaster absorbs the moisture from the clay, the bowl will slowly stiffen and shrink. You will see an even gap appear between the clay and the mold when it is ready to be removed. Tilt the mold to help push the pot out, taking care to support the bowl while you do so.

SEE ALSO
Preparing the clay, *pages 40–42*
Slab building, *pages 50–51*

MOLD MAKING

Hump molds

A hump mold is a variation of a press mold, but the soft clay slab is draped over the mold rather than pressed into it. This method is ideal if you intend to decorate the inside of the dish with inlaid colored clay or slips. Any raised parts of decoration will be pushed into the clay surface by the pressure of smoothing the clay against the mold with a rubber rib or metal scraper. Hump molds must be fairly shallow and have sloping sides. As the clay dries and shrinks, it will grip the mold and can eventually crack your pottery as the pressure increases across the sides and base. When making hump molds, you will need to use soft soap (sometimes known as potter's size) to seal the surface of the base mold so that the new plaster will not stick to it.

TOOLS
- Brush
- Sponge
- Bucket
- Metal trimming tool
- Metal scraper
- Rolling pin
- Cloth
- Rubber rib
- Wooden potter's knife

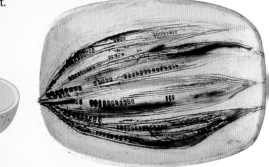

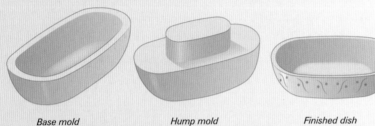

Base mold   Hump mold   Finished dish

PLASTER HUMP MOLD

1 Make a hollow, concave base mold in the required shape and allow it to dry thoroughly (see page 98). Use a brush or sponge to apply some soft soap to the surface of the mold to seal it, then wipe it with a damp sponge to remove any ridges or brushmarks in the soap. Repeat this process several times to ensure that the surface is totally smooth and sealed.

2 Mix some plaster (see pages 96–97) and gently pour it into the base mold. The level of the plaster should be slightly higher than the rim of the mold to give you some plaster to pare down after it has set. The plaster that you have poured into the base mold forms the hump mold.

3 When the plaster has set but not dried, carve some grooves into the surface with a metal trimming tool or similar item. These cuts will provide a good grip for the riser of the hump mold. The height of the riser can be whatever you want, but it should not be too high or the mold will be unstable and difficult to work with.

READY-MADE HUMP MOLD

Mollie Winterburn This curved dish was formed over a plaster hump mold, the edges were trimmed with a potter's needle, and then the piece was allowed to stiffen. The undecorated dish was bisque fired before glazing with a satin white, dolomite glaze. The artist's impression of the seed head was painted onto the powdery glaze surface using copper and cobalt oxides.

1 Many different objects can be used as ready-made hump molds. Here, a soft slab of clay is being shaped over a square wooden block. Lay the clay over the block and gently press the sides down to touch the base board. Allow the dish to stiffen so that it can safely be turned upright without the sides sagging.

2 Invert the dish and carefully remove the wooden block, which leaves a crisp, square center in the dish. In this example, stripes of contrasting porcelain were pressed into the slab before cutting and forming (see page 130).

SEE ALSO

Preparing the clay, *pages 40–42*
Slab building, *pages 50–51*

  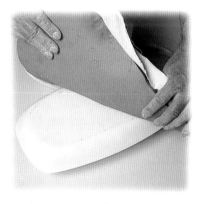

4 Place a clay wall around the scored central section of the plaster. The plaster will tend to dry out the clay quickly, so use soft clay coils to seal the clay wall to the plaster surface. Mix another batch of plaster and pour it inside the clay wall.

5 Remove the clay wall when the plaster has set. Once the plaster has dried, carefully remove the hump mold from the hollow, concave base mold. Scrape the bottom of the riser flat with a metal scraper and smooth and taper the edges to prevent chipping. Allow the hump mold to dry thoroughly.

6 Roll out a slab of clay on a piece of soft, clean cloth. Using the cloth as a support, place the clay over the finished hump mold. Smooth the clay into shape with a rubber rib and cut the excess from around the edges of the mold with a wooden potter's knife. Smooth all the edges with a damp sponge. When the clay has stiffened, gently ease it off the hump mold.

MOLD MAKING

Two-part molds

A one-piece mold will only allow open forms to be pressed or cast because the piece has to be able to drop out of the mold as it shrinks. By using two-part molds, it is possible to reproduce forms with simple undercuts. Joints in the plaster mold allow the two parts to be pulled away in different directions, enabling easier removal of the object. If you are pressing an object, the two elements must be pressed individually and joined by scoring and slipping the edges (see page 35). Slip-cast pieces can be made in one go by creating a pouring hole in the mold for the slip. Clay originals are the quickest to make, but often a plaster original, known as a model, is made so that several molds can be reproduced from the same original with greater ease. The model can be stored to remake damaged molds in the future.

CALCULATING JOINTS

It is important that you calculate exactly where the joint will occur because any undercuts will cling to your cast objects, preventing them from being released. The seam where the parts of the mold join will be visible on the finished piece and will require tidying up. You should therefore try to design the mold so that the joint occurs at places on your model where it will not be obvious—on changes in the contour of the form, for example.

1 FIELD

Inese Brants The body of this piece was made in a two-part press mold, the joining edges being scored and slipped prior to pressing them together to create a secure joint. The entire surface was incised with a herringbone pattern, emphasized by the soda-glazed wood firing.

2 ONI

Anna Malicka Zamorska Recurring images in Zamorska's work, these masked porcelain figures are 3 ft. (1 m) high. The torsos were slip cast in a large two-part mold and the hair and masks modeled separately and added after firing. Each piece was fired to 2520°F (1380°C) in an industrial tunnel kiln, with the masks receiving a luster firing to 1470°F (800°C).

MAKING THE MOLD

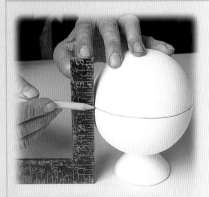

1 A plaster model of a sphere is used in this example. If the mold is for slip casting, as here, balance the sphere on a plaster cone; this will form the pouring hole for the slip and is known as a "spare." Use a set square to draw a line around the center of the model. It is important that this is exactly in the middle or an undercut will occur and the final cast will be difficult to remove.

2 Place the plaster model on a wooden bat and bury it up to the center line in clay. The easiest way to do this is to pack small pieces of clay around the model until the required height and width are reached. Smooth the top edge of the clay and use a brush or sponge to grease the model with soft soap.

3 Build a wall around the model. A length of rubber held together with clothespins and secured to the bat with clay is used here. Mix some plaster (see pages 96–97) and pour it over the model to a depth of about 1–1½ in. (3 cm) above the sphere. When the plaster has stiffened, remove the wall and invert the mold to remove the clay from beneath.

TOOLS

- Set square
- Pencil
- Wooden bat
- Smoothing tool
- Brush or sponge
- Length of rubber, clothespins, string, or similar items
- Bucket
- Small coin or commercially bought keys

SEE ALSO
One-piece press molds, *pages 98–99*
Slip casting, *pages 106–107*

4 Use a small coin to scrape two or more holes (called keys or natches) into the rim of the mold. These will form locating keys when the two parts of the final mold are placed together. Seal the surfaces of the mold and model thoroughly with soft soap.

5 Replace the wall and pour in a fresh mix of plaster. Continue pouring until the plaster is level with the top of the plaster cone. Allow the plaster to stiffen, then remove the wall, separate the two pieces of the mold, and remove the sphere and cone. Allow the plaster mold to dry thoroughly before slip casting any pieces in it.

6 This finished mold shows two types of keys: one scraped into the mold with a coin and three commercially bought keys. These are small plastic locating pegs that can be embedded into the rim of the clay in step 2 before casting the first half of the mold. They form long-lasting, secure keys that will not chip.

MOLD MAKING

Multi-part molds

Working with multi-part molds means that more intricate and complicated forms can be produced than would be possible using simple one- or two-piece molds. Ideally, forms should be designed with the fewest number of mold parts possible. The more pieces you have, the greater the danger of damaging the molds during use.

LARGE-SCALE PRODUCTION

Making items on a commercial scale may involve the use of several identical molds to enable efficient production of the pottery. These molds can become damaged over time, so a system of block and case molds can be used to ensure easily produced replicas. This system comprises four stages: positive, negative, positive, and final negative. The original positive model is first used to cast a negative mold, known as the block mold. The block mold is then used to cast a positive mold, known as the case mold. Finally, the case mold is used to produce a series of negative molds. These are identical to the block mold and are used to put the pottery into production—hence, they are known as working molds. For most studio potters producing only small runs of pieces, this system is rarely used, but you should keep at least the original model from which to cast replica molds should the need arise.

TOOLS
- Set square
- Pencil
- Wooden bat
- Smoothing tool
- Brush
- String
- Bucket
- Coin
- Surform
- Length of rubber or linoleum

SEE ALSO
Two-part molds, *pages 102–103*
Slip casting, *pages 106–107*

MAKING BLOCK AND CASE MOLDS

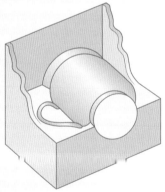

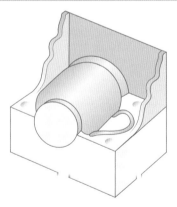

1 In this example, a model of a cup is used to make a three-part mold. The model has a spare at the top, which will create the pouring hole for the slip. Use a set square and pencil to mark the exact position of the halfway point on the model. This ensures that no undercuts will be created in the mold.

2 Place the model on a wooden bat and bury it up to the center line in clay. Build up walls of clay around the buried model. Smooth the inside edges of the clay and brush soft soap over the model so that it does not stick to the plaster. Tie string around the walls to keep them securely in place and pour in some plaster (see pages 96–97). When the plaster has stiffened, remove all the clay and invert the mold.

3 Use a coin to scrape a hole in each corner of the mold; these will act as locating keys to ensure the pieces of the mold fit together accurately. Allow the plaster to dry thoroughly, then brush the mold and model with soft soap. Build up walls of clay around the inverted mold and model and pour in another batch of plaster to form the second side section. Remove the clay when the plaster has stiffened.

MODEL AND MOLD

A solid plaster model and its three-section block mold. From this block mold, positive plaster casts would be taken to form case molds for the mass production of working molds. However, many studio potters would simply cast a series of working molds directly from the model.

1 Plaster model of cup.

2 The spare is turned from a separate piece of plaster and attached by nails cast into the top of the cup that fit into corresponding holes in the spare. Small amounts of fresh plaster floated into the nail holes hold the two pieces firmly in place.

3 Two side pieces of the mold, showing the pouring spare that will form the rim of the cup.

4 Base block, showing the section that makes the indented foot in the base of the cup.

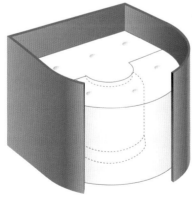

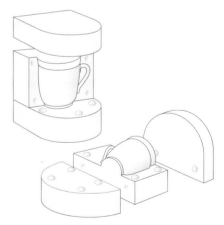

4 With the model still inside the two pieces of the mold, turn all three upside down. Use a surform to round off the sharp edges so that plaster does not chip off during use. Wrap a length of rubber or linoleum around the mold and secure it with string. Scrape holes in the base to act as keys, brush with soft soap, and pour in another batch of plaster to form the base of the mold. These three pieces are the block mold.

5 Build up a wall of clay around one side section of the block mold and pour in plaster to make the first side section of the case mold (this is the same process as step 3). When dry, turn both pieces upside down to make a base for this section of the case mold (as in step 4). Do the same to make a top section. Repeat with the other side section of the block mold.

6 You should now have a three-part case mold for one side of the cup and a three-part case mold for the other side of the cup. You can use these to make as many side sections of a working mold as you require. Repeat step 4 to make the required number of bases.

MOLD MAKING

Slip casting

Slip casting provides an exciting array of possibilities for the studio potter. Although it was developed for mass producing pottery cheaply and easily by largely unskilled labor, contemporary work shows increasingly inventive interpretation and slip casting is even used for one-off pieces. Slip casting utilizes the ability of plaster to absorb water from liquid clay slip when it is poured into a plaster mold. As water is absorbed from the slip, it begins to form a layer of solidifying clay on the inside surface of the mold. When this layer has reached the required thickness, the excess slip is poured out, leaving the deposit to stiffen and shrink away from the mold.

PREPARING THE SLIP

The slip used for casting should be smooth with no lumps. If there are any lumps, pour the slip into the mold through a sieve to collect them. Most commercial producers use slip blungers, which are large tanks with rotating blades inside that keep the slip constantly moving to ensure a smooth and creamy consistency. The slip is then poured through an outlet pipe and directly into the mold via a nozzle.

TOOLS
- *Rubber band*
- *Jug*
- *Bucket*
- *Bowl*
- *Slatted shelf*
- *Plastic or blunt metal knife*
- *Sponge*

SEE ALSO
Casting clay, *page 28*
Mold making, *pages 96–105*

CASTING A COFFEE POT

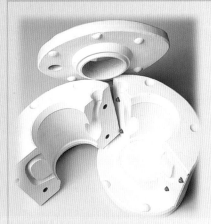

1 This example uses a four-piece coffee pot mold and a two-piece lid mold. Put the pieces of the mold together, using the keys to locate the individual parts correctly. Use a strong rubber band to hold the sides firmly in place so that they will not push apart under the weight of slip. The weight of the mold will hold it down on the base.

2 Pour the slip into the molds quickly and confidently. Try to pour the slip in one go without having to replenish the jug halfway. If you have to refill it, you may see a pour line on the outside of the pot when it is removed from the mold. This can be trimmed off later.

3 When full, gently tap the sides of the molds repeatedly with your fist to bring any air bubbles to the surface. If you do not, air bubbles will collect between the slip and the plaster mold and form small holes in the surface of the pottery.

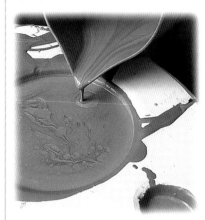

4 As the plaster absorbs the moisture from the slip, the clay forms a drying wall directly against the plaster surface of the mold. As it begins to dry, the level of slip in the mold will drop. Top up with more slip if required.

5 When the wall of the pot has reached the required thickness, pour the excess slip out of the mold back into your bucket of slip. Any spillage should be cleaned up before it dries and becomes dusty. Alternately, it is easy to clear up the slip when it has become leather-hard and can be scraped up with a tool.

6 Leave the molds upside down to drain any remaining excess slip from them. Here, the molds are placed on a wooden slatted shelf to allow the slip to drip through into a bowl below. Molds can be leaned one against another while they drain.

7 Allow the slip to stiffen a little. Once the clay is firm but pliable and not sticky to the touch, cut away the spares from the rim and spout using a plastic or blunt metal knife. This will ensure that you do not cut into the plaster mold.

8 The clay will shrink back from the surface of the mold and a small gap will appear all around when the mold is ready to be opened. Remove the top piece of the body mold and gently separate the sides from the base. Separate the two pieces of the lid mold.

9 Carefully clean up the cast. Gently scrape off the seam lines using a metal blade before smoothing down with a sponge. The clay will be very brittle and easy to break at this stage, so great care must be taken when handling the pottery.

MOLD MAKING

Agateware

This is the name given to pieces of work that use a combination of two or more colors of clay to make patterns. The name is derived from the agate stone, which displays multicolored layers when sliced. Certain techniques derived from carpentry, such as lamination, are also generally referred to as agateware.

COMBINING THE CLAYS

Different colored clays can be mixed together to produce agate patterns that run all the way through the clay. You can mix different clay bodies together or pieces of the same clay stained different colors, depending on the effect you wish to achieve. Rough, groggy clays mixed with porcelain will create natural, rock-like formations as the clay stretches and splits.

1 PORCELAIN AGATEWARE BOWL

Linda Caswell Layers of stained clay were inserted into cuts in a block of white porcelain. Slices were then cut from the block and rolled carefully into circles, trying not to stretch the clay and tear it. The sheet of clay was placed on a flat piece of foam and a hump mold pressed down onto it before inverting the mold with the clay on it. Gentle pressure formed the piece over the mold. Working in this way allowed Caswell to retain the naturally occurring folds of clay in the bowl. A small addition of bronze glaze emphasizes the rim.

1

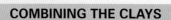

COMBINING THE CLAYS

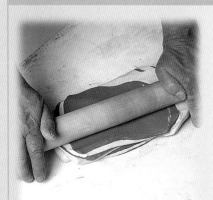

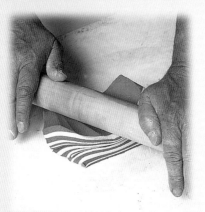

1 Sandwich several layers of contrasting colored clay together, lightly brushing each joint with slip (see page 35). Roll the layers together firmly with a rolling pin but do not flatten them too much.

2 Use a wire to cut the block in half and stack one section on top of the other. Roll the clay into a thinner lump. Repeat the process until you are happy with the number of layers.

3 The clay can be rolled out into a slab ready for forming, beaten into shape with a wooden mallet, or stretched into sheets (see pages 50–51). Depending on the method you use, the clay will either form restrained sheets or torn, fractured slabs.

USING CLAY STRIPS

Thin strips of clay can be laminated together to form slabs of patterned clay and millefiore pieces. The clays are rolled out and layered together, then cut into pieces and used to create patterns of multiple strata. You should always use a similar clay body, stained in different colors, so that the drying and shrinkage rate will be equal. The integral structure of the joints is quite weak with this method, so any differences in shrinkage would cause splits to appear in the final piece.

2 SLIP-CAST BOWLS

Sasha Wardell *Multiple layers of colored bone china casting slip were thinly poured into plaster molds to make these bowls. When leather-hard, the bowls were removed and small slices cut from the walls to reveal the various colored layers.*

TOOLS
- *Rolling pin*
- *Brush*
- *Wire*
- *Wooden mallet*
- *Knife*

SEE ALSO
Clay and pottery bodies, *pages 8–17*
Colored clay, *page 32*

USING CLAY STRIPS

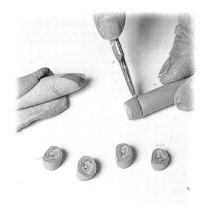

1 Roll out thin sheets of stained clay. Try not to use too many colors or the design could become too busy. It is always possible to achieve interesting designs using a limited palette of colors and, after all, the pattern itself is likely to be busy enough.

2 Layer several of the slabs, sticking them together with slip. Cut them into narrow strips, then cut these into smaller pieces. Reassemble the pieces to form different patterns, rotating the shapes to create new arrangements.

3 Roll a coil of clay and wrap a sheet of clay in a contrasting color around it, joining the edges with slip. Repeat the concentric circles until you have built up several layers. Cut slices off the roll. These pieces are known as millefiore and can be incorporated into the design of the piece.

MOLD MAKING

FORMING THE PIECE

Agateware made from colored clays mixed together by rolling can be formed using handbuilding or throwing techniques. If used for throwing, the pattern will spiral up through the entire pot. This technique has been popular for hundreds of years in Japan, where it is known as neriage, producing pottery with fascinating swirling patterns through the body of the pots. Most ceramics made from laminated strips of clay are formed in molds, but this is by no means the only method and laminated slabs can easily be built into objects. Care must be taken to join all the edges with slip, but you will be rewarded with exciting and innovative patterned pottery. Additions of millefiore pieces can often add further interest to your work.

USING AGATE SLABS

Agate slabs can be handbuilt or shaped in a mold. Here, a torn, variegated slab is draped into a wooden dish mold and allowed to go leather-hard. It can then be removed and cleaned up if required. The tears through the wall reflect the appearance of rugged landscapes.

EARRINGS

Linda Caswell Two techniques were used to make these earrings. The circular rings were made by rolling out mixed clay very thinly and cutting it to shape when leather-hard. The high-contrast striped pair (bottom left) were made by joining laminated strips of colored clay together before finally cutting it to shape when leather-hard. Caswell makes her own surgical steel findings to complement her fine jewelry.

USING MILLEFIORE

1 Use a sponge to dampen the inside of the mold and paint small areas at a time with a thin layer of white slip (see page 35). If the slip begins to dry too much, add a little more water or slip to soften it. Begin to build up patterns by pressing the millefiore pieces into the slip. Firmly join the slices together with more slip. Do not worry about keeping the inside of the bowl neat.

2 When the bowl is completed, allow it to dry until it is leather-hard, then clean up the inside with a flexible kidney-shaped metal scraper. Keep the bowl in the mold as a support because this type of work is fragile. Give the inside a final cleaning with fine steel wool, bringing up the final design and smoothing out any irregularities in depth. Make sure you wear a mask because you will be creating dust.

3 When dry, the pot will shrink away from the mold and can be carefully removed. Scrape away the white slip coating from the outside of the pot with the scraper and then some steel wool to reveal the finished decoration.

SLIP-CAST AGATEWARE

1 Cut various shapes from thinly rolled laminated clays and press them against the inside surface of a plaster mold. You can make regular patterns or abstract, irregular ones.

2 Pour casting slip into the mold to form a pot with the laminated shapes embedded in the wall. This part of the process must be done quickly before the shapes separate from the walls of the mold.

3 When the required thickness in the wall is reached, pour out the excess slip and allow the mold to drain. When nearly dry, scrape the humps down flat where the slip has built up over the laminated patterns. The colored shapes will be revealed. Leave the piece in the mold for support when you do this.

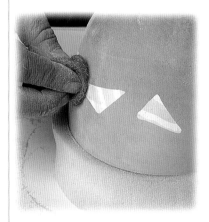

4 When dry, remove the bowl from the mold and refine the outside with steel wool. The designs on the outside of the pot will be clearly defined, while those on the inside will be slightly softer.

TOOLS
- *Sponge*
- *Brush*
- *Flexible kidney-shaped metal scraper*
- *Fine steel wool*

SLIP-CAST AGATEWARE

A development from simple slip casting is to combine it with methods of agateware. This can give an infinite variety of exciting possibilities for decorative expression. Try to be inventive and explore pattern and color to the full. One method involves casting pottery in multiple layers of slip, pouring out each layer before the next is cast to build up consecutive layers of colors, like a piece of laminated timber. When removed from the mold, carve through the layers to reveal areas of color in the surface. Another method, shown here, is to place specific shapes of laminated clay into a mold and consolidate them into the piece by pouring a thick layer of slip over them.

Following the making process, the pot should be allowed to dry completely before refining the surfaces with fine steel wool. After bisque firing, further refinement with wet and dry sandpaper would bring a natural sheen to the surface after the final firing. This refining process creates a considerable amount of dust and is obviously a hazardous process, so always wear appropriate masks and overalls and ensure good ventilation.

SEE ALSO

Casting clay, *page 28*
One-piece press molds, *pages 98–99*
Slip casting, *pages 106–107*

Mold-made ceramics

Many contemporary artists use molds as the starting point for creating works of great beauty and intricate form. Incredibly thin sections can be supported in the mold until dry enough to handle, giving ceramicists the ability to achieve lightness and translucency in their works.

1 PORCELAIN VESSEL

Arnold Annen *This fine vessel form was cast from high-temperature porcelain slip, which was removed from the one-piece mold when leather-hard and allowed to become almost dry. Using a fine-nozzled gas torch, the surface was heated until the clay began to explode off in small fragmented shards, creating areas of varying thickness and even making holes through the wall of the pot in some places. The variation in surface density produces intriguing patterns when the piece is illuminated after having been fired until the porcelain was translucent.*

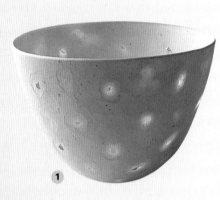

1

3 WIND

Pavel Knapek *The artist produced series of three-dimensional sketches and small paper maquettes before deciding on the form that would be made full size. The model for this large wall piece was constructed from cardboard with a slightly waxy surface. All the hard edges were scored and bent and the undulating surfaces were crushed and crumpled. A large plaster mold was then cast, into which porcelain slip or slabs could be poured or pressed. As light passes across the piece, shadows activate the surfaces, reminiscent of snowy, windswept landscapes.*

4 VIRÁG (FLOWER)

Éva Kádasi *The artist employs several techniques when making her wonderfully organic and exuberant sculptures. The large plant heads are cast by pouring different thicknesses of porcelain slip inside and over plaster molds, producing a natural, petal-like structure. Traditional techniques for pulling handles are used to form the intertwining stems, which are supported with pieces of foam until hard enough to be self-supporting.*

2   **3**

2 MOUNTAIN STORM

Steve Mattison *The original of this vessel form was thrown on the wheel and refined with metal scrapers until the intended form was accomplished. A one-piece mold was cast in plaster, allowing the artist to repeat the basic form many times. Although the initial shape remains the same, the method of laminating colored clays, combined with the dramatic cut rims, produces unique and individual pieces.*

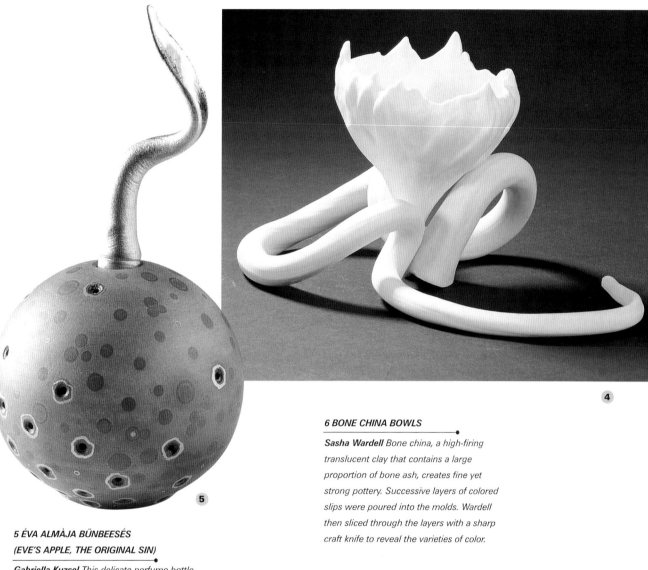

4

6 BONE CHINA BOWLS

Sasha Wardell Bone china, a high-firing
translucent clay that contains a large
proportion of bone ash, creates fine yet
strong pottery. Successive layers of colored
slips were poured into the molds. Wardell
then sliced through the layers with a sharp
craft knife to reveal the varieties of color.

5

**5 ÉVA ALMÀJA BÜNBEESÉS
(EVE'S APPLE, THE ORIGINAL SIN)**

Gabriella Kuzsel This delicate perfume bottle
combines a slip-cast porcelain body with a
handmade stopper. The beautiful, egg-like
form is smooth and sensuous to the touch,
while the lustrous gold stopper gives the
piece a rich and exotic appearance. The
surfaces were painted with solutions of iron
chloride, with thicker coatings giving darker
spots, before being fired to
2340°F (1280°C). This piece was
the jury prize winner at the 5th
Cairo International Biennial and
is now owned by the Egyptian
National Museum.

6

Large-scale Ceramics

Many clay artists make large-scale ceramic pieces, both for private clients and for public display. Making large works may involve the artist in many decision-making processes with prospective clients regarding design, siting, and installation. With any type of large-scale piece, the design, size, color, and texture must be appropriate for the location. Even the maintenance and cleaning has to be thought of, especially if sited outdoors where weather, erosion, and graffiti may take their toll.

FREESTANDING SCULPTURE

The way in which large sculptures are constructed depends on a variety of factors. The size of any single piece will ultimately be dictated by the size of the kiln, with anything larger than the chamber being made in sections. The physical weight of a single piece must also be kept in mind—if it is too heavy, you will have difficulty moving it to the kiln and manipulating it after firing. Many artists working in this genre have trolley kilns, where the base of the kiln is on a rail track. The sculpture is made directly on the kiln base and simply wheeled into the kiln for firing. When making a large sculpture, you must also consider the location in which it will be placed and how it will be installed. If the work is to be sited outside, it must be suitably resistant to weather and human attack, of a sufficient weight not to be blown over, or anchored to the floor in some way.

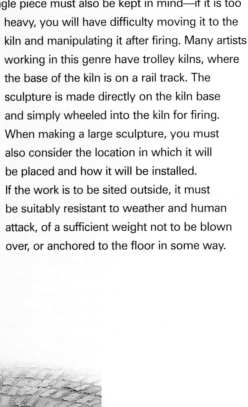

1

2

1 PAST AND FUTURE

Jim Robison *The artist worked with local children and featured their ideas about the past and future of their community in this large tower sculpture. For the final installation, metal screw-threaded bars were cemented into the ground and each section of the tower was lowered down over them, with the final section firmly bolted into place.*

2 VANTAGE POINT

Steve Mattison *This 7 ft. (2 m) sculpture was coil built in three sections for ease of maneuvering. Fired to 2550°F (1400°C) in a gas kiln, the high feldspar content in the clay fused to produce a stonelike quality, making it ideal for the outdoor setting in the sculpture garden at Panevezys City Museum, Lithuania.*

3 PORTAL

Michel Kuipers *Many of Kuipers' pieces are made in response to the environment and are site specific. The large gateway stands in front of a wall section made from glazed stoneware. The shape of the wall section reflects the negative space created by the gateway. Made in small sections and blocks, the individual pieces were finally cemented into place.*

4 MAYBE COFFEE?

Eugenijus Cibinskas *This large slab-built installation measures 125 x 95 x 48 in. (320 x 240 x 120 cm) and was made in several sections. The two cups are hollow, with the top surface painted to represent the reflection of a man and woman in the surface of the coffee. The tabletop was made in one piece and fired to 2550°F (1400°C) in an extremely large gas kiln with a chamber size of 13 x 10 x 7 ft. (4 x 3 x 2 m).*

3

4

SEE ALSO
Installation methods, *pages 118–119*

LARGE-SCALE CERAMICS

Tiles and murals

For thousands of years, tiles have been produced to decorate our homes and cities. We use them to adorn floors, embellish the facades of buildings, and enrich the domes of churches. Although they can be used individually, more often groups of tiles are installed together. Their flat surface provides an ideal canvas for decoration such as murals. Each tile may have an individual motif placed on it or an overall design can be painted across a panel of tiles.

MAKING TILES

Tiles have a tendency to warp when fired so you should use a grogged body to avoid this. There are several different methods of making tiles. They can be cut from slabs of clay, or pressed or slip cast in molds. Slow and even drying is important. Many potters dry tiles on wire racks so that air can circulate beneath as well as over the top.

LARGE-SCALE MURALS

Ceramic murals are frequently made using commercially manufactured tiles as the basic canvas because they simplify large-scale work. However, murals composed of individually made tiles often have more character and give the designer greater scope for personal expression. Once an overall design has been chosen, the size and shape of each tile needs to be calculated. Will all the tiles be square or should they follow the lines of the design? If square tiles are required, cardboard or wooden templates can be used to cut squares from flat slabs of clay. When using the design to dictate the cutting, there are two possibilities. The first is to draw the design lifesize on cardboard and then cut the cardboard into the relevant pieces and use these as templates to cut the tiles. This method is good if working space is restricted. The second method is to roll out one enormous sheet of clay, complete the panel, and then, using the outlines of the decoration as a guide, cut the panel into the individual tiles.

1

1 SELF-PORTRAITS

Meri Wells This series of raku tiles was hand-painted using oxides, slips, and stains over textured areas of impressed and modeled clay. A transparent low-temperature glaze was applied selectively, allowing the smoke of the reduction to blacken areas and give depth to the decoration.

2 SPRAYED MURAL (DETAIL)

Craig Bragdy Design Limited This detail from a large panel for a road tunnel uses commercially manufactured tiles. The tiles were already glazed and only required the design to be applied with enamels, which can be done by painting, sponging, or spraying. This design was sprayed by hand using cardboard stencils. The detail shows the variations of surface decoration possible from spraying. Such a design will only be viewed for seconds from a passing car and should be very different from the detail needed for a mural that will be viewed close up.

2

3

3 LARGE TILE PANEL

Craig Bragdy Design Limited This company
specializes in unique ceramic murals, panels,
floors, and swimming pools. Each panel
is designed to be site specific. Here, the
decorators are working on a panel for a
school. Using a wide variety of resource
materials, including sketches, photographs,
and books, an overall design has been
drawn and painted to scale. The grogged
stoneware clay has been hammered out into
long slabs on a floor covered with absorbent
plasterboard. Each artist works on a section
of the panel from scaled-down segments of
the original design. Using a wide variety of
tools and stamps, the images are impressed
into the clay. Each panel may take several
weeks to complete, so they must be
dampened and covered with a sheet
of plastic at the end of each day.

4 MUSEUM MURAL

*Edmun O'Avazian and Craig Bragdy
Design Limited* This long mural for the
National Museum of Riyadh in Saudi Arabia
was handmade using sculpted, impressed,
and modeled elements. Made from a single
large sheet of clay, the design was created
by the Craig Bragdy's artists in conjunction
with Islamic designer and calligrapher
Edmun O'Avazian. The brief was to create
an intellectually and aesthetically stimulating
mural that would interest a wide age group.
The picture on the left shows the mural being
reassembled after the glaze firing to check
that all the pieces fit before shipping and
installation. The finished mural (below left)
is installed on a pedestrian bridge joining two
parts of the museum. The success of working
to this type of brief depends on an excellent
design based on sensitive consultation with
the clients. The photograph shows how the
tiles have been cut to suit the design.

4

SEE ALSO

Clay and pottery bodies, *pages 8–17*
Low-shrink clay, *page 29*
Slab building, *pages 50–53*
Mold making, *pages 96–113*
Installation methods, *pages 118–119*

Installation methods

It is vital that large-scale ceramic work be installed securely, not only for the security of the work but also for the safety of the public. Each work may present a different set of problems and criteria, but generally speaking gluing or cementing and bolting or screwing are the most common methods of installation.

ATTACHING WALL PANELS

Wall panels can be installed in a number of different ways. The method you choose will depend on the size and weight of the individual tiles, the wall to which they are to be attached, the required finished look, and whether the panels need to be portable. They can be cemented directly to the wall, but this should be avoided if the individual pieces are very large and heavy. Setting metal rods or bolts into the back of the panels will allow them to be drilled into walls to ensure a secure attachment. It is also possible to screw them onto wooden boards and then screw or bolt the boards to the wall. Commercial adhesives and cements are available, such as those used in swimming pools, that set quickly and are weatherproof.

TOOLS
- *Scoring tool*
- *Boring tool*
- *Metal-working tools*

1 ABALONE SHELL

Jean Powell and Craig Bragdy Design Limited *The shell stands on a busy road junction on the Red Sea coast in Saudi Arabia. Supported by an internal structure of stainless steel and timber encased in a 1 in. (2.5 cm) thick envelope of glass-reinforced plastic, the ceramic elements were cemented into place.*

CEMENT OR ADHESIVE

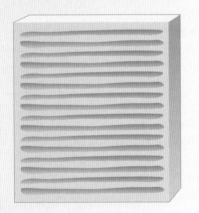

Tiles or ceramic blocks should be scored as deep as possible when leather-hard. This will provide a good key for cement or adhesive.

METAL RODS OR BOLTS

A series of holes bored into the back of the panels when leather-hard can have metal rods or bolts cemented into them after firing. These will provide good stability when cemented into holes drilled in the wall.

MIRROR PLATES

Ceramic tiles can be glued onto wooden boards, ready for attaching to the wall. Mirror plates are a good method of securely installing the boards on the wall.

SEE ALSO
Large-scale ceramics, *pages 114–115*
Tiles and murals, *pages 116–117*

INSTALLING SCULPTURE

Another set of problems arises for freestanding sculptures, especially if the pieces are tall. Generally, sculpture for outdoor installation is made heavier than sculpture intended for indoor use so that it has better resistance to wind. Some sculptures can be simply cemented into the earth, but tall sculptures may require vertical structures running through the body of the work to provide adequate support.

2 MAKING ABALONE SHELL

Jean Powell and Craig Bragdy Design Limited When embarking on monumental ceramic works, problems can be many and varied. They frequently require complex solutions that are unique to that particular piece. Much of this way of working is a process of investigation and discovery. This 20 ft. (6 m) shell form was made from a series of curved and sculpted ceramic blocks. Two temporary molds were made—one for the inside and one for the outside—and the clay formed to suit the complex curvatures involved.

1

SCREWS

Holes pierced through the ceramic slabs or tiles when leather-hard will allow screws to be inserted to attach the tiles securely to a wall. Do not over-tighten the screws or you may crack the ceramic. The holes can be filled with colored grout afterward to disguise the screw heads.

STEEL STRIPS

Bent steel strips can be made and screwed to the wall, with corresponding bent steel strips screwed to the backing board. The strips on the board can then be hooked over those on the wall so that the panel is literally hung from them. Theatrical equipment suppliers sell ready-made fasteners similar to this for flying stage scenery.

2

Ceramic sculptures

Clay provides unique possibilities for sculptors. The soft material can be molded into virtually any shape and then fired to render it permanent and solid. It is not without its difficulties, however. Pieces generally need to be made hollow, and the size of kiln will determine the dimensions of any individual part.

1

1 CLOUDS IN THE SKY

Michel Kuipers Much of Kuipers' work is large scale and architectural. Formed in sections from grogged clay, this piece was made solid and hollowed out when leather-hard. Working in this way, Kuipers is more akin to traditional sculptors than ceramicists, carving and forming his work from solid blocks.

2

2 CASSIOPEIA AND CEPHIUS

Robert Harrison The artist always works in response to the environment in which his sculptures will be situated. This site-specific architectural piece, commissioned for the Jundt Art Museum, Washington, was made from raw bricks, carved and stacked into shape, before being dismantled for firing. The reassembled piece was then cemented together and the galvanized steel pipe securely installed. Each brick was clearly numbered to make the assembly easier.

3 CONFUSION (DETAIL)

Mikang Lim Each of Lim's works carries a message personal to the artist and falls within the realms of conceptual art. Her large installation pieces are composed of numerous human forms, usually torsos made from coiled and pinched stoneware clay. Lim often combines metal, wood, and textile elements in her work.

3

4

4 SUBTERRANEAN MOONLIGHT

Hideo Matsumoto The artist creates intriguing worlds from clay, inviting his audience into his amphitheater of imagination. Made from many elements, both handbuilt and molded, his installations evoke theatricality with their dramatic lighting. The individual parts were cut and assembled from porcelain, stoneware, and iron-bearing clays, stained with subtle oxide washes, and fired to 2260ºF (1240ºC).

5 IE (HOME)

Itsue Ito This series of slab-built blocks is stacked into small tower constructions, commenting on contemporary life in Japan. Colored with commercial glazes applied by spraying with a fine airbrush, the piece stands over 7 ft. (2 m) in height on its base of ceramic bricks. The sculpture was fired to 2340ºF (1280ºC) in an electric kiln, keeping the colors bright and clean while making the piece weather resistant.

6 MACHOS

Anna Malicka Zamorska These mythical creatures were constructed from a variety of elements and clays. The torsos and feet were made from coiled, heavily grogged stoneware clay painted with oxides. Porcelain slip was poured onto plaster bats to produce the thin, folded, feather-like sheets that cover the bodies. The torsos were joined to the feet with metal rods and assembled after firing. The gold luster-painted masks and hair were also attached after firing.

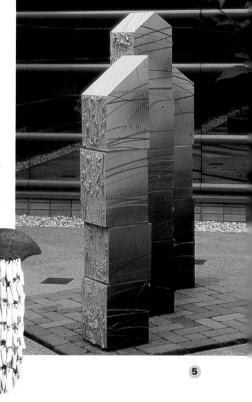

5

6

Chapter 4

DECORATING PROCESSES

Decoration can be applied at any time in the making of ceramics. It can be the simple impression of fingers on a wet clay surface or an intricate enamel painting on a glazed article. For the studio potter, the raw clay surface is like a painter's canvas, providing endless opportunities for creating individual pieces that express personal feelings and thoughts. All potters will develop their own visual language, both in terms of subject matter and the materials used. Decoration should be regarded as an integral part of any piece, rather than merely the application of color, pattern, or motif to a clay surface. It should be one of the first considerations when making a piece, growing throughout the making process so that the decoration enhances the form as well as embellishes the surface.

TYPES OF DECORATION

There are many decorative possibilities before you even handle a brush or color. Manipulating the clay itself by stretching, bending, or rolling provides excellent opportunities for experimentation. Soft, plastic clay in the potter's hands responds to any pressure. The earliest pots were decorated with simple fingermarks and impressions of sticks, providing an astonishing array of decorative possibilities. Korean Ongii potters use carved wooden tools to impress decoration into the surface as they paddle the clay to refine the shape. Japanese potters often use string or rope wound around a small stick to produce a continuous spiral pattern when rolled around the pot. Leather-hard pots can also be cut or faceted. Raw materials, including oxides, slips, and glazes, provide a wide palette of colors. Commercial suppliers produce an amazing array of underglaze and enamels colors. Decoration can also be printed onto clay, either using simple paper stencils or more sophisticated screen-printing techniques.

PRACTICAL CONSIDERATIONS

If an article is purely decorative, there is virtually no limit to the techniques that can be used. If the ware is to be utilitarian, however, the suitability of material and technique must be the prime consideration. When choosing how to decorate a domestic item—and, indeed, choosing the clay body and method of production—it is important to consider its function, the durability of the materials, and any hygiene and health regulations covering their use.

BRUSHES

Many types of decoration are painted onto the clay using brushes. Brushes come in a huge array of types. Soft oriental brushes like the hake and hakame are excellent for covering large areas with smooth slip as well as drawing thick and thin linear marks. Narrower writing brushes give wonderful variations of line when using pigments or glazes.

Design and Inspiration

The clay artist's ideas for decoration can be inspired by almost anything he or she sees, feels, or even hears. Since the first artists made marks in stone, nature has always been a rich source of inspiration, whether it be the colors in a landscape, the shape and feel of smooth pebbles, deeply eroded rock formations, or small leaves and shells. Everything you see around you can suggest decorative finishes for your pottery and sculpture.

LESS IS MORE

Great care and restraint is needed when decorating pottery. It is easy to be overwhelmed by the variety of materials available and over-decoration is a constant temptation. Simplicity is always best and decoration should never fight against the form of the work. If you want the decoration to be the main focus of the piece, simple forms with clean lines are best. Sometimes, however, it may be appropriate to let the form speak for itself with just a simple glaze over it.

LOOK AT YOUR ENVIRONMENT

All art is an interpretation of what we see and experience. Potters have the opportunity to re-create not only the colors and textures but also the form and structure of the environment. The geometric patterns of natural objects such as leaves and seeds or manmade structures such as the bricks and stones in a wall may suggest layered slip decoration on a plate. Cracked and crumbling plaster on buildings or fissures in a natural rock formation can be reproduced in paddled, scored, and torn clay, while fungus and lichen growth can be modeled onto surfaces. Dry copper raku glazes can re-create the sensation of rusting metal, while high-fired burnished porcelain has the appearance of beach pebbles pounded smooth by the tide.

1 KECSKEMÉT SERIES

Steve Mattison These illustrations show the development of an idea from the source of inspiration to the design sketches and the finished piece. Inspired by stone walls seen in Hungary, the artist developed a series of tall column structures with an eroded vessel balanced on the peak. By drawing a variety of heights, widths, shapes, and forms, the visual language of the piece was established. Experiments in surface treatments, including impressed textures and painted decoration, developed into the final slab-built structure. Textured clay was laminated into the walls of the slabs before construction, then layers of copper oxide were washed over the piece prior to raku firing to 1830ºF (1000ºC), resulting in dry, matte-colored surfaces—a personal interpretation of the source material.

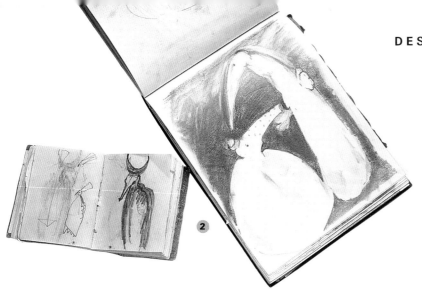

2

2 & 3 THE PROCESSION SERIES

Meri Wells *The artist captured these magical creatures on paper in quick pencil sketches, often taking only a matter of seconds as the image flashed into her mind, stirred by unrelated objects, sounds, or glimpses of animals around her farmhouse. Wells carries small, pocket-sized books whenever she goes out walking because she never knows when an idea will need to be drawn. She sees her mythical creatures moving as a processional group through the world they inhabit. After sketching, Wells created a series of hand-painted monoprints, trying to capture the atmosphere and imagery. The three final zoomorphic figures were coil built from grogged stoneware clay and decorated with slips, oxides, and selective glazing. They were fired in a wood-fueled kiln to 2370ºF (1300ºC) using soda to give lively and exciting surfaces.*

MAKING SKETCHES

Many studio potters paint and draw to record their ideas and thoughts for design and decoration. Drawing the chosen decoration before applying the final image to the work will also reduce the number of mistakes you make. Learn to select only the important elements of the design and make sure they relate to the form. With practice and patience, you will soon develop your own personal vocabulary of visual language that can be expressed through your ceramic work.

3

DESIGN AND INSPIRATION

PHOTOGRAPHIC REFERENCE

Photography is a useful tool for developing a range of reference material. It can be used extensively to record the objects, patterns, marks, and forms encountered on daily travels. Try to be aware of what is around you at all times, not only the big picture but also the minute details—always be inquisitive. While the objects you photograph should be interesting in themselves, try to consider the composition of the photograph so that you produce exciting and visually intriguing images. Photography is ideal for capturing abstract patterns that translate well into ceramic decoration. The colors and patterns of nature can all feed their way into your decoration and surface treatments of pottery. The use of this reference material in the final ceramic work will probably be implied rather than literal, often with several ideas combined. The idea is to create an impression of the moment or a feeling, so that the viewer of the pottery has the opportunity to make his or her own connection with the piece.

RAKU WARE

Steve Mattison *The illustrations shown here demonstrate the inspiration gained from photographic reference. The information has been distilled and only the impression of the resource material is expressed. For example, the piece on the far right, entitled Moving Sky, is a press-molded vase made from several pieces of colored and laminated clay. Inspired by cloud patterns in the evening sky turned pink by the setting sun, the vessel's rim was cut after removal from the mold when the clay was leather-hard. Dark lines emanating from the deep cut add dynamism and movement to the piece.*

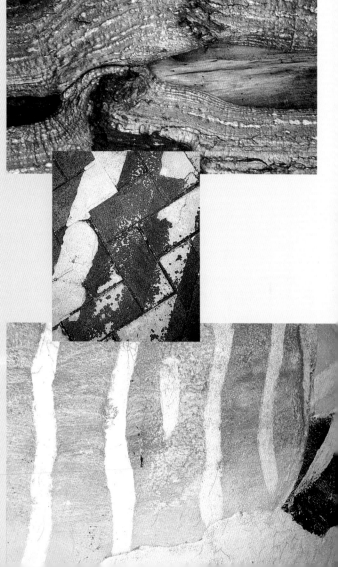

Decorative Use of Clay

Clay itself can provide its own decoration. Marks pressed into soft clay are one of the oldest forms of ceramic ornamentation. The first writings on clay tablets—lettering from impressed marks—are found in the earliest excavations. Bronze Age pottery has patterned marks pressed into the surfaces, ancient oriental vases with rolled rope marks are common, and fingerprints from the earliest potters are often seen on pots—signs where moist clay was lifted from a wheelhead. As well as texturing the clay in this way, there are countless other methods of adding interest to your pots, from incorporating modeled clay in the form of sprigs to cutting away shapes and patterns and inlaying them with contrasting colored clay.

1 STONES

Peteris Martinsons This detail of a large outdoor sculpture shows the range of impressed marks possible from just the hand. Thumb and fingertips, the side of a fist, and the palm of the hand were used to make bold, natural undulations in soft clay slabs, which were then cut and assembled into large, rocklike structures.

1

2

2 LANDSCAPE

Helle Videvik Here, Estonian artist Videvik is working on large slab constructions made from impressed and textured slabs. Thinner textured sheets are also applied to give a more three-dimensional surface quality to the angular box forms, reflecting the fractured nature of the landscape.

Impressing

The ability of clay to retain impressed marks can be exploited for decoration. Spontaneous gestures with the hands or fingers can produce lively, vigorous marks and tools of all descriptions can be used to embellish surfaces. Most potters acquire collections of found objects capable of making interesting marks in soft clay. Stamps made from plaster or bisque-fired clay can be used to impress motifs, and wooden rollers to give continuous patterns. Impressed marks can also be enhanced using slips, pigments, or glazes.

> **TOOLS**
> - Wood, bisque, or plaster stamps
> - Rolling tools
> - Textured materials

2 IMPRESSED PATTERNS

Vladimir Tsivin *Geometric impressions provide detail in Tsivin's sculptural forms. Rubber floor mats are used either in their entirety or cut into segments and pushed into soft clay, as shown on these test pieces.*

1 SUGAR TOWERS

Gwen Bainbridge *Plaster of paris casts were taken from textiles with appliqué designs, raised textures, and braiding. Bainbridge then pressed slabs of porcelain clay into these molds and used the textured slabs to form her delicate pieces.*

STAMPS

These stamps were all handmade from wooden blocks, bisque clay, or potter's plaster. You could use them as individual motifs or repeat them to create areas of pattern. When applying a stamp to a pot, make sure you support the inside of the pot with your other hand to prevent the pot from distorting under the pressure.

ROLLING TOOLS

Carved circular rollers, rope wound around sticks, and roulettes made from clay cylinders with impressed patterns can all be used to make continuous marks on pottery. When applying a roller to a pot, make sure you hold the pot steady to prevent it from toppling over or distorting under the pressure.

ROLLING CLAY

Slabs of clay can be pressed or rolled onto textured materials such as rough woven textiles and then used in decoration or the actual construction of work. In this example, a clay cylinder (with a support inside) is being rolled over a textured wooden mat to impress a series of grooves.

DECORATIVE USE OF CLAY

Inlaying

Incising marks into pottery and inlaying colored clay has been used as a decorative technique for thousands of years and is a versatile method of embedding contrasting colors of clay into the body of your pots. Clays of all colors can be used but often it is the simple contrasts that are the most effective. Cut your design when the pot is soft but firm enough to handle without distortion. Be sure to use clays of similar shrinkage or gaps may appear at the edges of your inlay. A good tip is always to mix your colored clay from the same clay as the body. Porcelain or white earthenware will give the cleanest color response but any clay can be used.

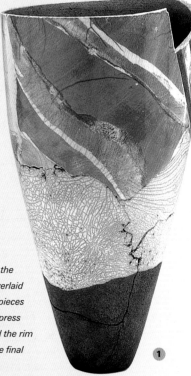

1 SKY SERIES VESSEL

Steve Mattison *Inspired by the patterns of clouds and the colors of sunset, this collage vessel was made from overlaid pieces of painted clay. Rolled together and retorn, the pieces were pressed and firmly joined inside a tall one-piece press mold. When leather-hard, the vessel was removed and the rim cut to shape before firing. The random crackle from the final raku firing creates additional decorative interest.*

1

SEE ALSO

Colored clay, *page 32*
Impressing, *page 129*
Slip decoration, *page 134*
Colored slip, *page 139*

INCISED INLAY

1 Incise lines into leather-hard clay using a metal trimming tool or similar item. Paint a contrasting colored slip thickly into the incised lines. The slip will shrink a little as it dries, so you may need to apply several layers to build up the inlay to surface level. You may also need to dampen the incised lines so the slip adheres well.

2 When the inlay has dried to the leather-hard stage, level it off with a metal scraper. This cleans up the inlaid lines and reveals the intricacy of the decoration.

PRESSED INLAY

A direct method of inlay is to press some contrasting clay firmly into the surface of your pots. The center of this flat dish is being decorated with lines of porcelain clay. Be sure to support your pots while doing this. Use a metal scraper to clean up the inlaid lines if desired.

TOOLS
- Metal trimming tool
- Brush
- Metal scraper
- Rolling pin
- Roulette

EXPERIMENTATION

Bold areas of color can be inlaid or fine lines cut and filled. Experiment with different combinations to achieve your own original designs. This is an excellent way of making well-defined lettering on commemorative pieces. Encaustic tiles are made using this method, where designs are cut to almost half the thickness of the tile, filled with clay of a different color, and then leveled. These decorative floor tiles may become worn down but the pattern will remain. Another sort of inlay can be obtained by rolling contrasting pieces of clay into a flat slab of clay. This type of decoration is rolled flat with the surface as opposed to being slightly raised and therefore does not need scraping back. The decorated slab can then be cut up and assembled into a three-dimensional shape or pressed into a mold.

2

2 SKY SERIES VESSEL (DETAIL)

Steve Mattison *Several layers of painted clay were overlapped and firmly rolled together, securely embedding the individual pieces. Where the clay stretched under the pressure of rolling, the color was broken to reveal striations of the raw white clay color. This natural occurrence adds depth to the surface.*

ROLLED INLAY

Arrange thin sheets of colored clay in a pattern on a soft slab of clay, then roll it firmly into the surface. The pattern will distort slightly as it stretches under the rolling pin, but this can be very effective. If the clays are soft enough, they will stick together easily, but you may need to wet them slightly if they are too stiff.

SURFACE PATTERN

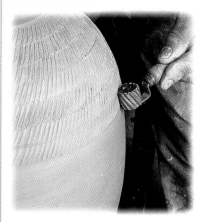

1 Use a roulette or similar tool to impress repeat patterns into a leather-hard pot. While slowly turning the throwing wheel, make sure you press down on the top of the pot to prevent it from toppling off the wheel under the pressure of the roller. Paint a layer of contrasting colored slip over the whole pot, making sure it goes into all the indentations.

2 Allow the slip to become leather-hard, then use a metal trimming tool to scratch off the outer surface of the slip. The slip will remain in the impressed marks, thereby emphasizing the pattern. Take care not to scrape away too much clay or you may lose some of the inlay pattern.

DECORATIVE USE OF CLAY

Sprigging

Sprigging is a method of applying small relief clay shapes onto the sides of pottery or into dishes. It involves making small molds into which clay is pressed to produce thin but solid clay motifs. Perfected as a technique during the 18th century, it has become synonymous with the work of the Wedgwood company in England, where white sprigs are applied to their blue-stained parian ware.

SPRIG MOLDS

The original model for sprigs can be made of clay or finely carved from plaster. You can even use real objects from which to make molds. The sprigs can then be produced by pressing small amounts of clay into the molds or by casting with slip. Generally speaking, the clay you use for sprigs should be the same as the body clay, or a stained version, to avoid possible shrinkage problems.

MOLDED SPRIGS

1 Here, a fossilized ammonite and a plaster cast of a trilobite are being used to create sprig molds. Embed the objects in a block of clay. Seal the clay around them, taking care not to create any undercuts or the models will not release from the molds.

2 Form a narrow clay wall around each object and firmly seal the walls to the clay base. Brush the objects with a good coating of soft soap to prevent them from sticking to the plaster as it dries. Mix a small quantity of plaster (see pages 96–97) and pour it over the fossils.

3 When the plaster has set, remove the clay and pull the fossils from the plaster molds. When the plaster has thoroughly dried, press soft, plastic clay into each mold and remove any excess clay with a metal scraper until it is level with the top of the mold.

STAMPED SPRIGS

Using stamped sprigs involves impressing small lumps of clay directly onto the surface of the pot with a small plaster or bisque-fired clay stamp. The stamp can be carved with a motif or pattern, which will be transferred into the clay. By this method you can work with softer clay as well as use a different clay from the body clay, since the pressure of the stamp usually embeds the motif firmly. A small amount of slip painted onto the pot will also help the sprig to stick, especially if your pots are leather-hard.

2 VESSEL WITH LUGS

David Frith This thrown jar was textured with rolled rope, then a plaster stamp was used to press porcelain disks into the leather-hard clay. These spots of light clay add points of interest to the random fly ash effects from the wood firing.

1 TEAPOT

Sarah Monk This thrown, white earthenware piece shows Monk's effective use of sprigged decoration. From a wide array of small plaster molds, she selects and applies motifs to add detail and interest to her work and enriches them with applications of honey glaze.

SEE ALSO
Impressing, *page 129*

STAMPED SPRIGS

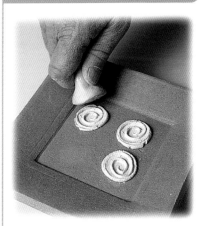

4 You can remove the sprig from the mold straight away. Press the flat blade of a knife onto the top of the sprig and draw the sprig cleanly out of the mold. Place it to one side and repeat the process until you have enough sprigs for your decoration.

5 Attach the sprigged motifs to the pot when both the sprigs and the pot are leather-hard to avoid distorting the shape of your work. Score and slip the edges to be joined (see page 35). Use a soft brush to clean up the edges of the sprigs and remove any excess slip.

You can apply a whole range of shapes, lumps, and pellets to clay surfaces. All will produce results similar to molded sprigging when pressed with carved stamps. Here, porcelain clay sprigs are being stamped onto a heavily grogged clay body. A small amount of slip has been used to adhere the stamps securely to the body.

Slip Decoration

Using different colors of liquid clay, or slip, as a decoration is one of the oldest but most expressive techniques. Dull brown clays can be transformed into smooth, light-colored pots or vividly exuberant pieces. Traditional slip-decorated pots are warm and rich in color, mainly with a red clay body, a white slip decoration, and a honey-colored transparent glaze. Engobes are a type of thick slip that usually contain flux to make them vitreous. They can be used without a glaze to produce a dry-looking surface finish. If you intend to use bright colors on your pottery, a light-colored body clay will give a good base for strong colors. Alternately, a dark clay body can be given a base coat of white slip first.

MIXING SLIP

The choice of clay for your slip is important because the shrinkage of the slip must be almost the same as that of the body; if not, it might peel or flake off as it dries. A good ball clay on its own will adhere well to most clay bodies and will be light in color. It is usually the base for most colored slips (see page 139).

TOOLS

- *Bowls*
- *Jug*
- *Stick or electric drill and metal mixing blade*
- *80-mesh sieve*
- *Stiff-bristled brush or rubber rib*
- *Flat brush*
- *Paint roller*
- *Open-weave textiles*
- *Paper*

BASIC WHITE SLIP

2¼ lb. (1 kg) ball clay
3½ pints (2 liters) water

MIXING SLIP

1 For small amounts of slip, add water gradually to the dry powdered clay, mixing until you reach a creamy consistency. Make sure you wear a mask because of the dust hazard. For larger amounts of slip, use the recipe above and add the water in one go. Using an electric drill and metal mixing blade will make the job easier.

2 Pour the clay slip into an 80-mesh sieve and stir it through with a stiff-bristled brush or rubber rib. Small amounts of water can be added afterward to adjust the thickness if required. If the slip is too thin, allow it to settle overnight and then pour off some of the liquid on the surface.

BRUSHING ON

Brush the slip onto the pot as evenly as possible. Use soft, flat brushes because they leave fewer brushmarks. In some cases, you may need a couple of coats to cover the body clay sufficiently.

APPLYING SLIP

The stage at which slip is applied to the surface of a pot is important. In practically all cases, slip is applied to leather-hard clay. The surface of the pot should be hard enough to handle easily and not lose its shape, but damp enough to absorb the slip slowly. If the pot is too wet, it can collapse as it absorbs the water from the slip and must therefore be supported in some way to prevent this (if the pot is still in a press mold, this will not be a problem). If the pot is too dry, the slip can crack off as the water is absorbed and the slip shrinks. Often a pot will survive the slipping stage only to peel off during a glaze firing, taking the glaze with it.

LARGE JAR

Kang Hyo Lee *One of the master Ongii potters of Korea, Lee throws using thick coils of clay on a traditional kick wheel, firing his pots in an anagama kiln over several days. The slowness of the wheel's rotation and the softness of the clay give his work simplicity and freshness. Slip was wiped on with his hands, retaining all the vigorous fingermarks.*

ROLLERING

If your pot is wide and shallow, you may be able to use a paint roller to apply the slip. This can often create an interesting texture in the slip that can be exploited in your decoration.

TEXTILE STENCILS

Try brushing on slips through open-weave textiles to create patterns on your work. Here, an ordinary dishcloth has been rolled into the soft clay and colored slips painted over it before peeling off the stencil to reveal the body color of the clay. Small areas of impressed textures are highlighted with thin layers of slip on the ridges.

PAPER STENCILS

This series of stencils cut from thick absorbent paper will make interesting shapes and patterns when used as resists for slip. This type of paper can be washed and reused many times. You can also use newspaper, but the stencil can only be used once.

SEE ALSO
Clay and pottery bodies, *pages 8–17*

SLIP DECORATION

SLIP TRAILING

Slip decoration has its traditional roots in the 17th century, especially in the Staffordshire potteries of England where master potter Thomas Toft perfected the technique of slip trailing. Fairly thick slip is squeezed onto the clay through a nozzle fixed into a rubber bulb. The pressure of squeezing the bulb controls the flow of slip. You may also be able to find slip trailers made from clay, like small bottles, with feather quills for nozzles, some even having multiple nozzles to draw parallel lines. When using clay slip trailers, blocking an air hole with a thumb controls the flow. Whatever type of trailer you use, the technique requires a little practice to ensure confidence and an even flow of slip. Start with a flat or open surface rather than a vertical one.

EXPERIMENTATION

Slip designs can be applied in many ways, including pouring, dipping, painting, spraying, sponging, and trailing. When several of these techniques are combined, lively and exciting surfaces can be achieved. Painted slip can be exuberant and handled almost like watercolor washes, with thin slips painted over thicker layers of color. The thickness or thinness of the slip will produce different effects, so experiment with all the possibilities to find your own personal expression.

TOOLS
- *Slip trailer*
- *Paintbrush*
- *Sponge*
- *Paint roller*
- *Wooden stick*

1 CUP AND JUG

Sitar Brothers These traditional drinking vessels from Baia Mare in Romania show a distinctive style of slip trailing. Thrown on a kick wheel from a local red clay, the pots were coated with black slip before the final details of trailed white slip were added. Raw glazed with a galena (lead) glaze, the pots were fired once in a wood-burning updraft kiln.

SLIP TRAILING	COMBINED TECHNIQUES

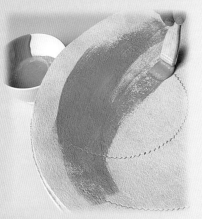

Rest the trailer on your fingers so that you can squeeze the rubber bulb with your thumb. Trailing requires slip of a fairly thick consistency, but if it is too thick, it will sit in peaks. If this happens, gently tap the pot on your workbench while the design is still wet to encourage the peaks to flatten. Keep the trailer fairly full to avoid spattering.

1 Apply a white slip over the whole surface and allow it to dry leather-hard so that it can support additional decoration without smearing. This dish has also been impressed with a roller to create small zigzag lines across the surface to liven up the "canvas." Paint a series of vigorous marks in a colored slip. While still in the mold, this pressed dish is safely supported.

2 Slips can be applied using a variety of sponges. Here, a natural sponge produces subtle textures. Sponges can also be cut into shapes for applying motifs. For accurate cuts, dampen the sponge, squeeze it out, and put it into a freezer overnight. You can cut extremely accurate and fine marks with a sharp craft knife while the sponge is still frozen.

2 UNTITLED VESSEL

David Miller This thrown vase form has been reshaped while still soft and cut with a wire at the rim and base. The enjoyment of decoration is ever-present in Miller's work, with the surfaces becoming canvases for his vigorous and immediate slip decoration. All of his pieces are made from red clay coated with a white slip onto which stained slips are painted. They are then wood fired to 2050°F (1120°C) with a thin matte glaze.

3 Define areas of the abstract design by painting on more colored slips. A paint roller is used here to apply thin washes of white slip to tone down areas of the decoration. The roller also adds texture to the piece and gives the appearance of misty tones of color.

4 Using a trailer with a narrow nozzle, trail lines of black slip to give definition to areas of color and emphasize edges of the design. You need to control the trailer with confidence to produce the flowing lines that are the essence of slip trailing. Mistakes or shaky lines are hard to correct at this stage.

5 Use the end of a wooden stick to apply dots of slip. Dip the stick after applying each dot to ensure they are evenly sized. Allow the decorated dish to dry gradually before bisque firing. A transparent glaze will add a sparkle to the surface.

SEE ALSO

Impressing, *page 129*
Colored slip, *page 139*

Sgraffito

Sgraffito is a form of incising into clay. It is usually used on pieces coated with a contrasting slip to the body clay, where you cut through the layer of slip with various tools to reveal the body color. Sgraffito can be carried out on wet, leather-hard, or dry slip, each giving a different effect. While the slip is still wet, a fluid-looking design can be made using a serrated tool or even the fingers. Confident strokes give the best results and a temptation to overwork the decoration should be avoided to retain the freshness of this technique. On leather-hard pots, the slip should be scraped away without digging into the body clay. Whole areas of slip can be removed using a broad tool, while knives, modeling tools, knitting needles, and wire-looped tools all give variations of line. Textures are easily achieved using sgraffito on dry slip, but it can tend to chip easily. It is advisable to use a sharp metal tool to produce a fine rather than broad line. This type of sgraffito looks best on burnished slip surfaces.

TOOLS

- *Wooden incising tool*
- *Serrated piece of plastic or soft rubber*

DISH

Ibata Katsue Made from red clay, this small press-molded dish was coated with white slip followed by black slip brushwork when leather-hard. Sgraffito details were freely drawn through the slips to varying depths, revealing not only the white slip but also the red clay.

INCISING	COMBING	FINGER WIPING

Use a wooden tool to cut through leather-hard slip to reveal the warm color of the body clay. You can make freehand, organic marks or use a ruler for straight lines. If you cut with a lot of pressure, you will also incise into the body of your pottery. If you are working on press-molded dishes, it may be easier to keep the dish in the mold for support while you decorate.	Using a serrated piece of plastic or rubber, comb a series of lines through slightly damp slip to produce patterns reminiscent of furrows in a field. Do not press too hard or you can gouge deep marks into the clay—unless this is an effect you desire.	Finger wiping can be found on the earliest pottery. While the slip is still wet, pull your fingers through it, leaving wavy lines in the surface. This creates soft, decorative contrasts of color with a human feel.

SEE ALSO

Slip decoration, *pages 134–137*
Colored slip, *page 139*

Colored slip

You can use either metallic oxides as colorants or commercially prepared stains. The amount of coloring agent required depends on personal taste and the intensity of the colorant being used, some being more powerful than others. If using oxides, add 0.5–2 percent for light shades; 2–5 percent for medium hues; and 5–10 percent for dark colors. This guide is for use with white or light-firing clays that give a purer color response. If using commercial colorants, add about 10–15 percent of the stain to a white slip. Always make up a sample batch because stains may vary depending on the supplier. If a small amount of very thick slip is required for high-relief work, add a few drops of a flocculent such as calcium chloride to increase the viscosity; a deflocculent such as Dispex will give the reverse effect (see page 28).

TOOLS
- *Bowl*
- *Jug*
- *Stick*
- *Sieve*
- *Stiff-bristled brush*

BLUE SLIP

White base slip	96.5%
Cobalt oxide	3.5%

GREEN SLIP

White base slip	97.5%
Copper oxide	2.5%

BLACK SLIP #1

Red clay base slip	93%
Iron oxide	3%
Cobalt oxide	2%
Manganese dioxide	2%

BLACK SLIP #2

Powdered red clay	70%
Cobalt oxide	15%
Manganese dioxide	15%

MARBLED STORAGE JARS

Bethan Lloyd-Davies Small amounts of colored slips were poured into molds one after another and swirled around to create the patterns on these jars. A final pour of thicker slip was used to bind all the layers together. After bisque firing, the inside was glazed and the outside was polished with wet and dry sandpaper to smooth the surfaces prior to a final high firing to intensify the color.

MIXING COLORED SLIP

1 To make a colored slip from scratch, add the powdered clay and colorant to the water and mix thoroughly. If you already have a base slip you wish to color, it is best to pre-mix the colorant with water to break down any lumps and disperse the color evenly. Use a stiff-bristled brush to push the mixture through a 100–120-mesh sieve, then pour it into the base slip and mix well.

2 Stir the mixture through a 200-mesh sieve. This prevents small particles of stain from speckling the slip when painting or during firing. The next day, remove any excess water from the top of the slip if desired.

MARBLING SLIP

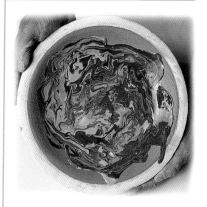

Pour areas of contrasting slip into a press-molded dish. Twist or shake the mold to move the liquid slips around to form variegated patterns. Be careful not to shake the mold for too long or the slips will begin to mix together.

SEE ALSO
Slip decoration, *pages 134–137*
Pigments and stains, *pages 176–177*

SLIP DECORATION

Burnishing

Polishing the leather-hard clay surface is known as burnishing. This traditional decorative technique was used before glaze technology was developed, giving pottery a slight surface shine and water resistance because it causes the clay particles to compact. Any fine clay body is ideal for burnishing, but if your clay is coarse or groggy, a coating of fine clay slip can be painted or sprayed onto the surface and polished. The clay needs to be in the correct state of dryness—too damp and the tools will stick to the surface, too dry and you will have to use more pressure, risking damage and scratching. The perfect slip for spraying and burnishing is terra sigillata (see page 141). Burnished pottery should not be fired above 1830°F (1000°C) or the effect will be lost. After firing, a clear wax can be applied and polished with a soft cloth for a glass-like finish.

BURNISHED VESSEL

Antonia Salmon *Stillness and movement have always interested Salmon and she explores these qualities in her strong, pure forms with subtle finishes. The delicate burnishing of the piece allows geometric sgraffito patterns to contrast with the polished smoked surface. The balanced blade of clay emphasizes the fragility of low-fired burnished ware.*

TOOLS
- Polished pebbles
- Stencil
- Paintbrush

USING PEBBLES

1 This bowl is being burnished with small polished pebbles. Other tools you can use include glass, metal, or even plastic spoons. Use a circular motion so that any marks in the clay surface will be less obvious. As the clay becomes smoother, many potters give it another polish with a plastic bag over the fingers or a soft cotton cloth.

2 As a decorative feature, areas of the burnished surface can be masked out and a contrasting colored slip applied. Make sure the slip dries leather-hard before burnishing it—too dry and it can be chalky, too wet and it can smear.

3 Burnish the decorative slip using the polished pebbles. If you want to keep a defined edge to the decoration, burnish along the join line before resuming a circular motion. If you polish across the join in a circular motion straight away, the mark will lose its definition.

Terra sigillata

Terra sigillata is an extremely fine clay, having been ground over thousands of years by rocks and water. The characteristic rust red surface sheen can be seen on Roman Samian ware in museums, and more rarely, as shards found in the earth. Terra sigillata will develop a dense, shiny coating when fired at earthenware temperatures, but if fired at a higher temperature the sheen may disappear. With unglazed, porous pottery, a surface coating of fine terra sigillata gives a dense layer of impervious slip, slowing down absorption of liquid through the body. Thin sigillata slip should be sprayed finely onto leather-hard pots, when it can shine immediately. You can also pour or paint the slip, and when it has dried to a matte finish, lightly buff it with a soft cloth to bring it to a satin sheen.

MAKING TERRA SIGILLATA

Most potters now make their own terra sigillata slips from white ball clay, which gives a good base for coloring oxides (see page 139). Add the clay to the water and mix thoroughly. Sprinkle some water softener, such as Calgon, into the mixture and stir well.

Leave for 24 hours until it separates into three distinct parts—water at the top, fine slip in the middle, and sludge at the bottom. Siphon off the water and carefully pour the middle section into a container—this is the sigillata. You may have to adjust the amount of water softener in the mix, depending on the natural softness of your water. In some areas, no softener is needed because the water has enough in itself.

BASIC TERRA SIGILLATA

3½ lb. (1.5 kg) dry white ball clay or powdered red clay

6 pints (3.5 liters) water

¼ oz. (10 g) water softener

---

1 SAMIAN WARE

Displaying fine molded decoration, these shards of Roman pottery were found while digging a garden. A fine coating of terra sigillata gives them a warm color and soft, unglazed sheen.

2 LANDSCAPE SCULPTURE

Alan Watt Working from solid blocks of clay, layers were cut with knives and torn away to create these natural-looking strata, heavily influenced by the rock formation of Watt's Australian landscape. The clay was hollowed from underneath to reduce the thickness. Terra sigillata slips were sprayed onto the surfaces, allowing rainbow colors to appear during a heavily reducing smoke firing.

3 COIL VESSEL

Sue King This coil-built vessel has been burnished and coated with a fine layer of terra sigillata slip before polishing with a soft cloth. Firing in a sawdust kiln made from house bricks has produced patches of smoke of undulating density. While still warm, a wax polish was applied and buffed using a soft cloth to give a natural sheen to the piece.

Slip-decorated ceramics

Slip can be used in many ways to make attractive decoration. It can brushed all over a pot, applied in abstract patterns, or painted in pictorial designs. Decorative marks can also be incised into the slip to great effect.

1

2

1 BOTTLE

Cseke Janos *This traditional wood-fired earthenware bottle has a hollow handle with an air hole. Closing or opening the hole with the thumb controls the flow of liquid. Lines of white slip were combed through as decoration, and the bottle was coated on the inside and partially down the outside with a transparent glaze. Janos throws his pottery on a left-sided kick wheel.*

2 STONEWARE VASE

Claude Varlan *Painterly application of engobe slips colored with stains and oxides creates a dry yet lively surface, with minimal highlights of glaze. Prolonged periods of wood firing allowed flashes and ash build-up to add color and texture variations to the exposed areas.*

3 DANCING GIRLS IN NATIONAL COSTUME

Florin Colibaba *This naive sgraffito-decorated plate is typical of the Kuty region in Ukraine and northern Romania. Painted white slip was drawn through to reveal dark lines of terra-cotta clay, while cobalt blue and copper green oxides were washed over areas to add variations of color. Colibaba's pottery reflects the daily life of village people, their traditions, and customs.*

4 DISH

Megumi Urwake *Thick coils of clay were pressed together to form small slabs and the edges softened with the palm of the hand. Broad geometric shapes were then painted in white slip and the corners of the slab lifted and supported on small balls of clay while it dried. After bisque firing, lines were drawn with underglaze pencils and chalks to add details and emphasis.*

5 SGRAFFITO BOWL

Jean Paul Landreau *The entire range of slip decoration techniques can be seen in Landreau's work. Areas are masked with stencils, brushwork sweeps across the surface, spatters of bright slip are flicked from toothbrushes, sponges speckle and add texture, while sgraffito lines cut through the blue background reveal lines of hard white.*

3

5

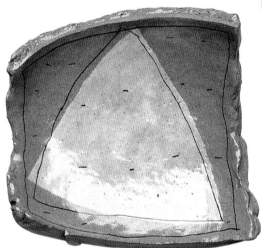

4

6

6 SQUARED DISH

Jim Robison This soft slab has stenciled slip decoration with square indents pressed into the clay, making small mounds of clay on the underside. Slashed with a knife, the deep cuts have been stretched open and the edges of the dish rounded over to soften them. Colored slips were painted and sprayed to build up the surfaces and the piece was reduction fired to 2340°F (1280°C) in a gas kiln with applications of dry ash glazes.

Glazes and Pigments

Pigments and glazes are the basic materials for many kinds of decoration. Ceramic pigments are derived from metallic oxides, carbonates, and dioxides mixed together in various combinations to give a variety of hues when fired. They can be applied on their own to raw or bisque-fired clay or added to glazes to give a richer palette of colors and tones. Glazing ceramics simply means adding a coating of ground raw materials suspended in water to the surface of the pottery. Glaze is commonly applied to bisque-fired work but can be applied to raw clay as well. When heated, the glaze melts to form a glass-like surface that is usually impervious to water. Glazing pottery adds another decorative dimension of color and texture.

METALLIC OXIDES

Ceramicists use many metallic oxides. The oxides of cobalt, copper, manganese, and iron are the most common and form the basis of most of the colors used in clay and glaze. They can be applied to soft, leather-hard, or bone-dry clay. They can be painted onto bisque or rubbed dry into the clay surface. They can also be mixed with water for painting. Sometimes a gum such as gum arabic or tragacanth is mixed into the liquid to adhere the oxide to the surface so that it is harder to rub off while handling and glazing. Oxides can also be added directly into the clay body to give alternatives of color. The higher the percentage of oxide, the darker the color will become. Oxides can be added to dry powdered clay before mixing with water to give an even dispersal of color, or they can be kneaded into plastic clay to give a more speckled effect. This can be especially interesting when the oxides flux and bleed into a subsequent glaze coating.

STAINS AND UNDERGLAZE PIGMENTS

If you do not wish to mix your own pigments from oxides, you can buy commercially manufactured stains in a wide range of hues. These are stable and reliable and can be obtained as body or glaze stains. Underglaze pigments are a more refined version of stains and are used for decorating a bisque clay surface prior to an application of transparent glaze. They can also be used on top of a dry glaze surface prior to firing and are the basis of majolica painting. They can be bought as dry powders, pencils, or crayons.

ENAMELS

Enamels are pigments that contain fluxes to allow them to melt and fuse onto a fired glaze surface. Some are spirit based and require great skill to use because the balance of turpentine and oil in the mixture can be critical. More commonly these days, they are obtained in water-soluble form. Enamels provide the potter with the greatest range of hues and colors. They are ideal for detailed work but more difficult for covering large areas.

BLACK STAIN FOR CLAY

Chrome oxide	*50%*
Red iron oxide	*25%*
Manganese dioxide	*20%*
Cobalt oxide	*5%*

This will give a consistent black stain for mixing into powdered or plastic clay.

Underglaze pigment

Iron oxide

Powdered and liquid enamel

GLAZES

Glaze ingredients are relatively cheap and the process of glazing is a simple one, but the results can be glorious when done well. For many potters, glazing is the most daunting pottery process and results can be disappointing, but with perseverance pleasing results can be achieved. Fired glazes span the entire spectrum of colors and textures. They can be transparent, translucent, or opaque; they can be glossy, semi-matte, or matte. Glossy glazes tend to run more during firing, whereas matte ones are usually more stable. However, all glazes will run if over-fired in the kiln. Glazes add durability and practicality to work, especially for domestic use, and will render clay surfaces impervious to water and enable easy cleaning.

Glazes can be applied in virtually any way you can think of. However, all application methods will leave traces when fired—brushmarks can still show and over-painted layers will have different finishes. It is therefore important that you choose a method that will give you the finish you desire. Multiple glazes can be applied to the same piece, giving variegated effects when fired together, and reactive glazes can break through in unexpected ways to add rich colors and textures. Specialty finishes such as crystalline glazes require greater care and experience but can be rewarding if used on smooth, white-firing clay such as porcelain. Whichever way you decide to use glazes, they can lift your work into the realms of beauty.

TESTING GLAZES

All glazes need to be thoroughly tested by firing them in your own kiln at the temperatures you work with and on the clays you use. Even if you buy glazes ready made from suppliers, they still need to be tested before you glaze all your work. Pictures in catalogs can be deceptive.

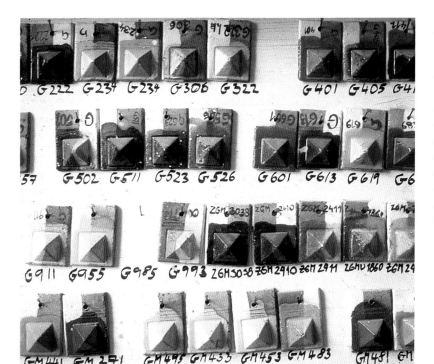

GLAZE TESTS

This extensive series of glaze tests has been carefully cataloged and numbered to enable students to select suitable glazes for their work easily. Recipes that correspond accurately to the test samples are listed in an accompanying book. For any glaze formulation and testing, thorough notes and records must be kept to enable successive batches of identical glaze to be made. It is surprisingly easy to forget which mix of materials created that wonderful glaze from the last firing, never to be repeated.

SEE ALSO

Colored clay, *page 32*
Preparing the clay, *pages 40–42*
Raw materials, *pages 170–187*

Underglaze decoration

Underglaze colors are commercially manufactured pigments that are stable during use and will generally fire to the same or similar color as the raw material. This quality makes them ideal for many decorative purposes and gives unprecedented control of color and artistic expression. Underglazes are made from mixtures of various oxides and frits, calcined at high temperatures to stabilize the ingredients, and then ground into powder form for use. When mixed with water, they can be applied directly to plastic or dry clay or to bisque ware under the glaze. Underglazes can also be applied on top of a dry, unfired glazed surface and will sink into the glaze as they melt together during firing (see pages 150–151).

USING UNDERGLAZE

When used on bisque, the liquid is quickly absorbed from the underglaze so that it returns to powder form, making it easily smudged. To prevent this, add a small amount of gum arabic or underglaze medium to the mixture to adhere the color to the surface. It may be necessary to bisque fire the piece again to burn out the impurities of the medium and make sure the glaze will not be affected by any vapor. Powdered underglaze is the least expensive form to use, but ready-mixed brush-on underglaze is a good substitute and already contains a suitable amount of medium for free-flowing application. Underglaze pencils and crayons are also becoming popular.

SELF-PORTRAIT

Meri Wells This raku tile, one of a series of portraits, shows the freedom and precision that is possible when using underglaze colors. The prepared stains and oxides on this piece were applied to the bisque tile mixed only with water. The carbonized black surface provides shadow and contrast to the subtle variations of color and tone achieved by the artist.

POWDERED UNDERGLAZE

An extensive palette of underglaze colors is available, giving you a considerable degree of choice and control. When mixed with water or underglaze medium, these colors can be used in a very painterly fashion. Take care when overpainting colors to avoid smudging previous layers.

UNDERGLAZE PENCILS

Detail can be added with underglaze pencils. These are a solidified version of the powdered form with flux added. The powdery finish of the pencil line is easily smudged, so take care. Pencils are usually only available in a limited range of colors.

UNDERGLAZE CRAYONS

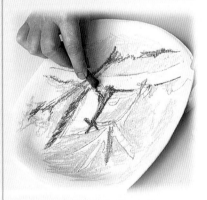

Underglaze crayons are softer and wider versions of pencils. They behave in a similar way to chalks, allowing larger areas to be covered in a variety of marks. Like ordinary drawing chalks, they create a fine dust around the drawn lines that can be blown away easily, but it is advisable to wear a mask if using crayons a great deal.

Enamels and lusters

Enamels are prepared colors composed of metal oxides and fluxes that are designed to melt at low temperatures. When applied to previously fired glazes and then fired to 1200–1440°F (650–780°C), they melt into the surface. Enamels are the brightest of all ceramic colorants and are available in a wide range of hues. Lusters are classified in the same range of on-glaze decorative finishes as enamels due to the similar firing temperature and their need to be applied to a pre-fired glazed surface. Luster is a fine metal coating deposited on the surface of pottery, traditionally created by firing in a reduced smoky atmosphere. Manufactured lusters can reproduce these metallic effects in an oxidation atmosphere by the addition of a thick oil medium that burns away during firing, creating a local reduction.

USING ENAMELS

Traditionally, enamels are mixed and ground on a glass plate (known as mulling) with fat oil or turpentine to ease the flow of the colors and to bind them to the glazed surface until firing. Many potters use commercially manufactured enamels that are already mixed with binders to form a thick liquid. This can be diluted with water if required. The firing of enamels is usually the final and lowest temperature firing of any ceramic and must be slow at first to allow the oil medium to burn off. Adequate ventilation is essential. If the firing is too fast, the oil will boil and bubbling will occur on the surface of the pot.

USING LUSTERS

Lusters are dark brown in color and very sticky to use. The color is deceptive and the true luster only appears after firing. It can be confusing to use lusters unless you are sure of the colors beforehand. Many potters fire each luster separately to be sure of the combinations of color. Precious metal lusters of gold, silver, platinum, bronze, and mother of pearl are most commonly used, but blues, reds, pinks, and other colors are also available.

ENAMELS AND LUSTERS

Enamels are available in liquid and powder form and are relatively inexpensive. If mistakes are made during application, they can be wiped off the glaze surface cleanly. Metal lusters (top left) come as a sticky liquid that can be thinned down to flow more easily. Certain lusters can be extremely expensive, depending on the quantity of precious metal involved. Both enamels and lusters can be applied by painting, spraying, sponging, stamping, or printing. They can also be diluted and used like watercolor washes.

2 ENAMELED DISH

John Maltby *This landscape-based decoration involves the use of thick engobe slips applied through paper stencils. After firing, red and black enamels were applied thickly to give deep, rich colors. The satin glaze gives the enamels a softer appearance than their characteristic hard gloss.*

1 UNTITLED SCULPTURE

Eva Tamas *The slip-cast egg lies on a poured porcelain slab, both covered in mother-of-pearl luster on a high-gloss transparent glaze. A spring of coiled porcelain exudes cord-like from the egg. Coatings of silver and 24-carat gold luster are expensive but give a delightfully rich finish.*

SEE ALSO
Glazes, *pages 178–187*
Kilns and firings, *pages 188–207*

GLAZES AND PIGMENTS

Resist techniques

A variety of materials and media can be used to mask off areas of a surface to create decorative effects. Anything held against the surface of the fired pottery will provide a resist, and the form of resist chosen will make its own contribution to the decoration.

WAX RESIST

Hot or cold wax provides resists on pottery at various stages of making. Used on leather-hard clay, it will resist poured and painted slips, while on bisque-fired items it is an excellent resist for glazes. Any design should be well planned out first and the wax should be applied swiftly because it sets quickly. Many potters add a small amount of vegetable dye to the wax, which allows the design to be seen more clearly but burns out during firing. For hot wax, you can purchase specially manufactured wax pots for ceramics or use textile batik pots. These have thermostat controls to prevent overheating. Kitchen slow cookers can also be used satisfactorily, or you can heat the wax in a small saucepan immersed in water in a larger pan; the heat from the water permeates the inner pan and melts the wax. Small amounts of paraffin should be added to the wax to make it flow more easily from the brush. Cold wax, known as emulsion, provides a slimy

1 SLABBED VESSEL

Peter Beard This large slab-built vessel utilizes matte and semi-matte glazes to achieve rich, textured surfaces reminiscent of cool, deep waters. Beard's work has become synonymous with latex resist techniques. Here, layers of latex were applied and peeled off after the final glaze coat.

WAX RESIST ON BISQUE	WAX RESIST ON GLAZE

Wax is commonly used to resist glazes from the base of pots. This can save time in a production pottery because it allows the entire pot to be dipped in the glaze bucket, the liquid running off the base on removal from the container. Wax can also be applied as a decoration to the bisque clay prior to a glaze coating. On firing, the wax burns away to reveal the raw clay.

1 Using a stiff-bristled household paintbrush, apply the wax to the glazed surface in the required design. A zigzag line is drawn here. Quick and assured movements are often best.

2 Apply a second glaze over the dish. The glaze will run off the waxed areas. During firing, the two glazes will melt and react with each other to create interesting effects.

SEE ALSO
Glazes, *pages 178–187*
Kilns and firings, *pages 188–207*

surface that repels liquid. Wax emulsions take longer to set and must be dry before continuing with the decoration or the effects can smear. Wash brushes thoroughly after use because any cold wax left in the bristles will set and ruin the brush. Brushes used for hot wax will become encased in wax over time and should be kept specifically for this use. The wax in the bristles will melt each time the brush is used.

PAPER RESIST

Paper stencils can be applied over bisque clay or a previously glazed surface and painted or sprayed through. Generally, if the area to be masked is large, paper resists are the obvious choice. Paper is a versatile tool for resisting glazes because you can draw the stencils before cutting them.

LATEX RESIST

Latex is a rubber solution that dries fairly quickly into a stretchy material that can be removed easily from dry surfaces. When intricate designs of overlapping latex are applied to bisque or glazed pottery, the latex can be removed in one mass, each piece stretching away and pulling off the next. Layer on layer of glaze and latex can be built up to achieve rich surfaces, especially where dry and shiny glazes are superimposed. Pulling off layers of dry glaze will create dust and suitable precautions should be taken. In addition, larger particles of glaze may contaminate other pieces of pottery by being flicked from the rubber onto other areas of your work.

TOOLS
- Paintbrushes
- Bowl
- Ladle
- Paper
- Knife
- Slip trailer
- Tweezers

2 BLASTED FORM

Peter Beard *Thick latex patterns were applied to the fired, unglazed clay and eroded with fine particles of sand blown by compressed air. Air-borne silica from the clay and dust from the blasting are hazardous, so Beard wears a full face mask with a filtered air supply to ensure none of the dust is inhaled.*

PAPER RESIST	LATEX RESIST

Draw the design you require and cut out the paper stencil. Position the stencil and brush glaze over it. You can also spray the glaze, but small amounts can bleed under the paper unless it is taped down. This overspray effect can be decorative in its own right, however.

1 Latex resist can be applied in narrow lines through a slip trailer or areas may be painted with a brush. Regular and precise patterns can be achieved and slight irregularities in the width of the line can add to the quality of glazing. Allow the latex to dry before applying the next coat of glaze. The drying can be speeded up with a gentle flow of warm air from a hair dryer.

2 When the resist has dried, immerse the pot in the second glaze. Alternately, glazes can be painted or sprayed, depending on the desired result. When the glaze has dried, pull off the latex with your fingers or a pair of tweezers. If the resist lines join up in some way, the design will peel off as a stretchy mesh of rubber.

GLAZES AND PIGMENTS

Majolica

Majolica was first developed in the Middle East and quickly moved to southern Europe, where the technique became famous and is typically found in Spain and Italy. In other parts of Europe it became known as faience and delftware. All these names refer to the technique of painting colors over an unfired dry glazed surface. When fired, the color melts into the glaze, fusing the design. This leads to its other name of in-glaze decoration, which describes the physical process involved.

BASE GLAZE

Originally, a transparent base glaze would have been applied over a white slip body, but in recent times an opaque white tin glaze has become the accepted base. However, potters may still use colored transparent glazes, depending on the desired result. When a white opaque glaze is used over a red terra-cotta clay body, the technique is commonly referred to as tin-glaze earthenware.

1 MUG AND A JUG

Italy These are two fine examples of patterned majolica pottery. Slip cast in white earthenware clay, these pots have been coated with transparent glaze before being handpainted with patterned lines of lively color. Broad brushmarks are detailed with fine, wavy lines of black pigment. This type of work is typical of handcrafted, mass-produced domestic pottery from the Italian majolica factories.

1

APPLYING COLORS

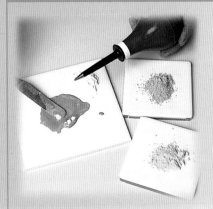

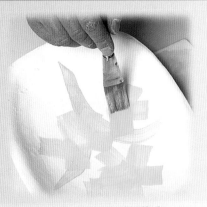

1 Mix some powdered underglaze colors with a small amount of flux and a little water. It is often best to add the water drop by drop from a slip trailer because it is difficult to thicken the colors if they become too watery. Use a palette knife for mixing; it will grind down any large particles of stain.

2 Use a large, springy bristled brush to apply large areas of color. The marks shown here will form slightly abstract flower petals. Broad brushstrokes need sufficient color in the brush. If it dries up mid-stroke, the marks may show when fired.

3 As the design becomes more intricate and detailed, start to use smaller brushes. Pure sable bristles, although more expensive, give a beautiful line. For accuracy, support and stabilize the wrist of your drawing hand with your other hand. This will allow the free and easy movement necessary for fine lining.

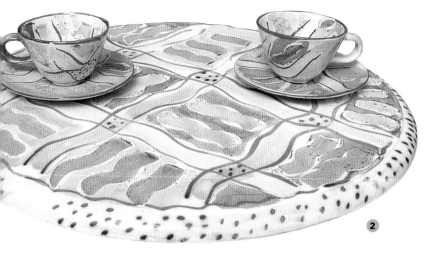

2 TEA SETTING

Majolica Works As the majolica painting melted into the base tin glaze, the color broke up slightly to give a beautiful mottled surface where specks of white break through the decoration. Thrown using red earthenware clay, the opaque white glaze provides a neutral ground that adds brilliance to the colors.

APPLYING COLORS

The color pigments are best used when finely ground and added to a small amount of flux, frit, or the base glaze. This allows the color to flow more freely from the brush. Practice is needed to become confident with the brushwork, and designs need to be planned carefully beforehand. Mistakes are difficult to rectify because the friable glaze can easily be damaged and flake off.

3 RUNNER BEAN CASSEROLE

Morgen Hall This is a classic piece of tin-glaze earthenware pottery. Areas of cobalt blue were painted over stencils of runner beans applied to the opaque tin glaze. Areas of thinner glaze reveal the richness of the terra-cotta clay breaking through the surface, while a speckling of rutile adds further depth to the decoration.

4 Rutile contains iron oxide and titanium dioxide and will produce broken textures. Sponge a thin solution of rutile onto the surface. When fired, it will sink into the glaze and give a lively mottling of subtle burnt orange to soften the decoration.

5 Apply highlights and details. Here, red and pink colors are dotted onto areas of the design using the end of a wooden dowel. Inventive applications of color lead to exciting results.

TOOLS
- Slip trailer
- Palette knife
- Selection of tools for applying paint, such as paintbrushes, sponges, and wooden dowels

SEE ALSO
Pigments and stains, *pages 176–177*
Glazes, *pages 178–187*
Kilns and firings, *pages 188–207*

GLAZES AND PIGMENTS

Glaze on glaze

Most potters develop their own palette of glazes, many of which produce interesting colors and textures on their own. When glazes are applied over glazes, however, surprising and exciting reactions often occur. An informed knowledge of the glazes and how they interact with each other during firing is crucial and usually a great deal of experimentation is needed to master the possibilities. Always place test pieces on broken or old kiln furniture, raised off the shelf, or sit them on a thick layer of alumina. This will prevent the work from sticking to the kiln shelf if mixtures of glaze become excessively fluid and the molten glaze runs down the pot. Using glazes with different viscosities will often produce more interesting effects, especially when overlaying glossy glazes with dry ones. The shiny glaze will tend to move a little, breaking through the surface of the dry glaze as it melts.

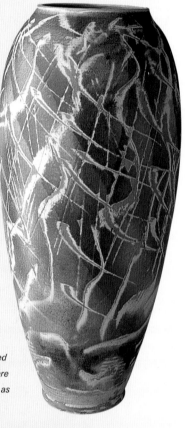

TOOLS
- Bowls
- Jug
- Glaze tongs
- Ladle
- Metal scraper

SGRAFFITO VASE

Jobb Heycamp *This tall thrown vase has been decorated with several glazes. When dry, the successive layers were randomly scraped away to reveal the underlying colors as the piece was slowly rotated on a banding wheel.*

POURED DESIGN		SCRATCHED PATTERN

 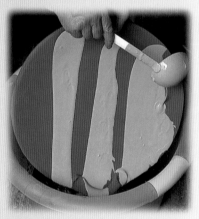 

1 Using a large jug that holds enough glaze not to need refilling, pour the glaze evenly over the pot. The handles on this platter give a good place to grip the pot and can be touched up with glaze afterwards. Alternately, you could hold the pot with glaze tongs or with spread fingers on the bottom rim, resting the base against your forearm.

2 Pour the second glaze in streaks down the face of the platter using a ladle. A contrasting ocher glaze is applied here. This type of expressive decoration has its roots in Japan, where layers of freely poured glaze are used to produce simple yet vigorous surfaces. The interaction of glazes will give a rich finish of variegated texture.

Two glazes have been applied one on top of the other on this small vase. Use a metal scraper to scratch areas of the top glaze away to reveal the glaze and even the clay beneath. The edges will soften slightly during firing.

SEE ALSO

Glazes, *pages 178–187*
Kilns and firings, *pages 188–207*

Tube lining

Tube lining is used to draw the outline of a design in a thick slip on leather-hard clay. After bisque firing, the slip is seen as distinct raised lines. The spaces between the lines are then filled with colored glazes, the raised lines containing each color and providing a white highlight when fired. Colored lines can provide interesting contrasts to the glazes as well. This technique is best used for flat ware and tiles where the glazes will not run down the firing surface. A more direct approach to tube lining is achieved by freely trailing glazes across the surface. Overlaying several glazes produces rich mixes of color.

GLAZE CHARACTERISTICS

The glaze used for tube lining needs to be thickened so that it is raised above the surface of the clay. The addition of ball clay will ensure that the mixture flows easily even when thick. China clay in the glaze will prevent the drying glaze from cracking, and soda content in the alkaline frit gives good adhesion. Dampen the surface of the bisque before tube lining to slow down the drying of the glaze. If any glaze begins to lift off the surface, float a little water onto it with a fine brush to renew adhesion.

RAKU MASK

Meri Wells This mask inspired by ritual body ornamentation has a dark theatrical presence. The trailed lines of alkaline glaze were applied to bisque-fired raku clay and subjected to a heavy post-firing reduction in sawdust after rapid raku firing. The mask is mounted on a 16th-century slate roof tile.

TUBE LINING

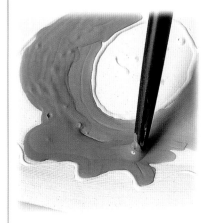

1 Use a slip trailer to draw lines of slip on the surface of the pot in the required design and then bisque fire the pot. Apply the first glaze color using a trailer with a wide nozzle. Various sizes are available, depending on the intricacy of the work. A wide nozzle ensures a good depth of glaze.

2 Apply a second glaze. As the glaze melts, it will run away from the tube lines, leaving them as highlights. It is possible to apply the glazes by brush but it is often difficult to achieve the right build-up of glaze depth.

TRAILING GLAZE

Use a slip trailer to draw lines of glaze onto a bisque-fired surface. These lines can be trailed across the surface of a contrasting glaze to give a softer result when they melt together. Combining matte and shiny glazes can result in highly textured surfaces.

SEE ALSO
Glazes, *pages 178–187*
Kilns and firings, *pages 188–207*

GLAZES AND PIGMENTS

Spraying glaze

Mass-produced ceramics usually have their
glazes sprayed on for speed and consistency
of effect. Spraying glaze involves far less direct
handling, and for some large pieces, can be a
viable alternative to dipping or pouring. In the
hands of the studio potter, a spray gun can become an instrument of infinite
creativity. Stencils can be cut from paper or cardboard to be sprayed
through, and masking tapes can be applied as resists to build up intricate
patterns. Thin coats of glaze can be blended with even graduations of color
across surfaces. Spraying glaze at a low angle to create shadows and
highlights can enhance textured clay.

TOOLS
- Spray booth
- Spray gun
- Stencils
- Scraping tool

SPRAY EQUIPMENT

Glaze can be sprayed with a hand atomizer, a garden sprayer, or a spray gun
powered by air from a compressor to give a continuous flow for even coats.
Spraying creates a great deal of air-borne particles and should ideally be
carried out in a spray booth with a filtered extractor fan. It is possible to
spray small amounts of glaze outdoors, but the dust created is extremely
dangerous and a mask should be worn at all times.

SECTION OF SWIMMING POOL

Craig Bragdy Design Limited *A variety of
handcut stencils were used to create the
coral designs for this swimming pool. The
commercially manufactured tiles were laid
out on a large raised floor the actual size
of the finished mural and the images were
sprayed in situ before being fired in a gas kiln.*

SPRAY BOOTH

Spraying should be done in a spray
booth with adequate means of
extraction of the glaze to the outside.
In addition, filters should remove the
particles from the atmosphere where
possible. Always wear a mask.

USING STENCILS

Here, commercially produced tiles are
being sprayed with glazes and enamel
colors. Using a series of cut stencils as
resists and masks, large areas can be
decorated with layers of even color.
The compressed air for the spray gun
is fed from overhead pipes for ease of
movement. A spray booth would be
too restrictive. Extractors in the ceiling
remove excess spray from the air.

REMOVING EXCESS GLAZE

Large single pots or a great number
of smaller pieces can be glazed evenly
using spray guns. Try to place the
pieces on an absorbent surface, such
as wood, plasterboard, or soft brick,
so that any overspray will not pool and
run onto the work. Wax resist can be
applied to the bases so that they will
not stick to the kiln shelf. Here, the
edges of sprayed tiles are being
scraped to remove excess glaze.

SEE ALSO
Glazes, *pages 178–187*
Kilns and firings, *pages 188–207*

Post-firing techniques

This type of decorative finish includes polishing with waxes and lacquers, grinding, sanding, and the application of glues and acrylics. Many potters enjoy the alternative possibilities offered by some of these methods. Natural waxes are best applied when the pot is slightly warm. The soft wax will be absorbed into the pores of the clay and give a subtle sheen after polishing with cotton cloths. Colored shoe polishes can also be used to add patina and age to sculptural pieces. Grinding can smooth surfaces and reveal integrated materials, such as stones and gravel mixed into the clay. Sand- and grit-blasting will cut through layers of clay to reveal different colors and carve patterns deep into the body. Some of these techniques will create dust or unpleasant fumes, so take precautions. Always wear a mask and be sure rooms are well ventilated.

POD FORM

Steve Mattison This smoked and raku-fired vessel was press molded in two pieces and joined. Made from porcelain, at low-firing temperatures the body does not fuse and is therefore still soft enough to absorb carbon from the post-firing reduction. Masking tapes were applied in linear patterns and the soft clay was sand blasted back through the smoke to bring out the pure white color of the piece, combining sharp cut edges with subtle gradations of smoke.

SANDING

Use wet and dry sandpaper to smooth and polish fired pottery to reveal and refine decorative clay effects. Use successively finer papers to achieve a glass-like finish. This can also be done after bisque firing and before giving the piece a final firing to high temperature to fuse the clay.

GRINDING

Use a commercial grinder to polish surfaces to a fine sheen. Some grinders can produce quantities of dust but the equipment shown here sends a constant flow of water across the grinding head and no dust is produced. The operator need not wear a mask.

GOLD LEAF

Gold leaf applied to scratched lines in a fired glaze produces a rich finish. Paint a thin layer of size into the scratched areas and allow it to become sticky. Press gold leaf gently onto the glue and then burnish to add jewel-like details to the glazed surface (see page 140).

Colored ceramics

Some potters treat their work as canvases for color and imagery, whether figurative, pattern based, or abstract. Colored decoration can be in the form of stains and pigments applied directly to the clay body or via glazes.

1 MUGS

Andrew McGarva *The artist has a considerable reputation for his freely decorated domestic pottery. Made from local stoneware clay glazed with feldspar from the Morvan hills of France, the pieces are firmly rooted in the European tradition, being reminiscent of early blue-painted wares. The painterly designs were created using cobalt, titanium dioxide, and rust pigments.*

2 COMEDIANS

Ekaterina Soukhareva *The artist combines the Russian tradition of ceramic figure making with her own contemporary vision. Soukhareva's work always has a feeling of theatricality, often implied by the costume she gives her characters, who here are caught in a tender off-stage moment. The figures were constructed from thin sheets of stoneware clay, folded and formed when very soft. The application of engobes, slips, and glaze combine to create subtle hues.*

1

2

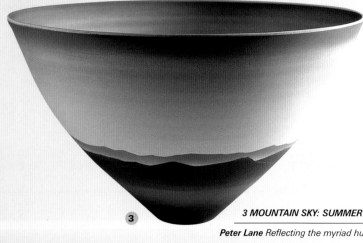

3

3 MOUNTAIN SKY: SUMMER

Peter Lane *Reflecting the myriad hues of the evening sunset, this thrown porcelain bowl was decorated using commercially prepared ceramic stains, applied in even sprays with a small airbrush. Areas were masked out using stencils to give crisp and hard edges depicting the silhouettes of the mountain landscape. Fired in an electric kiln to 2320°F (1270°C), the colors retain their brilliance and clarity.*

4 BOWLS

Mark Titchener Made from red earthenware clay, these bowls have an energetic brushwork decoration of cobalt blue and black pigments over a white slip. Thin washes of copper add tinges of color and richness to the transparent glaze. No two bowls are the same, which makes for wonderfully exciting and vivacious table settings.

5 FISH PLATE

Willie Carter Exuberant and expressive brushwork is a characteristic feature of Carter's work. This press-molded dish, made from red earthenware clay, has bold sweeps of cobalt blue highlighted with orange and rutile over a sgraffitto-marked white slip. Free and spontaneous outlines were painted with fine brushes to give a sense of shimmering movement, reflecting the rapid changes of direction made by shoals of fish. Coated with a transparent glaze, the plate was fired to 2050°F (1120°C) in an oil-fueled kiln.

6 FIGURATIVE VESSEL

Linda John The outlines of the decoration were incised into the clay surface when leather-hard, delineating areas for painting on the colored slips. After bisque firing, the carved lines were partially filled with white glaze before a transparent glaze wash was applied over the whole pot and fired in an oxidation atmosphere to 2340°F (1280°C).

6

5

4

Printed Decoration

Printing on ceramic, in all its varying forms, is not new. The motifs on early medieval floor tiles were, in effect, intaglio printed into the surface and then colored with contrasting slip. Carved wooden blocks were used to print colored slip designs onto clay and impressed decoration from stamps has been used since the earliest potters began producing their wares. By the 17th century, true transfer prints were beginning to appear, and with the rise in popularity of engravings, the quality of the printed image was greatly improved. Transfer papers revolutionized the decoration industry and soon multicolored prints could be found on everyday ceramic objects. Screen printing became popular for printing directly onto the raw clay surface, often using hand-cut paper stencils. Modern developments have led to photographic stencils.

USING COMPUTERS

In recent years, computers have revolutionized the way artists work with print on ceramic. Using laser printers and specially coated transfer papers, almost any image can be printed onto a ceramic vessel or sculpture. Software packages for image manipulation, such as Adobe Photoshop, allow complex pictures to be created on screen, incorporating text and photographs, to produce fascinating and exciting images. The digital information can also be transferred to plotter cutters, which allow stencils to be cut accurately from paper, vinyl, or rubber.

LIGHT-SENSITIVE EMULSIONS

With the advent of light-sensitive emulsions and gums, it is now possible to print photographs directly onto ceramic. The ceramic is coated with the emulsion and then photo-stencils are used to mask either the positive or negative areas of the image. When the emulsion is exposed to light, the photographic images are reproduced on the ceramic surface.

WHO WANTS TO BE MY ART DEALER? VIII

Thomas Sipavicius Equally at home with computers and design software as with ceramic processes, Sipavicius combines the two media in his printed ceramic imagery. His series Who Wants To Be My Art Dealer? explores the relationships between art and contemporary culture in his native Budapest through collages of juxtaposed images and text photographically transferred onto porcelain tiles.

Stencil printing

Printing through stencils can be as simple or as complex as you wish. In its most basic form, a drawing on paper is cut out by hand with a sharp craft knife and then slips, oxides, or glazes are either painted or printed through the paper stencil.

COMPUTER-DESIGNED STENCILS

Hand-cut stencils have their limitations, especially with regard to accuracy and fine detail. Designing stencils on computer and using a commercial plotter cutter allows you to create an infinite variety of detailed stencils that can be cut from paper, vinyl, or even rubber. Paper and vinyl stencils can be painted through, while rubber stencils can be impressed into soft and leather-hard clay. Enamel decal papers can be plotter cut to give highly accurate water-slide transfers.

TOOLS
- *Sharp craft knife*
- *Paintbrush*
- *Hair dryer*

SEE ALSO
Printed transfers, *page 165*

PRESSED PLATE (DETAIL)

Morgen Hall *The computer-designed runner bean decals illustrated below were laid color side down on the clay and pressed into the surface of this plate. Water was applied to the back of the decals, dissolving the gum layer on the backing paper. The backing paper was then lifted away cleanly, leaving the acrylic and enamel firmly adhered to the clay.*

HAND-CUT STENCILS

1 Draw your design on paper and carefully cut it out with a sharp craft knife. Dampen the stencil slightly so that it will adhere lightly to the clay and gently press it down with your fingertips. Apply the required slip, oxide, or glaze. Here, an iron-rich slip is painted over the paper stencil with a soft brush.

2 Dry the slip gently with a hair dryer until it is touch dry. Carefully peel off the paper to reveal the stenciled design.

COMPUTER-DESIGNED DECALS

Computers, microscope photography, and plotter cutters have been used to create these runner bean decals. Acrylic screen-printing medium mixed with on-glaze enamel was applied to a sheet of ceramic decal paper. A drawing of runner beans was scanned into a computer and the design output to a plotter cutter to cut out the runner bean decals.

PRINTED DECORATION

1

2

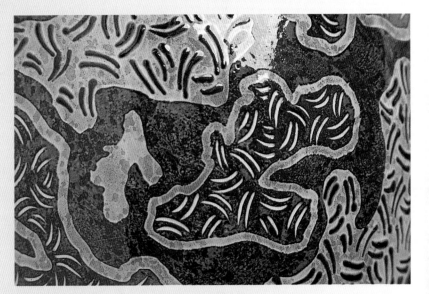

3

4

1 STENCILS OF MICROSCOPIC BROCCOLI CELLS

Morgen Hall The artist has a powerful microscope attached to her computer from which she can input images into design and drawing software for manipulation. A microscopic image of broccoli cells was then plotter cut into these intricate stencils.

2 TEA-LEAF TEAPOT

Morgen Hall Plotter-cut newspaper stencils of enlarged and outlined tea leaves have been applied to this thrown teapot. A cobalt slip was then sponged over the surface. Once the stencils are removed, the tea-leaf design will be revealed.

3 TEA-LEAF TEAPOT (DETAIL)

Morgen Hall This is a detail of the teapot in photograph 2 after glazing. The rich, orange-mottled surface was created by sponging on layers of slip with rutile. Such intricate stenciling could not have been achieved using hand-cut methods.

4 DISH

Morgen Hall This large salad bowl was thrown using red earthenware clay. Decorated using plotter-cut stencils of celery hearts, it has a lively and ornate feel.

PHOTO-STENCILS

The photographic process of using light-sensitive emulsions on ceramic surfaces involves adding gum arabic and ceramic pigment to a light-sensitive medium known as gum bichromate. This is thinly applied to the ceramic surface and allowed to dry. The required image is laser printed onto an acetate sheet to form a negative photo-stencil. This is placed over the gum bichromate and exposed to ultraviolet light, which hardens the exposed areas. The unhardened areas are then washed away with water, leaving the image to be fired on.

An alternative method that produces more subtle color variations and tones is to use a bichromate solution mixed with a sticky substance like sugar or honey instead of ceramic pigment. The solution is applied in the same way and allowed to dry. The coating is then exposed to ultraviolet light through a positive photo-stencil instead of a negative one. The areas least exposed to the light become slightly hardened and less sticky. Ceramic pigments can then be dusted onto the surface and will achieve a greater density where the emulsion is stickiest. When the surface is washed, the images are fully revealed.

5

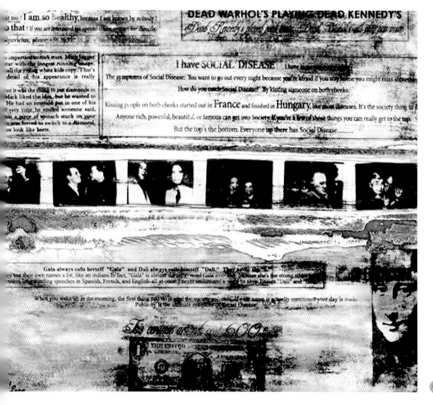

6

5 WHO WANTS TO BE MY ART DEALER? XXVI

Thomas Sipavicius These complex images were manipulated using Adobe Photoshop, a professional image-editing software package. They were then printed onto a sheet of acetate to form a photo-stencil. Ceramic pigment was dusted onto the porcelain tiles through the stencil and then washed away from the unexposed areas.

6 WHO WANTS TO BE MY ART DEALER? II

Thomas Sipavicius The images on this porcelain panel were built up from photographs, drawings, newspaper cuttings, and photocopies to create these remarkable collages. Fired onto porcelain panels, they have a highly textural quality.

PRINTED DECORATION

Monoprinting

Monoprinting is a direct and simple way of transferring drawn images onto a raw clay surface while still retaining the spontaneity of the sketch. The process involves painting oxides onto a board and allowing them to dry. You then draw the desired image onto a piece of paper placed on top of the oxide-covered board. The oxides adhere to the reverse side of the image and this can then be transferred onto clay. In the example shown below, a freely drawn portrait is transferred onto a slab of porcelain for a wall tile. You can also reproduce images onto the sides of pots in this way.

USING OXIDES

Using a variety of painted oxides, the whole range of colors becomes possible. You can paint different colored oxides onto different areas of the board to change the color of the drawn line that will be applied to the clay. A variety of tools can be used to create a range of marks and rubbing with your finger will give softer areas of color. After the initial image has been transferred, you can work into the surface of the clay with additional oxides, slips, stains, or impressed textures. Be inventive and experiment with the technique, combining other decorating methods to achieve highly individual results.

1 FLATTENED VESSELS

Fiona Thompson These delicate slab-built vessels are made from a white, grogged earthenware clay. When leather-hard, selected areas were brushed with slip decoration. More slip was painted onto cut pieces of newspaper and pressed onto the clay surface to transfer the colored areas. Monoprinted imagery and text was painted and drawn onto more newspaper using a mixture of oxide and glycerine, pressed onto the clay, and the paper peeled away to reveal the printed image.

SINGLE-COLOR PRINTING

1 Paint an even layer of thick oxide on the face of a smooth melamine-covered board. Allow the oxide to dry thoroughly. You can use a hot-air gun to speed up the process if you wish. The board must have a nonabsorbent surface so that the dry oxide will lift off onto the paper.

2 Place a sheet of paper onto the dry oxide and draw the image on the paper with a pencil or tool. Make sure you hold the paper down firmly so that it does not move while you draw.

3 Carefully peel off the paper, removing it cleanly from the oxide to avoid smudging the image. You will be able to see the clear lines of oxide of the reverse side of the drawing.

①

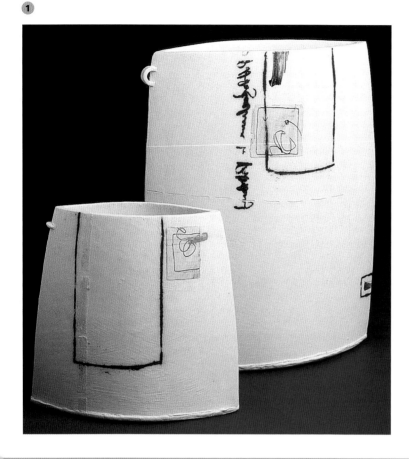

TOOLS
- Paintbrush
- Melamine-covered board
- Paper
- Pencil or drawing tool

②

2 SELF-PORTRAIT

Meri Wells *A unique variation of monoprinting was used to create this effect. A line drawing of the artist was drawn with high-temperature glaze onto a smooth plaster bat using a slip trailer. When the glaze has dried, a soft sheet of porcelain clay was pressed onto the plaster bat and the trailed glaze was impressed into the porcelain's surface. When leather-hard, the porcelain slab was removed from the bat and cut to shape before being raw fired in a gas kiln to 2400°F (1320°C). The glaze melted into the clay, creating a shiny line drawing that contrasts with the matte white background of the tile.*

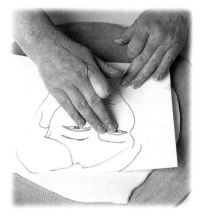

4 Place the paper oxide side down onto the damp surface of a clay slab and rub your fingers over the paper. The oxide powder will stick to the damp clay beneath.

5 Peel off the paper to reveal the transfer print. At this stage, you could paint the image with oxides or slips or leave it as a line drawing.

SEE ALSO
Glazes and pigments, *pages 144–145*
Pigments and stains, *pages 176–177*

PRINTED DECORATION

Intaglio printing

Intaglio is a printmaking term, from the Italian word *intaglione*, meaning to engrave or cut. In ceramics it refers to the technique of cutting an image into a block and transferring it to a clay surface. The most common method is to carve a design into a slab of plaster and press clay firmly onto the image so that it is transferred to the clay. However, a more versatile method is to cut the design into a block of linoleum, which can then be pressed into the clay. Working in this way can give highly distinctive and accurate repeat images, ideal for creating a series of plates or tiles. The raised lines of intaglio printing produce wonderful patterns for borders, simple repeat motifs, and intricate drawn designs. After bisque firing, underglaze colors, stains, or oxides can be painted onto the surface.

TOOLS
- Linoleum block
- Pencil or ink pen
- Lino-cutting tools
- Rolling pin
- Paintbrush

SEE ALSO
Glazes and pigments, *pages 144–145*
Pigments and stains, *pages 176–177*

CUTTING A LINO BLOCK

Draw your design onto a printer's lino block in pencil or ink (ordinary vinyl flooring will also work well, but it cannot be cut as deeply). Use lino-cutting tools to engrave the design into the surface, following your drawn lines.

PRINTING AND COLORING

1 Lay the lino block onto a slab of soft clay and firmly roll over it so that the image is transferred successfully. Lift off the block and inspect the image. If further detail is needed, you can cut into the block a little deeper. The impressed clay slab can then be formed into dishes, pots, or left as tiles.

2 After bisque firing to 1830°F (1000°C), paint the design with your chosen colors. Here, underglaze colors are mixed with plain water and painted onto the surface. When using commercial stains such as these, you can see the hues and tones build up, but you could use oxides for richer colors if you prefer.

3 When dry, lightly rub off some of the color with your finger to create a more subtle effect. Deeper shades will build up around the raised lines, emphasizing the decoration. Fire to a higher temperature to bring out the full intensity of the colors.

Printed transfers

Transfers, or decals, have historically been used for applying drawn designs to functional pottery, epitomized by the willow pattern. A transfer is basically a layer of ceramic pigment printed onto a specially developed paper coated with a soluble gum, which releases the print from the paper when immersed in water. A plastic cover coat printed over the image acts as a carrier until it burns off during firing. The most popular methods of making transfers are screen printing and lithography. Commercially printed transfers of flowers, patterned borders, and colored textures are widely available and inexpensive. Sheets of flat single colors can also be bought and cut up into highly individual shapes. Intricate designs and motifs can be printed in their entirety or more simple transfers can be overlaid and juxtaposed to create new and exciting combinations. Ideally, decals should be applied to glazed ware, the gum providing a good adhesive until the color is fired and melts into the glaze. Decals are usually fired in the 1260–1400°F (680–760°C) temperature range.

LASER-PRINTED TRANSFERS

Recent developments in printing technology have produced Lazertran paper, designed to be used with color laser printers and photocopiers. Images can be drawn or painted onto paper, or created using computer image-editing software to produce unique, exciting, and complex designs that can be printed or copied onto Lazertran paper. These decals are used in the same way as printed ones but the final firing is only to a temperature of about 360–390°F (180°–200°C). Unlike ceramic printed decals, Lazertran transfers are less durable and can easily be scratched.

TOOLS
- *Scissors*
- *Sponge or flexible rubber rib*

SEE ALSO
Stencil printing, *page 159*
Screen printing, *pages 166–167*

BORDER DESIGN

Commercially produced decals come in every shape and size possible. Interesting patterns and borders can be created from repeating the same motif or combining different images on the same piece.

ALL-OVER PATTERN

1 Roughly cut out the decals and soak them in warm water until the printed image begins to separate from the backing paper. Lift the decal from the water and gently slide it into place on the pot. The decal has a certain amount of movement on the glazed surface and can be repositioned. Firmly press the decal into place with a small sponge or a flexible rubber rib.

2 This plate, based on motifs by Matisse, utilizes a combination of home-printed decals and commercially produced gold luster stripes. The luster decals work in exactly the same way as pigment ones. Make sure that no air bubbles remain under the decals.

PRINTED DECORATION

Screen printing

Screen printing involves forcing ink or ceramic pigment through a stretched mesh screen onto clay or paper. For studio potters, it is the most versatile and flexible method of printing decals. The technique uses wooden or metal frames with a fine nylon, silk, or polyester mesh stretched across one face. Mesh is measured in threads per inch or centimeter. The ideal for ceramic printing is between 100 and 250 mesh, depending on the detail required in the image. Designs are then cut from a variety of materials to create stencils that block out areas of the screen. The ceramic pigment is pushed through the mesh with a rubber squeegee to transfer the design onto the ceramic surface or decal paper.

STENCILS

The simplest form of stencil can be cut from paper and stuck to the underside of the screen with water-soluble glue or tape. Masking tape can create strong linear designs when stuck to the mesh or cut into shapes. Blocking-out mediums can also be bought and are painted directly onto the screen mesh, or photosensitive screen emulsions can be used for extremely fine detail and are capable of reproducing photographic images. The emulsion is applied to the mesh and exposed to ultraviolet light shone

ROUSSEAU'S GARDEN

Mária Geszler-Garzuly This large figurative sculpture was press molded from sheets of porcelain directly printed with cobalt oxide. The piece was cut and altered after removing it from the mold when leather-hard. One of a series of homage portraits by this leading ceramist, the piece was fired in a wood-burning salt-glaze kiln to 2370°F (1300°C), creating melted ash deposits and a subtle sheen on the surface.

INDIRECT PRINTING

1 Mask off the area around the stencil to prevent any pigment from seeping around the edges. Use water-based gummed paper tape for this so that it can be cleaned off easily. Apply the tape to the top side of the mesh and the stencil to the underside. Allow a sufficiently large masked area for the pigment to be poured without affecting the print area and for the squeegee to rest when not in use.

2 Place the screen over the decal paper. Mix some pigment with water or oil (depending on the type of pigment you are using) and pour it along the top edge of the screen. Pull a wide rubber squeegee across the screen, pushing the pigment through onto the paper below.

3 Lift the screen to reveal the printed image transferred onto the decal paper. The handcut paper stencil can be clearly seen on the underside of the screen. This is the simplest method of screen printing and is ideal for studio potters working with limited resources.

through an acetate positive of the design. Wherever the light passes through, the emulsion is exposed; the unexposed areas are then washed out with a lukewarm water spray.

PRINTING TECHNIQUES

Two techniques are used: direct and indirect printing. An indirect print is where the image is printed onto a carrier paper or material that is then transferred to the ceramic piece. The process of direct printing can be applied to virtually any ceramic surface, whether raw plastic or dry clay, paper clay, bisque-fired ceramic, or glazed pieces. Using the same screen, the image can be printed directly onto the work using slips, oxides, pigments, glazes, or enamels. The way that the printing medium is pushed through the screen may have to vary, depending on the state of the ceramic. For example, brushes may be the best option if the clay is soft because the pressure from a squeegee could damage or distort the surface.

REGISTRATION

Many potters use direct printing to apply several designs to the same piece. It may be important that multiple colors are registered to each other; masking tape marks on the screen will allow consecutive prints to be aligned. Check that each screen is lined up carefully before printing. This is especially important if a series of tiles is being printed, where the first color will be applied to all of the tiles before the second color, removing each tile from the print bed before applying the next print.

TOOLS
- *Mesh screen*
- *Stencil*
- *Gummed paper tape*
- *Squeegee, piece of cardboard, or stiff brush*

SEE ALSO
Printed transfers, *page 165*
Pigments and stains, *pages 176–177*

DIRECT PRINTING

1 Always check the screen before printing. The image on this screen was photocopied onto a sheet of acetate and a layer of photosensitive emulsion applied to the screen. The screen was then exposed to ultraviolet light through the acetate stencil to transfer the image to the screen. A large porcelain slab is on the table ready to be printed.

2 Place the screen on top of the slab and apply the ceramic pigment directly to the clay, pushing the thick oxide through the mesh with a small piece of cardboard. This gives control of the pressure needed without affecting the soft clay. Allow the print to become touch dry on the surface of the clay before shaping the slab.

3 Alternately, use a stiff brush to paint the oxide through the screen onto the plastic clay beneath. This will allow you to vary the position of the image on the clay by moving the screen, as well as give you greater control over the amount of pigment being deposited.

Printed ceramics

Print has been used to decorate ceramics for many years, but recent advances in print and decal technology and the use of computers for creating imagery have opened many new opportunities for ceramicists to create lively and exciting decoration.

3

3 MARIA

Thomas Sipavicius *This flat porcelain panel has oxide ingrained into the textured background. It was coated with light-sensitive emulsion and exposed to light to transfer the photographic image onto its surface. The high-contrast, iconographic image was created by lightly dusting oxides onto the sticky emulsion.*

1 VESSEL

John Maltby *This vessel form was handbuilt from a grogged clay body. Thick slips and colored clay pastes were applied thickly through paper stencils. Drawing on his experiences of life in a seaside town, Maltby has designed the abstract nautical imagery to depict fishing nets, boats, lighthouses, sea birds, and the coastline.*

2 KECSKEMÉT

Paul Scott *A leading exponent of print techniques on ceramics, Scott's work often features witty historical references. Here, his hand-printed decals depict modern scenes with aircraft, city buildings, and power station cooling towers—contrasting markedly with the idyllic willow pattern plates of traditional English printed tableware. The idyll is further disturbed by the effect of the decals being offset, almost sliding off the plate.*

2

4 PORCELAIN VESSELS

Fiona Thompson The artist draws her inspiration from a wide variety of sources, particularly the rural landscape and travel. The surface imagery was built up through successive applications of colored slips and areas of monoprinted text and slips. Matte or glossy glazes were applied and, in some places, decals for additional interest. Handbuilt from a porcelain paper clay, Thompson's work is intended to be viewed as three-dimensional paintings, yet still involving craft-based concerns.

5 RIGA FASHION

Inese Brants These two slip-cast porcelain vases are Brandts' comments on the popular fashions of her native Riga, capital city of Latvia. After an initial glaze firing to 2340°F (1280°C) in an electric kiln, figurative imagery was applied by a combination of on-glaze enamel painting and luster decals, which the artist silk screen prints herself. These decals are of various views of the city, cut into the shapes of dresses and applied over the painted figures prior to firing at 1470°F (800°C). The vases stand on dark stoneware bases.

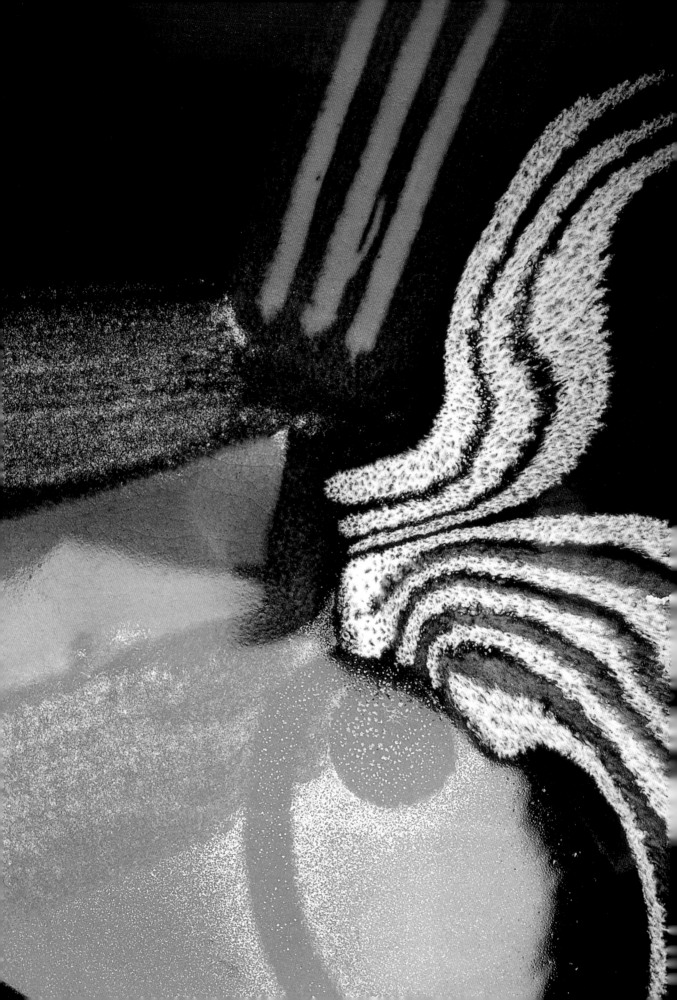

Chapter 5

RAW MATERIALS

A potter is far more than just a clay artist. A basic knowledge of chemistry and an understanding of the effects of extreme temperatures on the many raw materials at our disposal are an advantage. All potters and ceramic artists need to develop a palette of colors and glazes. Whether this palette is created from combinations of raw materials or purchased ready made from suppliers will depend on the individual, but the interaction of several colorants and glazes in different types of firings and kiln atmospheres will still need to be investigated.

TESTING YOUR MATERIALS

Clay has a natural color that can be beautiful in its own right, but many potters change that color either by coloring the clay body or adding color to the surface in the form of oxides or glazes. Oxides can be combined in different quantities to produce a wide range of hues. It is essential that you test the mixtures and note the results carefully so that you can repeat it in future. Metallic oxides are the coloring agents in most glazes and can be problematic in this context, because the oxides react differently depending on the glaze constituents. Formulating and testing glazes requires a methodical approach but is a fascinating and challenging exercise.

COLORING OXIDES

Metal oxides can be purchased from suppliers in varying quantities, some much more expensive than others. When added to glazes in small percentages, they yield a wide range of colors.

CERAMIC CHEMISTRY DEFINITIONS

The following list of chemical definitions is designed to provide a basic understanding of the chemistry of ceramics in relation to the raw materials. Even a limited understanding will prove useful when experimenting with glazes and pigments for coloring and decorating pottery.

Element *This is a substance that, as far as it is known, cannot be chemically broken down into simpler substances. There are few pure elements; most are combined with other elements or compounds.*

Atom *The smallest particle of an element that can take part in a chemical change. It cannot exist on its own, but combines immediately to form molecules.*

Molecule *The smallest part of an element that can exist in a free state. It is rarely found in its pure form, but diamond, being carbon, is the nearest to a pure element.*

Chemical compound *The result of the chemical union of two or more elements.*

Mixture *A mixture of elements, rather than a new compound. A physical change occurs in a mixture and it may take on different properties, but it does not form a new substance or change weight. This may often be reversed, such as the freezing or melting of water.*

Chemical change *This occurs when substances combine to make a new substance with new properties, appearance, and weight.*

Atomic weight *This represents the relative weight of one atom of hydrogen (being the lightest) compared with one atom of an element.*

Bases and acids *In pottery, the term basic means something that is not an acid. However, although all alkalis are bases, not all bases are alkalis. Bases in glazes are often referred to as fluxes.*

Salts *Compounds formed by the combination of an acid oxide and a basic oxide (e.g., silica and lead).*

Oxides *Elements combined with oxygen. Most ceramic raw materials consist of them. The basic oxides are metals and the acid oxides are nonmetals.*

Formula *The chemical composition of a glaze.*

Recipe *The raw materials used in a glaze and their quantities.*

Definitions

Raw materials is the term given to all the materials used for making glazes and colorants and can be subdivided into two general groups: glaze and clay materials, and pigments. Most raw materials used by the potter come from natural rocks and minerals. These have usually been ground down and refined by the ceramic supplier into powders. This gives the potter a reasonable consistency of result, which is essential in a busy studio. Many potters prefer to obtain some of their material directly from the mine because it is often cheaper. It may be less reliable but this is a feature that many artists desire for more lively surfaces and decoration.

CLAY AND GLAZE MATERIALS

1 China clay

2 Ball cay

3 Cornish stone

4 Sand

5 Feldspar

6 Flint

These six materials will produce a variety of clay bodies and glaze finishes when used in different combinations and varying amounts. When other materials are added to the recipe, infinite variations of color, texture, and surface quality can be achieved. Above all, be prepared to experiment and remember to annotate all your investigations carefully for future reference.

TOXIC RAW MATERIALS

Many raw materials contain toxins or can form poisons. You should be aware of their composition and properties and take adequate precautions. Always wear a mask when handling dry materials to reduce inhalation and wear gloves to prevent absorption through the skin. Please consult the health and safety guidelines on pages 214–215. If you are in any doubt about the safety of any materials, always contact your supplier for information.

Basic material	Variations and compounds
Aluminum oxide	Feldspar, clay
Antimony	Antimony oxide
Barium	Barium carbonate, barium oxide
Boron	Borax, sodium borate, boric acid, calcium borate frit, colemanite
Cadmium	Cadmium compounds
Calcium oxide	Whiting, dolomite
Chromium	Chrome or chromium oxide
Cobalt	Cobalt oxide, cobalt carbonate
Copper	Copper oxide, copper carbonate
Fluorine	Fluorspar, calcium fluorides
Lead	Lead carbonate, lead oxide (red lead), lead sulfide (galena), litharge (yellow lead)
Lithium	Lithium carbonate, spodumene, lepidolite
Magnesium oxide	Magnesite, dolomite, talc, magnesium carbonate
Manganese	Manganese dioxide
Nickel	Nickel oxide
Selenium	Selenium compounds
Silicon	Quartz, flint, cristobalite, clay
Sodium oxide	Soda feldspar, pearl ash
Titanium	Titanium dioxide, rutile
Vanadium	Vanadium pentoxide
Zinc	Zinc oxide

COMPOUNDS USED IN CERAMICS

Compounds	Formulae	Molecular weight
Alumina	Al_2O_3	102
Antimony oxide	Sb_2O_3	291.6
Barium carbonate	$BaCO_3$	197.3
Bauxite	$Al_2O_3\ 2H_2O$	138
Bentonite	$Al_2O_3\ 4SiO_2\ 9H_2O$	364.4
Bone ash (calcium phosphate)	$Ca_3(PO_4)_2$	310.3
Boracite	$6MgO\ MgCl_2\ 8B_2O_3$	893.9
Borax	$Na_2B_4O_7\ 10H_2O$	381.2
Calcium carbonate (whiting)	$CaCO_3$	100
Calcium sulfate	$CaSO_4$	136.2
China clay (kaolin) or plastic clay	$Al_2O_3\ 2SiO_2\ 2H_2O$	258
China stone (purple) (variable)	$0.012MgO$ $0.157CaO\ Al_2O_3\ 6.82SiO_2$ $0.340K_2O$ $0.244Na_2O$	569
China stone (white) (variable)	$0.048MgO$ $0.204CaO\ Al_2O_3\ 7.5SiO_2$ $0.280K_2O$ $0.040Na_2O$	594
Colemanite	$2CaO\ 3B_2O_3\ 5H_2O$	411
Cryolite	Na_3AlF_6	210
Dolomite	$CaMg(CO_3)_2$	184.4
Feldspar (lime)	$CaO\ Al_2O_3\ 2SiO_2$	278
Feldspar (potash)	$K_2O_2\ Al_2O_3\ 6SiO_2$	556
Feldspar (soda)	$Na_2O\ Al_2O_3\ 6SiO_2$	524
Flint	SiO_2	60.1
Fluorspar (calcium flouride)	CaF_2	78.1
Lead bisilicate	$PbO\ 2SiO_2$	343
Lead sesquisilicate	$2PbO\ 3SiO_2$	626
Lithium carbonate	Li_2CO_3	73.8
Magnesium carbonate	$MgCO_3$	84.3
Magnesium sulfate	$MgSO_4\ 7H_2O$	138.4
Nepheline syenite	$2(Na_2OK_2O)\ 4Al_2O_3\ 9SiO_2$	1130
Petalite	$Li_2O\ Al_2O_3\ 8SiO_2$	612.6
Plaster of paris	$2CaSO_4\ H_2O$	290.4
Potassium carbonate (pearl ash)	K_2CO_3	138.2
Sillimanite	$Al_2O_3\ SiO_2$	162.1
Sodium bicarbonate	$Na_2CO_3\ 10H_2O$	286
Sodium carbonate (soda ash)	Na_2CO_3	106
Sodium silicate (waterglass)	Na_2SiO_3	122.2
Talc	$3MgO\ 4SiO_2\ H_2O$	304
Wollastonite	$CaOSiO_3$	116.2

ELEMENTS USED IN CERAMICS

Element	Symbol	Atomic weight	Melting point °F	Melting point °C
Aluminum	Al	27	1220	660
Antimony	Sb	120	1166	630
Barium	Ba	137.4	1299	704
Bismuth	Bi	208	516	269
Boron	B	11	4082	2250
Cadmium	Cd	112.4	609	321
Calcium	Ca	40	1566	852
Carbon	C	12	volatizes above 5432	volatizes above 3000
Chlorine	Cl	35.5	−217	−103
Chromium	Cr	52	3328	1831
Cobalt	Co	59	2718	1492
Copper	Cu	63.6	1983	1084
Fluorine	F	19	−435	−224
Gold	Au	197	1945	1063
Hydrogen	H	1	−495	−257
Iron	Fe	56	2779	1526
Lead	Pb	207	621	327
Lithium	Li	6.9	367	186
Magnesium	Mg	24.3	1200	649
Manganese	Mn	55	2268	1242
Nickel	Ni	58.7	2651	1455
Nitrogen	N	14	−410	−210
Oxygen	O	16	−426	−219
Phosphorous	P	31	111	44
Potassium	K	39	147	64
Selenium	Se	79	423	217
Silicon	Si	28.3	2579	1415
Silver	Ag	108	1760	960
Sodium	Na	23	208	98
Strontium	Sr	87.6	1422	772
Sulfur	S	32	241	116
Tin	Sn	119	450	232
Titanium	Ti	48	3268	1798
Vanadium	V	51	1270	690
Zinc	Zn	65.4	786	419
Zirconium	Zr	90.6	3373	1856

DEFINITIONS

COMMON RAW MATERIALS

The raw materials listed here are the common materials in everyday use. For a comprehensive list of what is available, contact your supplier.

Alumina hydrate or calcined alumina A refractory additive for glazes. Alumina's reaction in glazes is complex. It can aid stability in a mobile glaze but by itself will not melt until it reaches a temperature of 3630°F (2000°C). The melting temperature is considerably lowered when small amounts are used in combination with silica. When added to clay, alumina will increase the fusing temperature of the body, making it less likely to melt. It is also used in a grainy sand form for embedding into fine bone china to act as a support during firing. Alumina can also be sprinkled onto kiln shelves or combined with china clay in a 50:50 mix and applied as a wash to the kiln shelves to protect them from glaze runs.

Ball clay A highly plastic clay that is generally added to other clays to increase their plasticity. It improves the mechanical strength of clay bodies and casting slips and is excellent for use in glazes. In its powdered form it is good for making slips. Usually it is pale ivory in color, making it a good base for decorating slips where a good color response in required.

Barium carbonate A secondary flux used in stoneware and porcelain glazes to produce a matte, vellum-like surface. It is poisonous in its raw state.

Basalt A ground volcanic lava used in glazes that melt at stoneware temperatures. It is useful as a base for tenmoku glazes.

Bentonite Weathered and decomposed volcanic ash that is a highly plastic material. It greatly improves the plasticity of clay bodies when added in amounts up to 5 percent. Bentonite is also highly colloidal and absorbs large quantities of water to form a jelly-like substance that is excellent as a suspension agent in glazes (up to 3 percent additions), especially for the heavy particles in a raku glaze.

Bone ash A secondary flux in glazes prepared from the calcined bones of animals ground into a fine powder. Bone ash contains calcium and phosphorous, which is a glass former, and is the essential constituent of bone china, giving translucency to the body. Bone china typically contains up to 50 percent bone ash, and when fused with china clay and Cornish stone, forms one of the thinnest and hardest ceramic bodies. It is sometimes used as a glaze opacifier to reduce the amount of tin needed.

Borax An extremely vigorous low-temperature flux for glazes that contains boric oxide and soda. On its own, it is soluble in water, so it is introduced into glazes in a fritted form with silica to render it food-safe. Otherwise, it is poisonous.

China clay A pure white, residual primary clay, ideal for making white earthenware and stoneware bodies. China clay is also used in the composition of many prepared clays, especially white-firing clays such as porcelain and bone china. China clay is also used in earthenware clays to counter the high shrinkage rate of the plastic ball clays, thereby reducing the overall shrinkage of the clay during drying. It is also used in glazes to provide alumina and silica. If larger quantities are added, it will act as a matting agent.

Cornish stone A decomposed granite used as a secondary flux in glazes. It is composed of feldspar, quartz, mica, and fluorspar and contains fluxes such as soda, potash, and calcium. Cornish stone is also used to give whiteness to clay bodies and glazes because it is almost free of iron. It is used as an alternative to feldspar in clay bodies and glazes but is not as fusible as feldspar because of its higher silica content.

Cristobalite A powdered, fired form of silica used to improve craze resistance in slips. It is hazardous when inhaled.

Dolomite A combination of calcium and magnesium carbonate that occurs naturally and is used as a secondary flux in high-temperature porcelain and stoneware glazes. When used in high quantities of between 10 and 20 percent, dolomite will produce a beautiful silky matte surface.

Feldspar The major flux in clay bodies and high-temperature glazes, some of which contain up to 70 percent feldspar. Feldspar tends to be milky due to fine bubbles in the glaze body. There are three main feldspars, each name referring to the principal, but not the only, flux present. Potash feldspar (orthoclase) is the one generally used and recommended but soda (albite) and lime feldspar (anorthite) are also common.

Fire clay A refractory material used as an additive in stoneware clay to produce a more open texture and speckling in reduction. It is also commonly used as a mortar when building kilns.

Flint A highly refractory material that provides silica in clay bodies and glazes, increasing the firing temperature but reducing the plasticity and shrinkage of the clay. It also increases craze resistance in glazes. Prepared from calcined flint rock, it is ground into a fine powder and is the form of silica preferred by most potters. It is hazardous in dust form if inhaled.

Fluorspar A vigorous flux in glazes. At low temperatures, fluorspar can cause bubbling in the glaze surface as it volatizes.

Frit Certain forms of materials such as lead have a low melting point and are also highly soluble in water, making them poisonous for use. Fritting involves the melting of these materials together with glaze ingredients such as silica to produce a compound that is either insoluble or has a low solubility. The constituents of frits are melted together and poured into water when molten. This causes the frit mixture to shatter and makes grinding it into a fine powder easier. Seldom used in their pure state as a glaze, frits need the addition of alumina, usually from china clay or a similar compound. The common frits are lead bisilicate, lead sesquisilicate, standard borax frit, soft borax frit, calcium borate frit, and high-alkali frit.

Grog Pre-fired clay that is ground down into various particle sizes (categorized by the size of sieve mesh they will pass through) and added to clay bodies. The addition of grog to clay bodies reduces shrinkage and warping because the grog has already been fired and is inert.

Lithium carbonate An alkaline flux used as a substitute for soda and potash when craze resistance is needed. It gives a typical alkaline color response to oxides.

Magnesium carbonate A secondary high-temperature flux that produces a satin matte surface when used in quantities of up to 10 percent. If used to excess, crawling and pinholing may occur. At lower temperatures of up to 2120°F (1160°C) it acts as an opacifier, but above that it becomes an active flux. On cooling it may cause crystals to form, creating an opaque matte finish.

Molochite Calcined china clay used as a pure white grog, commonly in white-firing clays. Fine grades can be used in engobes as a substitute for the clay to reduce shrinkage.

Nepheline syenite A similar mineral to feldspar but containing less silica and more alkaline flux. It is used in both earthenware and stoneware glazes. It is more fusible than feldspar and can therefore be used to reduce the maturing temperature of glazes.

Quartz A pure form of silica that can be used as an alternative to flint in glazes. It is hazardous if inhaled.

Silicon carbide Used to achieve local reduction in glazes in electric kilns. As a glaze constituent, it creates bubbly, lava-like finishes.

Soda ash (sodium carbonate) Used in the making of casting slips combined with sodium silicate.

Talc A secondary flux high in magnesium that is used in both glazes and clay bodies. In glazes it improves resistance to crazing but can form opaque surfaces. In clay it acts as a flux and is especially useful for making flameproof pottery for cooking.

Whiting A mixture of chalk, calcium carbonate, and limestone. It is the main source of calcium in glazes and is used extensively as a flux. It is prepared by finely grinding chalk originating from shells. It helps to increase the hardness and durability of a glaze and in larger quantities produces a matte finish.

Wollastonite (calcium silicate) An alternative to whiting in glaze formulations, containing both calcium and silica. It is a good source of lime in stoneware glazes and is useful where pinholing is a problem.

Pigments and Stains

Metallic oxides, dioxides, and carbonates provide the basic palette of pigments used in ceramics. Oxides are used in all stages of the ceramic process—additions to clay bodies, making colored slip, washing onto bisque ware, painting under or over a glaze, and mixing into a recipe to create colored glazes. When added to glazes, a wide range of colors can be produced from single oxides or by using them in combination. The color will be affected by the other constituents in the glaze, the firing temperature, and the kiln atmosphere. The intensity of any oxide depends on the particular material and the form in which it is being used—carbonates and dioxides are weaker forms of the pure oxide. When used in glazes, the oxides should be finely ground to give even distribution of color. Stains are commercially manufactured pigments. They are relatively stable and will always give a good color response, making them ideal for staining clay bodies and coloring slips.

BODY STAINS

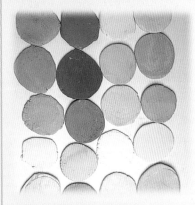

Adding 5–10 percent stain to a clay body will give a good variation of colors. Try a series of test batches, increasing the amount of color in each test to achieve a range of tones of the same color. Swatches of colored porcelain are a useful reference when working with agateware. In this example, two samples of each color have been mixed, one sample with 5 percent stain and the one next to it with 10 percent. This gives an indication of the color difference that can be achieved.

UNDERGLAZE PIGMENTS

A range of commercially manufactured stains and colors is available in a variety of forms. Powdered color can be mixed with water to produce a fluid paint, while ready-mixed colors come with a gum added to adhere the color to the surface of the pot to prevent smudging while working. Underglaze crayons and pencils provide additional decorative possibilities.

COLORED SLIPS

A range of colored decorating slips can be made by adding quantities of stain or underglaze pigment to a basic white slip. Make sure that the base slip suits the clay body and fits well without crazing. Additions of between 5 and 10 percent stain will usually give fairly strong colors. These slips will appear dull at the bisque stage (as shown in the central section of the test tile), but brighten considerably after glazing with a transparent earthenware glaze.

COMMON METALLIC OXIDES

SEE ALSO
Definitions, *pages 172–175*

These metallic colorants vary in strength, with carbonates always weaker than the pure oxide form.

Antimony oxide 2–10% produces a yellow color when added to a high-lead glaze.

Chromium oxide 0.5–3% normally gives a green color. When used in combination with tin oxide, it can produce pink.

Cobalt compounds The most powerful of all the coloring oxides, cobalt compounds produce strong blues even when used in low percentages. If manganese is present, cobalt may form purples.
Black cobalt oxide: 0.1–2% gives
    a deep blue; it tends to blacken
    in higher amounts.
Cobalt carbonate: 1–3% gives a
    blue glaze.

Copper compounds These strong fluxes produce apple green colors in normal conditions but in alkaline glazes give rich turquoise. In reduction atmospheres, they produce the characteristic copper red glazes.
Copper carbonate: 3–7% produces
    a more even color than the
    oxide with less risk of speckling.
Copper oxide: 0.5–5% is the usual
    added amount.

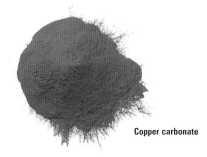

Copper carbonate

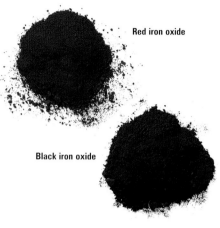

Red iron oxide

Black iron oxide

Iron compounds Iron oxides give a wide range of honey yellows, brown reds, blacks, and yellows in oxidized firings. They produce blues and greens in reduction, as in celadon glazes.
Black iron oxide: 4–8% gives darker
    shades than red iron oxide.
Purple/crocus martis iron oxide:
    4–8% produces speckled effects
    due to its impurity.
Red iron oxide (ferric oxide):
    0.5–10% gives honey yellows to
    dark browns; this is the most
    popular form of iron oxide.
Yellow ocher iron oxide: 3–8%
    produces yellow to light brown
    due to the oxide containing clay.

Manganese compounds
Manganese gives a brown color but can produce purple and plum colors in alkaline-based glazes. When mixed with cobalt it will give violet.
Manganese carbonate: 1–5% will
    produce pink to brown.
Manganese dioxide: 0.5–8% also
    gives pinks to browns but
    stronger than the carbonate
    form produces.

Nickel oxide 1–3% produces brownish greens or grays. When added to high-zinc glazes, a yellow color is produced in oxidation and blue in reduction.

Opacifiers Oxides such as tin, zirconium, and titanium make transparent glazes opaque—a characteristic feature of the white tin earthenware glaze. These materials are known as opacifiers and will also react with other oxides to produce a wide range of glaze colors.
Tin oxide: 2–10% gives the best-
    quality white.
Titanium dioxide: 5–15% produces
    a creamy color. In its impure
    form, known as rutile, it gives
    a pale brown color.
Zirconium: 6–15% produces a
    milkier white than tin oxide
    and requires greater
    concentrations.

Rutile An ore containing titanium dioxide and iron that is used to produce soft browns and mottled surfaces.

Rutile

Vanadium pentoxide 2–10% gives a yellow or orange in most glazes.

Glazes

Many studio potters prefer to put all their energy and time into building and making the ceramic pieces and are perfectly happy to buy ready-formulated glazes from suppliers. Mixing and formulating your own glazes, however, will give you an intimate knowledge of the most challenging area of the ceramic process.

GLAZE CONSTITUENTS

In simple terms, glaze is like a coating of glass applied to a ceramic surface in the form of a diluted powder. When fired, the raw materials melt and form a glaze that can be transparent, matte, shiny, opaque, or colored, depending on the recipe used. Glaze is composed of three basic ingredients: silica to form the glass; a flux to control the melting point of the glaze; and alumina to stabilize the glaze and bind it to the clay body. These three main ingredients may be derived from a more complex assortment of raw materials, depending on the effects required, and care needs to be taken to select the best combination of ingredients to prevent excesses of one particular oxide. Glaze contains a combination of oxides—the fluxes are known as the acid oxides, and alumina is the neutral oxide that balances the acid ones.

TESTING GLAZES

There has always been a mystique surrounding glaze formulation, especially because it involves so much chemistry. Thorough testing and experimentation will give you an excellent grounding in this complex area. Once you understand what the basic raw materials add to glazes, formulating your own becomes easier and more enjoyable—not denying, of course, that you will have failures along the way. For potters and students new to glaze formulation, the best approach is to experiment with the materials themselves. It is a good idea to make a series of small test tiles and put a teaspoonful of each material onto a separate tile, firing them to stoneware temperature and examining the results. You will soon see which materials melt, which ones are dry, which ones craze, and so on. You are already on your way to glaze formulation. You will discover many important points when carrying out glaze tests. Some materials will have opacifying effects, some will craze or crawl away, some will bubble and blister, some will be smooth and glassy. Above all, you will learn about the relevant raw materials and their effects. Glaze formulation can be a tedious but essential part of ceramics, but if carried out methodically, can be extremely rewarding and satisfying.

1 50:50 BLENDS

The simplest test is the 50:50 mix of glaze materials. Here, a series of small clay boxes are used to contain the mixtures in case any become extremely fluid. In each box there are two 50:50 tests—one at each end. Simply mix the glaze materials together in a small amount of water, sieve the mixture, and pour it into one end of the box. Fire all of the tests to earthenware temperature and examine the results. Some will be wonderfully melted and others dry, some crawled and some smooth, some opaque and others transparent. Always keep accurate notes of everything you do. There is nothing worse than achieving an interesting result and not knowing what you did. Select any tests that have not melted and refire them to stoneware temperature to ascertain the difference.

2 QUAD-AXIAL BLENDS

A more detailed method of understanding materials is to use a quad-axial blend of four materials. Here, ball clay, nepheline syenite, flint, and whiting have been used. Each side of the square represents one of the materials in various quantities. For example, top left is 100% nepheline syenite, and as the tiles progress along the top row, increasing amounts of ball clay are added to the mix. Each tile has been double dipped in the mixture to see how a single coat differs from a double coat. The results vary considerably, being shiny at top left and very dry at bottom left where there is only 100% flint, a refractory material. Somewhere on the board there will be a satisfactory glaze finish. The matte glaze containing 35% nepheline syenite, 65% ball clay, 65% whiting, and 35% flint was chosen from this series of tests to make additional experiments with color in the line blend example below.

3 LINE BLENDS

Using a glaze formulated in the quad-axial test above, a series of small mixtures of glaze were made with increasing quantities of coloring oxide added. Here, the tiles show increasing amounts of cobalt oxide, again double dipped, ranging from additions of 0.5% to 2.5% in 0.5% increments and tested on two different clays.

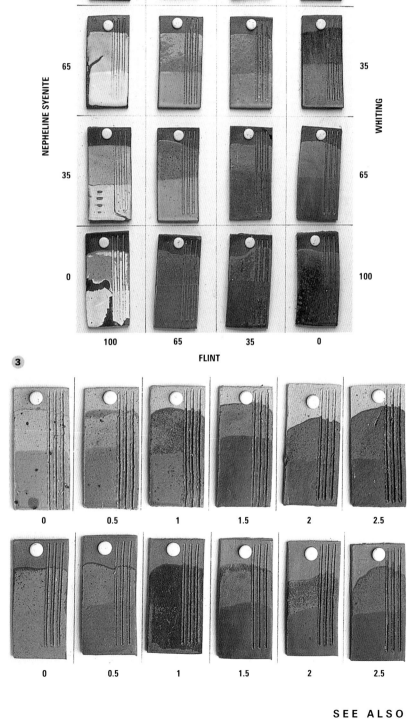

2

BALL CLAY
0   35   65   100

NEPHELINE SYENITE
100 ... 0
65 ... 35
35 ... 65
0 ... 100

WHITING

100   65   35   0
FLINT

3

White stoneware
2340°F (1280°C)

COBALT OXIDE   0   0.5   1   1.5   2   2.5

Iron stoneware
2340°F (1280°C)

COBALT OXIDE   0   0.5   1   1.5   2   2.5

SEE ALSO
Definitions, *pages 172–175*
Firing kilns, *pages 194–195*

GLAZES

Mixing glaze

Whether you are using commercially produced glazes or developing your own, the principles of mixing are the same. The only variant will be the amount of water you add to the dry, powdered material and this will depend on the type of glaze, the method of application, and the firing temperature. Experience will help you determine the best consistency of the glaze.

EQUIPMENT

A good set of scales is essential when mixing glazes. Kitchen scales can be used to measure small amounts of glaze, but ideally scales weighing up to 11 lb. (5 kg) would be the minimum for larger quantities. Using bathroom scales is a cheap way to weigh bulk glazes. You will also need sieves in a range of different mesh sizes, depending on the method of application. For most purposes, 80 and 100 mesh will be used, but if the glaze is to be sprayed onto the work, 120 mesh will ensure that the particles are fine enough to pass through the nozzle of the spray. Most glaze materials will pass easily through the sieve using a stiff-bristled brush, but in some cases it may be necessary to use a stiff rubber rib to push the material through the mesh. This is especially the case when using low-temperature fritted glazes that have a larger particle size.

1 CUT-SIDED JUG

Jim Malone This robust thrown pitcher, with its strong, wide base, owes much to medieval European wares. The rich, dark tenmoku glaze breaks into rust colors over the edges of the cut facets, the rim, and the handle.

MIXING GLAZE

1 With commercially prepared glazes, you will only need to weigh out the one material. If you are formulating your own glaze, you will need to weigh out a combination of materials, depending on the recipe you are using. Put the glaze constituents into a clean, dry bowl.

2 Cover the ingredients with water and allow to soak for about 30 minutes. This makes mixing much easier because any lumps will be slaked down.

3 Use a stick to stir the ingredients to mix them together and allow to soak for a short time again.

STORING GLAZE

Store the mixed glaze in a clean plastic bucket with an airtight lid. It will stay in good condition for a considerable time. If larger quantities of glaze are needed, plastic tubs from garden centers make good containers. Use wooden lids and stack them in a corner of the workshop when not in use.

SAFETY PRECAUTIONS

Using dry glaze materials can be hazardous so you should take adequate precautions. Always wear a mask, and with some glaze ingredients rubber gloves may be necessary. While it will be impossible to prevent dust, by adopting safe working practices risks can be reduced to a minimum.

2

2 PLATTER

David Frith When one glaze is used over another, interesting and exciting effects can be created. The platter was first covered with a lustrous brown kaki glaze, then a vigorous line of wax was painted on to resist the second thickly poured glaze, an icy blue/white chun glaze. The reactions between the two glazes create swirling patterns where they crawl and melt.

3 FLUTED BOTTLE

Phil Rogers A leading authority on ash glazes, Rogers achieves many rich and varied glaze surfaces. This nuka glaze was applied thickly over the entire pot, pooling on the shoulder and breaking over the fluting. All of Rogers' work is either reduction stoneware or salt glazed in his oil-fired kilns.

3

4 Pour the mix through a sieve of suitable mesh size. Push any leftover deposits through with a stiff-bristled brush or rubber rib. Here, the sieve is supported on pieces of wood suspended over a bowl.

5 Check the consistency of the glaze. For most uses it should be like a thick cream, and if you have used the glaze before, you will know how thick it should be. If you need to thin it down, add some more water. If it is too thin, allow it to settle overnight and then decant some of the excess water from the top.

TOOLS
- Scales
- Bowls
- Jug
- Stick
- Sieve
- Stiff-bristled brush or rubber rib
- Pieces of wood
- Ladle

SEE ALSO
Glazes, *pages 178–179*
Glaze recipes, *pages 182–183*

GLAZES

Glaze recipes

Mixing your own glazes is the best way to learn about the effects of heat on ceramic materials and you will gain the confidence and experience to make the adjustments needed for specific finishes. Variations can occur between different batches of materials and, undoubtedly, between different potters' firing conditions and clay bodies, so it is always wise to test samples of these recipes thoroughly before applying them to your work. Unless stated otherwise, the quantities of raw materials in the recipes are given as proportions of dry weight (not volume). So, if a recipe states 4 parts china clay and 6 parts ball clay, you could decide that 1 part is equal to 1 lb. (450 g) and therefore measure out 4 lb. (1.8 kg) of china clay and 6 lb. (2.7 kg) of ball clay. The basic weight unit will depend on the quantity of glaze you wish to produce and you will need to experiment to get this right.

EARTHENWARE GLAZES

All glazes falling into the 1760–2080°F (960–1140°C) temperature range are classified as earthenware and usually incorporate commercially fritted compounds, rendering lead safe to handle and alkaline materials in a nonsoluble form. Generally speaking, fritted lead and additions of copper oxide to lead should be used with caution on functional vessels (see box).

Lead warning

All of the earthenware glazes listed have passed current U.S. and U.K. lead release standards. However, potters who use these glaze recipes on functional ware should always have them tested for lead release because variations in materials from different areas or the individual firing method used could affect the levels of lead release.

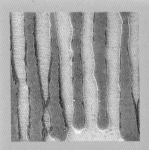

Transparent earthenware glaze overlaid with turquoise matte stoneware glaze. Although the earthenware glaze is usually fired only at earthenware temperatures, it can produce interesting effects when fired to higher temperatures with stoneware glazes. Here, the turquoise stoneware glaze seems to float on the shimmering low-temperature earthenware glaze.

TRANSPARENT GLAZE

1940–1980°F (1060–1080°C)

Lead sesquisilicate	
	22 lb (10 kg)
China clay	5½ lb. (2.5 kg)
Flint	3 lb. (1.3 kg)

Adding a teaspoon of calcium chloride (you could use a product such as Calgon) will prevent the glaze from settling in the container. This is a good all-around glaze, suitable for slip-decorated ware and as a base for colored transparent glazes. You can add oxides to color it. Add 4% iron oxide for golden orange; 1% cobalt oxide for strong blue; or 2.5% copper oxide for bottle green.

HONEY GLAZE

1940–1980°F (1060–1080°C)

Lead sesquisilicate	
	6½ lb. (3 kg)
Powdered red clay	
	2¼ lb. (1 kg)

This works well over white slip on red clay pots. Try to use the same powdered red clay as the clay body of the wares to ensure a good glaze fit. It is excellent on bisque ware, and by adding a small amount of bentonite, will work well as a raw glaze.

TIN GLAZE

1980–2050°F (1080–1120°C)

Lead bisilicate	26
Borax frit	7
Ball clay	6
China clay	4
Tin oxide	3
Bentonite	1

This produces a good, stable white tin glaze that is ideal for red clay and majolica work. Where the glaze runs thin, it breaks over throwing lines to reveal a rich red color.

RAKU GLAZES

Raku glazes have to melt at very low temperatures and become smooth and glassy during the extremely short firing cycle. Consequently, they are all frit-based. Even when using a pyrometer to indicate the temperature, you will still need to judge how even the glaze melt is by eye.

SEE ALSO
Definitions, *pages 172–175*
Pigments and stains, *pages 176–177*
Mixing glaze, *pages 180–181*
Kilns and firings, *pages 188–207*

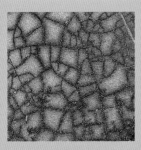

Turquoise luster glaze with smoked crazing. *Areas of copper red appear where reduced heavily.*

SOFT CLEAR GLAZE

1830°F (1000°C)

Borax frit	60
Calcium borate frit	40
China clay	10
Bentonite	10

Add 7 parts tin oxide to produce a good white crackle glaze.

TURQUOISE LUSTER GLAZE

1830°F (1000°C)

High-alkaline frit	50
Borax frit	20
Copper oxide	4
Bentonite	3

Produces a good turquoise where thick, with copper red luster where heavily reduced in sawdust.

COPPER MATTE GLAZE

1740–1830°F (950–1000°C)

Copper oxide	95
Alkaline frit	5

Produces the entire range of lusters when reduced.

STONEWARE AND PORCELAIN GLAZES

Glazes fired over 2190°F (1200°C) are usually classified as stoneware glazes. At these temperatures, the clay actually fuses to the glaze and becomes integral. Most stoneware glazes will work on either porcelain or stoneware clay, but with different finishes. The large variation in stoneware clay bodies will also produce different results. Always test these glazes to see if they are suitable for a particular clay, temperature, and type of firing, whether reduction or oxidized.

TENMOKU GLAZE

2340°F (1280°C) reduction

Feldspar	62
Flint	19
Whiting	10
Ball clay	9
Red iron oxide	8

A typical tenmoku glaze giving a good, dark black, breaking to rust over the edges.

Tenmoku with iron decoration. *Red iron oxide has been splashed across the tenmoku base before firing. The richness of these rusty colors gives a beautiful variegation to the surface.*

CELADON GLAZE

2300–2340°F (1260–1280°C)

Feldspar	40
Flint	30
Whiting	20
China clay	10
Talc	5
Red iron oxide	1

A classic celadon glaze for porcelain. This glaze gives a good subtle blue over white-firing clay bodies.

DOLOMITE WHITE GLAZE

Feldspar	64
Dolomite	13
Whiting	13
China clay	12
Tin oxide	5

A stiff, matte, white glaze. Fires well in oxidation or reduction.

TURQUOISE MATTE GLAZE

2300°F (1260°C)

Feldspar	50
Barium carbonate	20
Ball clay	10
Whiting	9
Zinc oxide	8
Copper carbonate	3
Titanium dioxide	2
Cobalt carbonate	0.5

A deep, matte, turquoise glaze where applied thickly. Becomes semi-matte when fired to 2370°F (1300°C). Produces subtle copper reds and pinks in reduction.

GLAZES

Applying glaze

Glazes can be applied to pottery in many ways—dipping, painting, pouring, or spraying. The method chosen depends on the shape of the pot and how it can be held, the size of the object, and the decorative effect intended. Combinations of different application methods on the same piece can result in interesting surfaces, especially when different glazes are used with each other. Glazes will settle over time and should be thoroughly stirred before use. This will ensure that all of the glaze constituents are in suspension and no deposits are left at the bottom of the container. It is also a good way to check the consistency of the glaze.

EARTHENWARE

Generally speaking, when earthenware pottery is fired, the clay itself will remain porous. The underside of the pot will therefore need to be glazed if it is to be used for food preparation or drinking. If the base is left unglazed, liquid and food will be absorbed over time, making the pot unhygienic. To prevent these pots from sticking to the kiln shelf, support the bases on small three-pointed stilts; these can be tapped off after firing. The scars left by stilts must be ground down because they will be razor sharp to the touch.

1 STONEWARE PLATE

Brian Gartside Inspired by the rich landscape of New Zealand, Gartside uses an extensive palette of glazes. They are poured, trailed, painted, applied with palette knives, and scratched through to produce highly individual pieces. The environmental symbols he uses in his work are developed with the use of painting software on a computer, which becomes his sketchbook of ideas.

DIPPING AND POURING

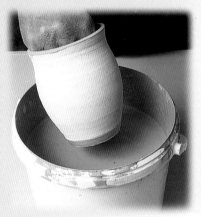

1 Fill a jug with glaze and, holding the pot upright, fill the inside to just above halfway. After tilting and twisting the pot to cover most of the inside, pour the remaining glaze back into the glaze bucket while rotating the pot to coat the inside of the rim evenly. Put aside to dry before continuing.

2 Make sure the bucket contains enough glaze so that the pot can be fully immersed. Grip the inside of the pot with an opened hand. The fingers will provide adequate bracing to hold the piece stable. Alternately, pots may be held upside down and immersed; the pressure of trapped air inside will keep the glaze from flowing in.

3 Lower the pot into the glaze bucket up to the rim of the piece, making sure no glaze runs inside. Hold it there for a few seconds so that enough glaze will build up on the surface. A certain amount of water will have been absorbed when the inside was glazed and this will slow down the absorption of glaze on the outside.

STONEWARE

Stoneware pots are packed directly onto the kiln shelf with only a thin layer of bat wash or powdered alumina to prevent the pots from sticking. The bases of these pots must be unglazed or they will become firmly attached to the shelf when the glaze melts. Glaze can either be wiped off the base prior to firing or the base can be coated with wax to prevent the liquid glaze from adhering.

3

2 LARGE BOTTLE

Jim Malone *Drawing inspiration from the best of oriental pottery, Malone makes classic shapes such as this bottle. A copper glaze was poured expressively over a base glaze of tenmoku. The ridged shoulder caused the glazes to break over its edge, creating the emphasized line.*

3 SPIKY BLUE

Catrin Mostyn Jones *Several layers of sprayed blue/green glaze over wax resist areas contrast with the orange and red glazes in the hollows to give these small pieces vitality. All of Mostyn Jones' work is handbuilt, using pinch pots as the starting point before adding modeled elements.*

2

TOOLS
- *Jug*
- *Bucket*
- *Large, soft brush*
- *Banding wheel*

SEE ALSO
Resist techniques, ***pages 148–149***
Spraying glaze, ***page 154***
Glazes, ***pages 178–183***
Kilns and firings, ***pages 188–207***

POURING

Grip the bowl between the thumb and spread fingers, with the thumb gripping the base. Fill a small jug with glaze and pour it slowly and evenly over the outside surface. Any fingermarks can be cleaned up afterwards. If the pot is too big to hold in your hand, place sticks across the bucket to support the rim of the pot while pouring the glaze.

PAINTING

1 Use a large, soft brush that will hold plenty of glaze. Place the bowl upside down on a banding wheel so that it can be rotated as the glaze is applied. The base of the pot can be waxed to give a clean edge to the glaze, but with experience this may not be necessary. Paint the outside first so that the banding wheel will not damage the inside glaze.

2 Allow the outside to dry before painting glaze onto the inside. Brushmarks may be visible after firing, so paint the glaze in short strokes, continually reloading the brush and applying several even coats to build up the thickness.

Glazed ceramics

Glazes are often considered to be the most magical area of ceramics and can be applied in a variety of ways to create thick, juicy coatings or fine layers. Many potters rely on the build-up of natural ash on the surface during wood firing to melt and create the glaze, producing characteristic runs and flashes.

1

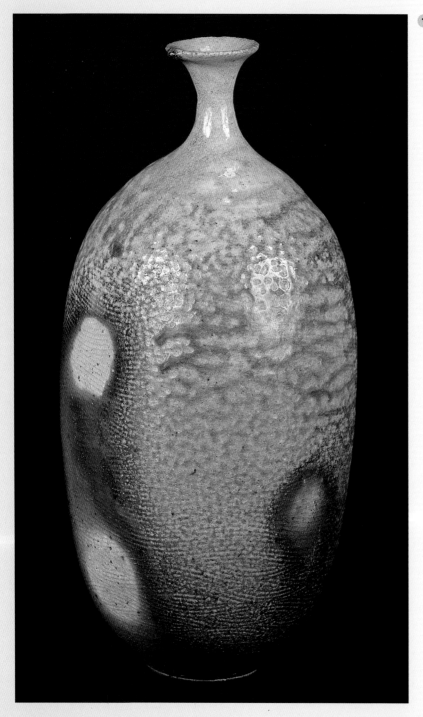

2

1 BOTTLE

Frederick Olsen *This bottle displays a strange asymmetry. The body was thrown and then the pot moved off-center on the wheel before throwing the narrow neck, resulting in a change of direction at the shoulder of the pot. It was fired on its side in a large wood-fired kiln and soaked for up to 12 hours at the top temperature of 2370ºF (1300ºC) to allow a heavy build-up of fly ash on the surfaces, which melted and ran around the bottle. Three distinctive marks on the piece show the position of the wadding used to raise the bottle from the shelf to prevent adhesion.*

2 SZIA KEDVESEM

Steve Mattison *Inspired by visits to eastern Europe, this blue tower block has delicately lit coral windows as if sunrise or sunset has flooded its façade with color. The female figure suggests a feeling of affection as she leans toward the male; the slope of the legs and the angle of his torso show a more tentative, shy connection. Selective areas of applied turquoise glaze run and thicken in the regular square impressions, turned copper red by reduction, while the soft sheen of soda-glazing vapor on the porcelain clay add depth and softness to the figures.*

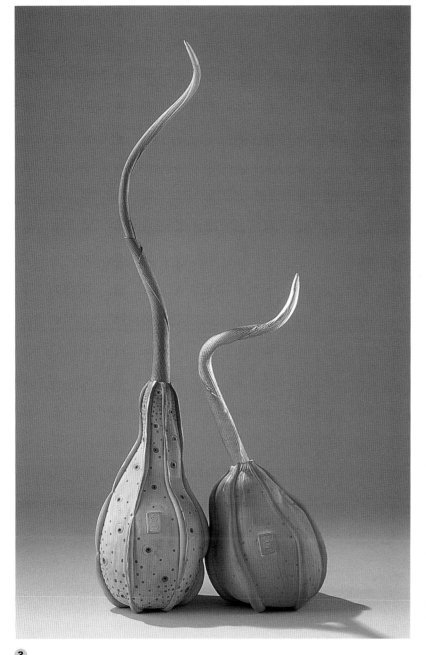

3

3 BOHÒCOK (CLOWNS)

Gabriella Kuzsel Inspired by the natural forms of plants, seeds, and fruit, Kuzsel created these distinctive pieces from thrown sections, cut and altered into pod-like forms. The newly fertilized stems grow from the body of the seeds into a form of life unlike any seen before. They were colored with washes of iron chloride of varying thickness and fired to 2340°F (1280°C) to create the rust-colored finishes.

4

4 JUG

Jim Malone This robust cut-sided jug was thrown on the wheel and then coated with an iron-bearing ocher slip. A rice-husk ash glaze was boldly poured over it before firing. The subsequent intermingling of glaze and slip creates a stunning and captivating effect as the glaze breaks over the edges of the rim, the handle, and the decorative facets.

5

5 CUPS

Brigitte Penicaud These small cups were thrown off the hump. The thinness of the walls gives them a delicate feel that contrasts with the exuberant trailed glaze over the outside. Several colored glazes were freely applied with brushes and slip trailers over a base color of stained engobe. The cups were fired in a wood kiln to 2340°F (1280°C) with a reduction atmosphere.

Chapter 6

KILNS AND FIRINGS

Before any clay object can become truly ceramic, it must be fired in a kiln. Firing is the most fascinating part of the process for any potter. No matter how you choose to fire your work, all potters share the same sense of excitement and uncertainty when opening a kiln after a firing. Extreme temperatures will have transformed the raw clay into a permanent artifact, an enduring personal mark of the artist.

EARLY KILNS

Firing clay can be traced back to the beginnings of civilization. Theories abound as to how humans first thought of firing pottery. One interesting proposition is that clay was used to line woven baskets to make them waterproof and, when placed too close to the cooking fire, the baskets caught alight and baked the clay. The real reason is probably that the ground was discovered to harden under the cooking pit, giving rise to early pottery being fired in the bonfire used for cooking food. In many cultures around the world, bonfire firing is still the most common form of baking pottery. The Chinese were the first to build kilns capable of high temperatures of around 2370°F (1300°C), and also the first potters to understand the relationship between heat color, kiln atmosphere, and the resulting ceramic glazes produced. In essence, not a lot has changed since then.

FIRING PRINCIPLES

In any kiln, the principle is to supply enough heat over a specific length of time to create chemical and physical changes in the clay body and glazes. Modern kilns have temperature gauges, pyrometric cones, and even computer controllers to manage and monitor the firing, but there is still a degree of unpredictability. It is this factor that adds excitement to the creative process. Electric kilns produce more predictable results than live-flame kilns, and in recent years, many potters have returned to using live-flame kilns, especially wood-fueled ones, for this reason. Modern technology handed down from the space missions of the 1960s and 1970s has revolutionized kiln design with the advent of ceramic-fiber blanket. It enables potters to make lightweight, thermally efficient kilns that operate from any fuel.

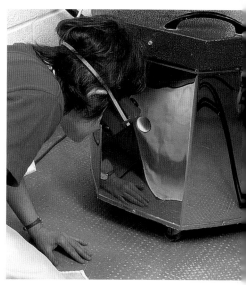

EYE PROTECTION

Looking through a spyhole when the kiln has reached a high temperature can damage your eyes, and the glare from the kiln usually makes it impossible to view the pyrometric cones inside that indicate the temperature of the kiln. View the cones through a piece of green glass, a special cone viewer, or best of all, protective goggles. Shine a flashlight into the glare as you look through the goggles to make the cones stand out as dark shadows.

Types of Kilns

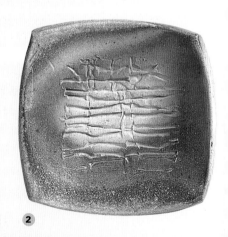

In its simplest form, a kiln is merely an insulated box for retaining heat. It is the careful control of fuel going in and the balance of heat escaping through the vents or chimney that increases the temperature at the correct speed, whether for a bisque or glaze firing. Most kilns work on similar principles, but differences occur depending on the type of fuel used and the atmosphere created within the kiln. The studio potter has to learn at what temperatures the different effects on clay and glaze occur and how the prolonged heat transforms clay into ceramic.

BASIC CHOICES

Front- and top-loading kilns are available in a number of sizes. The style you choose should depend on the type of work you are making, the ease of packing the kiln, and the rate of production you intend to achieve. Balance these factors carefully before purchasing your kiln—it will certainly be the single most expensive outlay you make in the studio. The choice of fuel for your kiln will be governed by several factors: its cost, availability, and the type of effects you are seeking. Electricity is perhaps the most expensive of the fuels, and although considered clean, you must balance this against the possible environmental damage created by nuclear power generation. Wood, on the other hand, is the cheapest and most efficient fuel if calculated in thermal units per quantity of fuel used. Wood can be labor intensive but the fired results will make it worthwhile. Many types and designs of kiln can be purchased from manufacturers or you can experiment and build your own. Building kilns is not difficult and can be extremely rewarding, not only in the knowledge you gain but also in the effects you can achieve.

ELECTRIC KILNS

Electricity offers the most controllable and straightforward way of firing. Electric kilns are clean, efficient, have automatic temperature controllers, and can be used in cities and built-up areas where smoke emission may be a problem. Results from electric kilns tend to be fairly uniform, making them an ideal solution for production wares because the atmosphere inside the kiln remains constant throughout the process. Electric kilns transfer heat by radiation from the elements, always fire in an oxidizing atmosphere, and no oxygen is needed for combustion of fuel. The drawback of electric kilns for many potters is that their predictability makes them less exciting.

Electric kilns are usually constructed from brick in a metal casing. In recent years, ceramic-fiber technology has revolutionized kiln efficiency. Always investigate the efficiency of any kiln you intend to buy—the more fiber used

1 VIEW INTO A GAS KILN

This small brick-built raku kiln has a removable lid to allow access to the pots when heated. Fueled by bottled propane gas through two small burners, temperatures of 1830°F (1000°C) are reached in about an hour. Firing in this way gives potters a valuable insight into what happens to clay at these temperatures.

2 SLAB DISH

Coll Minogue *This small dish bears all the hallmarks of wood firing. The light patch in the center is created by another pot, probably a small cup, placed there to create a shadow spot as the flame and ash swirl around it. Areas of heavier ash build-up on the edges of the dish nearest the flame source give a wonderful variation of surface.*

in its construction, the better. Before installing an electric kiln, make sure you have the necessary supply of electricity. Large kilns require a three-phase electric supply, but with modern fiber technology the consumption of fuel is reducing. Also check that your floor will withstand the weight of any kiln you are installing, especially if it is sited on an upper floor.

GAS AND OIL KILNS

Small, mobile kilns fueled by bottled propane gas have become popular with studio potters and beginners alike. A whole range of firings can be achieved, from low-temperature raku and luster firings to high-temperature stoneware and porcelain. Larger kilns may also be fueled by natural or town gas. Adequate ventilation is needed around the kiln and an efficient chimney to remove the waste gas. Take precautions to prevent the build-up of unfired gas and check regularly for leaking pipes or joints that may cause an explosion. Oil kilns can be fueled by diesel oil from automobiles or domestic heating oil. The fuel is usually introduced by a gravity feed system into a burner and the oil is vaporized into the kiln by a forced air supply. This fine spray of air and oil droplets produces long and intense flames, capable of raising the kiln temperature quickly if required.

As with any live-flame kiln, pottery fired in gas and oil kilns should not come into direct contact with the flames or damage may result from heating too quickly or from over-firing at the end. Gas and oil kilns allow a greater variation of effects on the clay and glazes than electric kilns because a smoky atmosphere (known as reduction) can be created by decreasing the amount of oxygen present in the kiln chamber.

WOOD-FIRED KILNS

Wood is relatively cheap, especially if you live near forested areas, or it can be obtained as scraps from timber mills, and when dry can give a fierce heat. Potters traditionally build wood-fired kilns from brick themselves and there are many schools of thought about the best design. In Japan, large multiple-chambered kilns are the norm, needing many thousands of pots to fill them and long periods of around a week to fire them. Smaller single-chamber kilns can be fired more frequently and more quickly, giving potters a faster turnover of work and more opportunities for increasing their knowledge of firing. The quality of fired pots is greatly enhanced by wood firing. The reduction created by the smoke-filled chamber and the deposits of ash on the glazes give a softness and richness to pottery surfaces.

3 *3 TOP-LOADING ELECTRIC KILNS*

Top-loading kilns are convenient for small-scale workshops because they are cheaper to buy and easier to install. Some potters feel that top loaders cool too rapidly, having a detrimental effect on their work. Others consider this an advantage because they are able to have a very quick firing cycle.

4 FRONT-LOADING ELECTRIC KILN

This type of kiln has a more solid metal framework and thicker walls than a top loader, which means it retains heat for longer. It is also more expensive to buy and install, but is harder wearing. Front loaders are heavy, so you will need to think carefully about how to maneuver the kiln into position.

4

SEE ALSO
Firing kilns, *pages 194–207*

TYPES OF KILNS

Kiln temperature and furniture

The most important factor for a successful firing is the control of the temperature. Traditionally, this was done by eye, judging the temperature at a given point by the color within the kiln. Many potters still fire this way, but it can be inaccurate, especially for inexperienced potters.

PYROMETRIC CONES

The most accurate method of measuring the temperature is to use pyrometric cones. These small triangular cones are composed of ceramic materials that have been pressed into shape. They are formulated to melt at specific temperatures, indicated by a number on the side. Be careful because different manufacturers' cones may vary slightly in the temperatures at which they melt. Always try to use the same make of cone so that you can fire time after time with confidence. Clay and glaze depend not only on temperature to mature successfully but also the amount of time

1

USING PYROMETRIC CONES

1 Place the cones in manufactured holders or in wads of clay, leaning them at a slight angle. If you stand the cones on a flat surface, you will see the direction of lean indicated. Place the set of cones in line with the spyhole of the kiln so that you can see them clearly as the firing progresses.

2 By looking through the spyhole into the kiln, you can clearly see the cones bending. Here, cones 8, 9, and 10 are placed in order from left to right. Cone 8 (2300°F/1260°C) has already bent over, cone 9 (2340°F/1280°C) is halfway down, and cone 10 (2370°F/1300°C) is beginning to follow. When cone 10 is fully down, the firing will be stopped.

3 It is always useful to keep sets of cones from successful firings to act as a guide for future firings. The two sets of cones on the right, from a successful firing, have fully melted. The dark cone 4 (1940°F/1060°C) denotes a period of reduction and is totally molten as it continued to melt with the increasing temperature. Cones 8 and 9 have also melted, denoting a final kiln temperature of around 2340°F (1280°C). These two sets were placed at the top and bottom of the kiln and show an even firing. The cones on the left are underfired, the results of a cool spot in the kiln.

SEE ALSO
Firing kilns, *pages 194–207*

exposed to the heat (known as heat work). Pyrometric cones are developed to reproduce this factor and are therefore the most accurate way of gauging clay and glaze maturity.

Cones are usually used in sets of three. The central cone is the important one, with the cones on either side melting at a temperature just above and just below the required temperature. These cones will give a warning when the correct temperature is approaching and if there is a danger of over-firing. Some potters include another cone at a lower temperature to denote when a period of reduction should commence, for example.

THERMOCOUPLES AND PYROMETERS

Pyrometers accurately indicate the rise and fall of temperature inside the kiln. They consist of two parts. The thermocouple or probe, shielded in a ceramic tube, that protrudes into the kiln through a hole drilled in the top or side. The thermocouple is connected by cables to the pyrometer on the outside of the kiln and indicates the temperature on a dial or screen. Pyrometers may have analog or, more commonly, digital displays. Many potters use both systems together for accuracy, especially when firing wood kilns. The thermocouple accurately denotes the rise of temperature and the cones indicate the heat work and final temperature.

KILN SITTERS

Kiln sitters are used mainly on electric kilns. A small trip switch is placed inside a box on the outside of the kiln, with a tube containing a set of plungers that protrude into the kiln through a drilled hole. The plunger levers are kept apart by a pyrometric bar, similar to a cone but smaller and thinner. When the specific temperature of the bar is reached, it bends, causing the lever to drop and operate a trip switch that cuts the power to the kiln.

KILN FURNITURE

Kiln furniture is the name given to the shelves and props used to support the pottery when packing the kiln. Unfired pots, especially if they are thrown, are usually capable of supporting each other as long as the weight is distributed evenly. If the work is of varying sizes and shapes, you will need to use a series of shelves. Kiln furniture is made from refractory fire clay and intended to withstand high temperatures. Ideally, the smallest work should be placed at the bottom of the kiln so that short props can be used to lift the next shelf over them. Larger props are generally used higher up the stack where they do not have to support heavy weights. It is always a good idea to fire as many different size articles as possible. Making a tighter pack and filling all the small spaces will be more economical.

2

1 KILN FURNITURE

A whole range of kiln furniture is available. Small stilts and spurs are available for supporting individual pots, especially useful in earthenware firings where pots may have glazed bases. Shelves come in different sizes and thicknesses, depending on the work and the firing temperature. Props may be simple tubes of varying diameters or castellated to give greater grip when stacking them.

2 THERMOCOUPLES, PYROMETERS, AND KILN SITTERS

On the right is a portable digital pyrometer and below is a typical standard thermocouple. Above left is a kiln sitter, which automatically shuts off the electric supply to the kiln when a specific temperature is reached.

3 APPLYING KILN WASH

Protect you shelves by always using a kiln wash. This is a 50:50 mixture of china clay and alumina. Paint it onto the shelf in an even coat. After firing, it will be hardened onto the shelf and will prevent most pots from sticking if glaze runs are a problem.

3

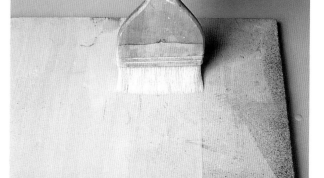

Firing Kilns

All potters develop their own firing patterns and there are no hard and fast rules. The main thing is to monitor the firings continually and keep accurate charts and kiln logs so that you can compare results from consecutive firings. Kiln firing is a slow learning curve with many frustrations along the way, but with perseverance it will be an exciting and enjoyable experience.

BISQUE FIRING

The first firing is known as the bisque or biscuit firing, during which clay is changed through an irreversible chemical process into hard and permanent ceramic. As the name suggests, the clay has a biscuit-like appearance and is still porous. Pots must be completely dry before going into the kiln. If the pots are unglazed, they may be stacked on top of or inside each other; it does not matter if they are touching. Bowls can be stacked rim to rim and base to base as long as the weight is distributed evenly. Do not wedge the base of pots inside the rims of others or they will crack when the clay shrinks during firing.

Bisque firings should be started slowly, ideally increasing at a maximum of 210–300°F (100–150°C) per hour. Leave bungs and spyholes fully open to let out the steam as the chemically held water in the clay molecules evaporates. Chemically held water is usually driven off by 930°F (500°C) and the rate of temperature rise can then be increased to reach the final temperature quickly. Studio potters usually bisque their work to between 1760 and 1830°F (960 and 1000°C) to ensure that any carbon deposits in the body have been burned out.

1 PACKING A KILN FOR A BISQUE FIRING

Some of the work is stacked on top of each other for economy of space. The series of bowls at top right are stacked rim to rim and base to base.

GLAZE FIRING

After bisque firing, pottery is usually glazed and returned to the kiln for a glaze firing. This firing differs from the bisque firing in several ways. The temperature achieved will be higher to melt the glazes, and when packing the kiln no work can touch each other. If pieces do come into contact, they will stick and fuse together when the glaze melts. Glaze firing should be started off slowly to ensure that any residue of water absorbed from the glazes is evaporated. Once the kiln has reached approximately 840°F (450°C), the firing can be accelerated to the required temperature. The temperatures of different glaze firings denote the maturing point of the glazes and fall

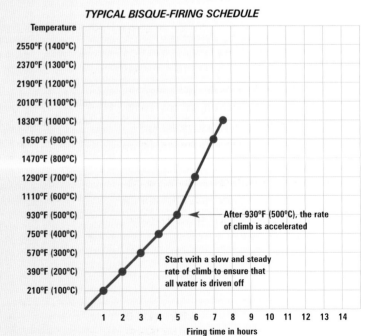

TYPICAL BISQUE-FIRING SCHEDULE

Temperature

2550°F (1400°C)	
2370°F (1300°C)	
2190°F (1200°C)	
2010°F (1100°C)	
1830°F (1000°C)	
1650°F (900°C)	
1470°F (800°C)	
1290°F (700°C)	
1110°F (600°C)	
930°F (500°C)	← After 930°F (500°C), the rate of climb is accelerated
750°F (400°C)	
570°F (300°C)	
390°F (200°C)	Start with a slow and steady rate of climb to ensure that all water is driven off
210°F (100°C)	

1 2 3 4 5 6 7 8 9 10 11 12 13 14

Firing time in hours

roughly into two categories: earthenware 1870–2050°F (1020–1120°C), and stoneware and porcelain 2190–2400°F (1200–1320°C).

EARTHENWARE

Most clay bodies fired to earthenware temperatures still remain porous and pottery may need glazing all over, including the base, especially for food use where hygiene is paramount. In this case, small triangular stilts or spurs will be needed to raise the work from the shelf during firing to prevent it from sticking. After firing, the spur can be tapped off and any sharp glaze residue ground from the pot. If you look at most commercial domestic pottery, you will see three small indentations on the base from these spurs.

STONEWARE AND PORCELAIN

When firing to stoneware temperatures, all the pots should have clean bases and feet, with any traces of glaze thoroughly removed. The pots should be placed directly on the kiln shelf to give adequate support and prevent bending at these extreme temperatures. A good coating of kiln wash on the kiln furniture should protect it from glaze drips or runs. If you know your glazes have a tendency to run slightly, remove any glaze within ¼ in. (5mm) of the base to be on the safe side.

REDUCTION STONEWARE

Normally the atmosphere in a kiln is oxidizing, meaning there is enough oxygen present to burn the fuel cleanly. In a live-flame kiln, it is possible to reduce the air supply by closing dampers in the chimney, creating the dirty, smoky atmosphere known as reduction. This has the effect of changing colors in the clay bodies and glazes. Reduction should normally start at about 1830–1870°F (1000–1020°C) before glazes have begun to stiffen and set. If reduction is started too soon, it may result in carbon becoming trapped beneath the glaze, possibly causing blistering. As the kiln reaches its maturing temperature, the dampers should be opened up for a short period to reoxidize the kiln and clean up the glazes and kiln chamber. Many potters maintain the final temperature for 30–45 minutes to even up any cool spots and ensure an even glaze melt. Reduction will cause fumes to emanate from the kiln and small flames to appear at the spyholes and between brickwork as they try to search out oxygen to burn efficiently. Always ensure there is adequate ventilation in the kiln room when reduction firing.

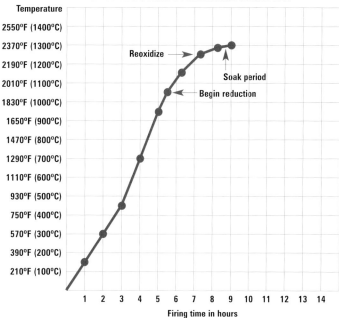

2 PACKING A KILN FOR A GLAZE FIRING

This wood-fired kiln is packed for a glaze firing. Although pots should not normally be touching, the bowls seen here have no glaze on the rims and therefore can be stacked successfully. In some cases, the rims may need to be separated with batting to prevent ash from sticking them together.

TYPICAL REDUCTION STONEWARE SCHEDULE

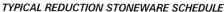

Temperature

2550°F (1400°C)
2370°F (1300°C)
2190°F (1200°C)
2010°F (1100°C)
1830°F (1000°C)
1650°F (900°C)
1470°F (800°C)
1290°F (700°C)
1110°F (600°C)
930°F (500°C)
750°F (400°C)
570°F (300°C)
390°F (200°C)
210°F (100°C)

Reoxidize →
Soak period
← Begin reduction

1 2 3 4 5 6 7 8 9 10 11 12 13 14
Firing time in hours

SEE ALSO
Types of kilns, *pages 190–193*

Wood firing

Wood was the first fuel to be used for firing pottery and wood-fired kilns can be found all over the world. They range in style from the multichamber noborigama and single-chamber anagama kilns of Japan and the climbing kilns of China and Korea to the simple updraft Iberian kilns of the Mediterranean and smaller, more efficient downdraft catenary and sprung-arch kilns used by many potters today. With the advent of gas and electric kilns, many potters turned away from wood firing, but in recent years wood firing has seen a renaissance and is now extremely popular among studio potters.

KILN CONSTRUCTION

There are a few things to keep in mind regarding kiln construction if you are to fire successfully with wood. The fire-mouth must be large enough and have a grate on which to burn the wood, with air being drawn under and up through the embers without obstruction. A large, high chimney will create a good draft to pull the flames through the kiln chambers. The kiln flue should be smaller than the fire-mouth to increase the draft.

PREPARING THE WOOD

Wood firing can be a highly physical and arduous activity, especially if timber needs to be sawed and logs split, but the benefits of prolonged wood firing for the pots far outweigh this. If there is a good site and an ample supply of wood locally, wood firing can be the cheapest alternative to the other fuels. A large amount of wood may be required to achieve the high stoneware temperatures, but more modern kiln designs have reduced this greatly. Soft wood burns hotter and more fiercely than hard wood, but it also burns more quickly. An ample supply of cut and dried wood should always be at hand—there is nothing worse than having to cut more wood at the end of a tiring day firing, just to get that extra 50°. Wood should be tinder dry so that it ignites readily and cut to a size that will generate instant heat in the firebox rather than smolder. Most potters cut, stack, and store their wood for 10 months to 2 years before using it.

①

1 UPDRAFT WOOD-FIRED KILN

The simplest type of wood-fired kiln is styled on a bottle form. The fire hearths are under the floor and the flame passes upward through the work, exiting via a narrow flue at the top. This example from the pottery village of Magyarszombatfa in southern Hungary has three fire-mouths equally placed around the base. Typically, the work here is unglazed or partially glazed earthenware. Ceramic roof tiles act as the kiln floor and shelves.

SEE ALSO
Types of kilns, *pages 190–193*
Firing kilns, *pages 194–195*

2 TWO-CHAMBER WOOD-FIRED KILN

This noborigama kiln at the International Ceramics Studio in Kecskemét, Hungary, has two chambers, the first used for stoneware glaze firing and the second for salt glazing. The firebox at the front is of a bourry design. The flames travel up into each chamber and are then drawn down through a low exit flue into the next chamber. When the first chamber is at temperature, small pieces of split timber are stoked through a small hole in the second chamber until that reaches the required temperature. This is basically the same design as oriental noborigama kilns but the latter often have between five and seven chambers.

3 SPRUNG-ARCH WOOD-FIRED KILN

This wood-fired, soda-glaze kiln is based on a design by American potter Frederick Olsen. The flame path is downdraft, with two opposing fireboxes and a central exit flue running between them. The packing space is 3 x 3 x 6 ft. (1 x 1 x 1.8 m) and reaches cone 10 (2370°F/1300°C) in 12 hours, including soaking. It is extremely fuel efficient, requiring only 53 cubic ft. (1.5 cubic m) of wood.

4 PACKING A LARGE WOOD-FIRED KILN

Frederick Olsen built this unusual design of kiln during a three-week symposium at the International Ceramics Studio in Hungary. Known as the Fire Magic kiln, it has an internal dimension of 10 x 10 ft. (3 x 3 m) and a low domed roof. It has two entrance doors that become the fireboxes when bricked up, and four exit chimneys. At the end of its 24-hour firing, the kiln is soaked at 2370°F (1300°C) for 8 hours to create a heavy ash build-up on the work. By closing dampers in the chimney, flame paths can be altered, causing unusual ash deposits on the surfaces of the pottery.

FIRING KILNS

ASH EFFECTS

During the firing, wood ash will be carried into the kiln chamber, where it will settle on the surface of the pottery. This ash melts at high temperatures, creating speckles and lustrous marks on the glazes; these are sometimes referred to as fly ash effects. If the firing is prolonged enough, the ash will be produced in sufficiently large quantities to form a glaze itself. In these circumstances, pots will need to wadded off the shelves to prevent them from sticking. Many potters only glaze the inside of their pots, relying on the effects of the flames and ash to create lively and rich outer surfaces.

1 HOUSE

Itsue Ito *Slab and coil built from grogged stoneware clay, this sculptural piece was decorated with layers of slip and engobe before wood firing. The extensive ash build-up over the 36-hour firing adds richness and depth.*

2 VASE

Nic Collins *This splendid example of an ash-glazed piece was fired in a single-chamber wood-fired anagama kiln over a period of 3–4 days. The resulting build-up of ash melted on the pot, creating the magnificent surface. This particular piece was packed in the kiln on its side, the telltale wad marks resisting the effect of the fire.*

3 PLATTER

Charles Bound *This large platter has been freely decorated with trailed glaze. Fired in an anagama kiln to 2370ºF (1300ºC) over a period of a week, the ash build-up increased, adding to the excitement and exuberance of the dish.*

1

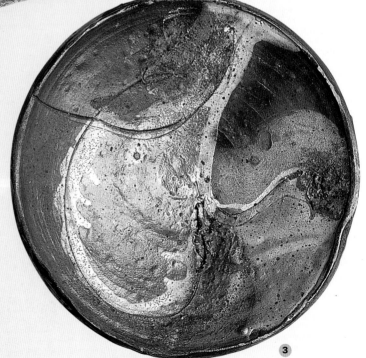

2

3

Salt and soda glazing

Salt glazing has been used extensively for many years in the ceramics industry for glazing drainpipes, bricks, chimney pots, and sanitary ware. The process is reputed to have begun in Germany in the area around the Rhine, where it certainly became popular for glazing all kinds of decorative stonewares, flasks, and bottles. Soda glazing produces similar results but is safer to use. The effects of this type of glazing can range from flashes and blushes on pots to the deeply pitted, characteristic orange-peel finish. When combined with slips and engobes, some interesting and exciting effects can be achieved.

SEE ALSO
Types of kilns, *pages 190–193*
Firing kilns, *pages 194–195*

SALT GLAZING

Salt glazing is a method of achieving an integrated glaze on the surface of an unglazed pot. Salt is introduced into the kiln either through the firebox or poured in through the spyholes from small metal boxes on rods. This is done at high temperatures, when the salt immediately volatizes and breaks down into its constituent parts: sodium and chloride. The sodium combines with the silica in the clay body to form the glaze coat, while the chloride is emitted from the chimney as hydrochloric acid in gas form. These emissions can be harmful and kilns should ideally be situated away from buildings and people. Wind direction must also be considered.

SODA GLAZING

Substituting soda (washing or baking soda is cheap and readily available) for salt decreases the harmful emissions from the kiln without altering the glaze surface. Soda has the added advantage of breaking down at lower temperatures, so many earthenware potters use small amounts of soda to liven up colors on their work. Soda may be introduced into the kiln chamber in a variety of ways. It is common to make a solution of the soda in warm water and spray it through the spyholes in the kiln, but soda itself will become a liquid if warmed on a hot plate. The liquid can be painted onto the split wood for stoking at the end of the firing. The soda recrystalizes as it cools, and when the wood is stoked, the soda gently volatizes and is carried around the kiln with the flames.

SODA-GLAZED WARE

Steve Mattison and Meri Wells *This wood-fired kiln is being unpacked after a soda firing. The pieces all bear the marks of the flames and the characteristic flashes from soda.*

FIRING KILNS

Raku firing

The term raku is derived from the Japanese expression meaning enjoyment or happiness and is the name now given to a particular pottery technique. Of all the firing techniques, raku is probably the most exciting and spectacular. As a medium, however, raku is more decorative than utilitarian.

FIRING PROCEDURE

Raku pots are given a normal bisque firing to 1830°F (1000°C) before being glazed and placed into a raku kiln. After rapidly reaching a temperature of between 1650 and 1830°F (900 and 1000°C), usually in 20–30 minutes, the glazes have melted and the pots are removed with tongs, red hot and glowing from the kiln, and usually placed in drums of wood shavings. The pots undergo intense thermal shocks because of the violent and rapid changes of heat. This causes the glazes to craze and reduce, while smoke penetrates the clay body and enhances the crackles. Copper-bearing glazes will reduce and flash rainbows of colors that constantly move across the surface of the pot until cooled or quenched in water to seal the effects.

FIBER-LINED WIRE MESH KILN

A wire mesh cage can be formed and welded at the joints to make a kiln. Cut holes for the burner ports, exit flue, and a spy hole. The spy hole needs a flap wired over it so that it can be closed during firing. Line the cage with 1–2 in. (2.5–5 cm) of ceramic fiber insulation held in place with bisque-fired clay buttons wired to the frame with nichrome (heat-resistant) wire. When handling ceramic fiber the particles are hazardous, so make sure you wear gloves and a mask. A base made of insulating bricks with a layer of fiber on top is required. The fiber gives a good seal for the kiln. When your pots have reached temperature, the entire kiln can be lifted from the base, giving good access to your hot pots.

GAS-FIRED BRICK KILN

①

High-temperature insulating bricks are best. Leave a two-brick gap on opposite sides of the kiln for the burner ports. Use kiln shelves for the roof, leaving a small opening of about 1 in. (2.5 cm) between the shelves to form an exit flue. Place a smaller kiln shelf inside the kiln supported on short props to lift the pots above the direct flame path.

RAKU KILNS

Raku kilns vary in sophistication. Traditional kilns were built of brick and fired with wood or charcoal, with pottery being placed inside a saggar (a fired clay box) to protect the glaze from direct contact with the flame. However, it is this flame action that many potters wish to exploit. Simple raku kilns can be built from insulating bricks or, for more rapid firing, from metal drums or cages of wire mesh lined with ceramic fiber insulation. Commercial gas burners are widely available and provide quick, clean, and easy firings. The raku kiln is often seen as a symbol of experimental involvement with heat and ceramic, in contrast to the production kiln and its repetitious control. The popularity of raku has grown rapidly in recent years and the introduction of more controllable, efficient, and portable ceramic fiber kilns has made this technique more accessible to potters.

SAFETY PRECAUTIONS

Raku firing involves working directly with hot pots in extreme temperatures. With all the associated hazards, adequate gloves, clothing, masks, goggles, and tongs must be used. With common sense, however, a raku firing can be a thoroughly enjoyable experience.

3 RAKU FIRING

Martin Mindermann Master raku potter Mindermann fires his large vessels rapidly in a gas kiln before removing them, glowing hot, for reduction in heaps of sawdust. The explosion of flame creates intense smoke that permeates the crazing glaze. The pots are then covered with earth to cool slowly, reducing the risk of cracking.

4 RAKU VESSEL

Martin Mindermann This stunning thrown vessel displays all the characteristics of raku-fired work. Green, yellow, and turquoise colors caused by oxidation of the glaze are overlaid with a dark varied crackle, while areas of reduced pink and copper red formed where direct contact with the smoldering sawdust occurred and oxygen was burned away.

2 LUSTER VASE

Martin Everson-Davis The copper matte luster glaze on this vase is perhaps the most fugitive of effects to achieve. The red-hot pot was placed on a small bed of dry sawdust and covered with a metal bin just a little bigger than the pot. The flaming sawdust was extinguished and the oxygen burned from the air. After about 20 seconds, the bin was momentarily raised and the reoxidation caused the colors to appear. The bin was then left over the pot until cool.

1 TWO TALL VESSELS WITH LINES

David Roberts These elegant coiled vessels demonstrate a confident control of the raku technique. A grogged china clay resist slip was applied over the bisque and a low-fire raku glaze brushed over this and incised through to the body. Rapidly fired in a gas-fueled kiln, the pots were removed hot and placed on pads of sawdust in metal containers to smoke through the cracking glaze. When cool, the glaze was scraped off and the pieces polished to a soft sheen.

SEE ALSO

Types of kilns, *pages 190–193*
Firing kilns, *pages 194–195*

FIRING KILNS

Saggar and pit firing

A saggar is a fired clay box capable of withstanding high temperatures and was originally developed to protect pottery from the flames of the kiln. These days many studio potters use saggars for the opposite reason—to protect the kiln from combustible materials packed around the pots in order to produce decorative effects, many of which could attack the brickwork of the kiln or the electric elements. Pit firing also involves using combustible materials but the pots are placed in a pit in the ground rather than in a saggar in a kiln. Saggar and pit firing cry out for experimental materials to be wrapped around the work. Kitchen waste can provide some interesting effects as they volatize and flash colors onto the work. Damp seaweed, banana skins, and string soaked in salt solutions can all have unexpected and wonderful results.

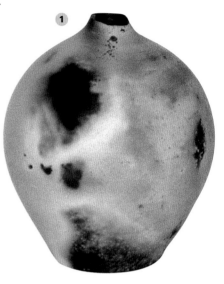

SAGGAR FIRING

Pots are placed in the saggar and surrounded with a variety of materials, such as sawdust, charcoal, salt, and copper oxides. The saggar is then closed with a kiln shelf lid and sealed with a clay coil. During firing the

SAGGAR FIRING

1 Place the pots in a saggar and pack combustible materials around them. Here, sawdust, salt, washing soda, string, and copper carbonate are packed around the pots. During firing these materials will burn, causing incidental effects on the surfaces of the pots. You can experiment with a wide range of materials.

2 Press the kiln shelf lid firmly onto its seal of clay. Any airway through to the saggar will lessen the effects of the combustible materials as well as allow gases to escape and affect the kiln interior.

3 When the kiln has cooled, remove the lid of the saggar to reveal the finished pots nestling among the remnants of the combustible material, now reduced to ash.

materials inside the saggar will volatize and flash colors onto the pots and produce areas of intense carbonization. As long as the saggar is airtight, it can be packed into the kiln with other normal glazed pots and should have no effect on them.

PIT FIRING

Pit firing is a more extreme version of saggar firing, where many pots can be packed into large holes dug in the ground and surrounded with materials and wood for firing. When blazing suitably, cover with a metal lid to retain the heat. If the fire dies down, lift the lid a little and throw more wood onto the embers. Remember that working this way has inherent dangers and suitable protective clothing, goggles, and gloves must be worn.

1 SEA BOTTLE

Paul Brimcombe *This small thrown bottle was smoothed with a rubber rib while still on the wheel to compact and semi-burnish the surface. Wrapped in swathes of seaweed and then buried in a sawdust-filled saggar, beautiful pink blushes have flashed onto the bottle from volatizing salt and nitrates from the seaweed.*

2 PIT FIRING

Ray Rogers *Here, Rogers is packing one of his giant pit kilns reading for a firing. The pottery is laid on a 6 in. (15 cm) bed of sawdust to produce dark black areas, and then surrounded with charcoal and sprinkled with salt and copper carbonate to produce pink colors. The pit is gradually filled with wood and lit from the top to burn down over a number of hours. Restoking the pit during firing will increase the temperature.*

3 SAGGAR-FIRED BOTTLE

Meri Wells *The subtle blue hues come from a thin cobalt oxide wash all over the pot. Small packets of salt and copper oxide were strategically placed alongside the piece to flash reduced copper red colors onto the surface. The clay was smooth but left unburnished to retain the dry, matte finish.*

SEE ALSO
Types of kilns, *pages 190–193*
Firing kilns, *pages 194–195*

Sawdust firing

This is a simple but effective way of firing pottery, especially if it has been burnished before bisque firing. These kilns can be made of ordinary house bricks or an old metal refuse bin because the temperatures are not high enough to affect the bricks or metal. The pots are packed on a 4–6 in. (10–15 cm) bed of fresh sawdust, with more sawdust sprinkled around and over them. Salts and copper oxides can be added in small paper packets for coloration. If there are several layers of pots, place some metal chicken wire between the layers so that they will not fall onto each other and break as the sawdust burns away. Light the top of the sawdust with a paraffin-soaked cloth and cover with a metal sheet or lid. The kiln will smolder for many hours. Only remove the work when cool or sudden exposure to cold air may cause it to crack.

SAWDUST-FIRED POT

Sue King *This rounded, coil-built vessel is the most appropriate form for sawdust firing because its large, burnished surfaces show the gentle smoking to its best advantage. Made from sanded red terra-cotta clay, it has a robust warmth.*

SAWDUST FIRING

Pack a small brick box with layers of pots and sawdust. Leave small gaps between some of the bricks to provide air inlets. These will raise the temperature in the kiln but can be blocked if the kiln begins to burn too fast. Use a large kiln shelf to form the roof. Light the kiln from the top, and once well lit, cover with the lid. The kiln should smolder happily for several hours until all the sawdust has been burned away. Remove the pots and wash them with a soft cloth. If you wish, apply a coat of wax, which gives a beautiful sheen when polished.

SEE ALSO
Types of kilns, *pages 190–193*
Firing kilns, *pages 194–195*

Smoke firing

SEE ALSO
Types of kilns, *pages 190–193*
Firing kilns, *pages 194–195*

Smoke is easily created when a fire is lit in a container with insufficient oxygen to burn cleanly. The source of the smoke is usually sawdust, straw, or newspaper. For many smoke effects the temperature does not have to be very great and the pottery must be bisque fired no higher than 1830°F (1000°C) so that the body is still porous enough to absorb the carbon. When smoking is combined with burnishing and clay slip resists, dramatic patterned decoration can result. Softer areas of light smoking will occur where light wafts of smoke creep under the fractured and shrinking slip.

1 SMOKED VESSEL

Ashraf Hanna *The surface of this handbuilt pots was burnished to a glass-like finish before bisque firing. For the final smoke firing, sgraffitto lines were drawn through a resist slip, allowing the smoke to penetrate the cracks and carbonize the surface in linear patterns. Smoke also bleeds under the slip, creating subtle tonal areas as the clay slip shrinks and peels away from the body.*

SMOKE FIRING

2 DISH

Jacqui Atkin *A press-molded dish forms the base for this piece, to which coils were added to widen the shape. The flat, open form was then covered with an intricate pattern of masking tape lines to form a resist for the painted slip. When the tape was removed, the raw clay body was exposed to the smoking process in a newspaper-filled container.*

1 Place the pot in a small metal container (such as a trashcan) and loosely pack crumpled newspaper or a similar combustible material around the pot. Ignite the paper and allow it to burn down. Cover the top of the container with wire mesh to prevent flaming paper from floating into the air. More paper can be added to smoke the piece more strongly if necessary.

2 When fairly cool, remove the pot and rub off the loose soot. Natural beeswax can be applied to the still warm surface and buffed with a soft cloth.

FIRING KILNS

In-situ firings

Many kilns are made from clay in one form or another, whether it is fired clay bricks, adobe mixtures, or ceramic-fiber blanket. In many countries, itinerant brick makers will set up business where natural deposits of clay occur, make a kiln from raw bricks, fill it with raw bricks, and wood fire it all at the same time—the work becomes the kiln. The sequence below shows the work of Danish ceramic artist Nina Hole, who takes this simple idea of clay object as kiln and creates extraordinary sculptures of great beauty, both during and after the firing. The firings of these large structures are an awesome sight—ceramics as theater. Working in collaboration with American artist Frederick Olsen, an expert in kiln technology, these pieces can be fired in situ to high temperatures, making them permanent artifacts.

OXIDES

Various oxides can be mixed with salt and placed in small paper packets. When thrown onto the surface of the sculpture when the firing reaches its highest temperature, they will produce different colors and effects.

IN-SITU FIRING

1 The sculpture is constructed from a series of clay slabs bent into U shapes and laid on top of each other in opposing rows. This creates pathways through the clay walls for the flames to penetrate. Built on a raised base of brick, which also forms the fireboxes, these structures are considerably high. The surfaces will be painted with engobes and mixtures of oxides.

2 When the building work is completed, the entire structure is loosely covered with ceramic blanket and held in place with nichrome (high-temperature) wire. The structure narrows toward the top to provide the necessary draft for the flame from the two opposing fireboxes. When handling ceramic-fiber, gloves and masks must be worn.

3 After firing for 1–2 days, the sculpture has reached its final temperature and the spectacle really begins. The ceramic blanket is removed, revealing the intensely hot, glowing sculpture.

FIRING PRINCIPLES

In recent years, many artists have experimented with this way of working, constructing hollow sculptures from coiled clay or stacked raw clay modules. This allows sculptures from clay to be built and fired virtually anywhere without the need for a separate kiln. Basically, these structures are simple updraft kilns, fired from below, usually with wood. The flames are sucked upward through the sculpture. A covering of insulating ceramic-fiber blanket retains the heat within the structure, raising the temperature.

SAFETY CONSIDERATIONS

Of all the ceramic working practices, this has to the most exciting and visually stunning. It is, however, not for the faint-hearted and great care must be taken when working in this way. Fire does have its dangers, but with common sense and an awareness of the risks, this type of work is extremely rewarding and need not always be on the scale of Hole's work, which is illustrated here.

SEE ALSO
Types of kilns, *pages 190–191*
Firing kilns, *pages 194–195*
Wood firing, *pages 196–198*
Salt and soda glazing, *page 199*

4 The entire audience watching the firing is illuminated in orange from the radiating heat as sparks drift upward into the night sky.

5 The hot surface is bombarded with sawdust and wood shavings and small newspaper packets filled with mixtures of salt and oxides. These ignite and volatize, promoting wide variations of color to form on the piece. The sculpture erupts in a final blaze of sparks before cooling slowly over a number of hours.

6 The final sculpture, entitled Torre de Lua, has cooled and remains a testament to its birth through fire. It is located in Montemor-o-Novo in Portugal.

Chapter 7

TOOLS AND EQUIPMENT

Whatever type of pottery you are making, you will require certain tools and pieces of equipment. The amount of expensive equipment you will have to buy will depend on the type of work you intend to make. The tools required for pottery making can be roughly split into two categories: hand tools and studio equipment, the latter being the most costly. Handbuilding obviously requires the least amount of equipment, while for throwing you will need at least a wheel.

HAND TOOLS

Whatever pottery you are making, you will need hand tools for cutting, scraping, and modeling clay. You may also need a series of wooden beaters for paddling clay into shape and refining surfaces. Hand tools are very personal items and all potters will have definite preferences, often styling and adapting homemade tools to their purpose. Tools from specialty suppliers can be expensive and many alternatives can be found in kitchen or hardware stores, often for a fraction of the cost. Making your own tools from wood, plastic, or steel can be rewarding, and this way you get exactly the tool you want. Use a good-quality wood with a close grain, such as boxwood, because it can be cut and sanded finely and will not wear down quickly, which is particularly important if you are using a coarse, groggy clay. Metal tools can be made from sheet metal or the banding tape around packing cases. They will need regular sharpening because they can quickly become blunt with use.

STUDIO EQUIPMENT

All potters need to fire their work and the kiln will be the single biggest capital outlay. With recent fiber technology, kilns have become less expensive and you may only need a small hobby variety to begin with. Top-loading kilns are generally cheaper than front loaders, but not as easy to load. Large studios often have several kilns of varying sizes—small kilns for firing tests and larger ones for the production work. Wheels can also be expensive, especially high-performance production wheels. Cheaper alternatives are available and are adequate for most uses. You will also need a whole range of ancillary equipment, such as tables, small banding wheels, sieves, jugs, buckets, and bowls.

BOUGHT AND FOUND TOOLS

You can often use items found around the home and studio as pottery-making tools. Here, you can see the different sgraffito marks that can be produced using purchased tools (right) and household items such as pens and forks (left).

Hand Tools

Hand tools can be categorized into scraping and cutting tools, forming tools, and decorating tools. The more techniques you use, the more tools you will need. Potters are great collectors and will hoard scraps of wood and metal that will substitute for expensive commercially produced tools. Many tools you buy will seldom be used, and with experience, you will soon find yourself discarding some in favor of the essential ones.

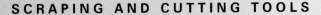
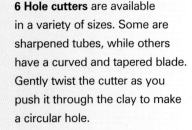
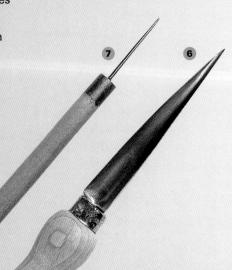

SCRAPING AND CUTTING TOOLS

These basic tools will enable you to cut and create forms, and refine the surfaces of your pottery.

1 Twisted wire is essential for wedging, dividing blocks of clay, and cutting thrown pots from the wheel. The wire is usually about 18 in. (45 cm) long and attached to wooden toggles for easy grip. A cheap substitute is model aircraft control wire, which is stainless and available at a fraction of the cost. One roll should last a lifetime.

2 Metal or plastic scrapers are used for refining and shaping clay. They come in a variety of shapes and sizes, some with serrated edges for scraping down rough edges. Discarded credit cards also make useful scrapers for smoothing soft clay.

3 Soft rubber ribs are flexible and give smooth, compacted surfaces.

4 Potter's knives usually have thin, narrow blades to prevent clay from sticking. An excellent alternative is an old hacksaw blade, which can be sharpened and ground down—you get a serrated edge as a bonus.

5 Rasp blades will quickly pare down leather-hard surfaces when handbuilding.

6 Hole cutters are available in a variety of sizes. Some are sharpened tubes, while others have a curved and tapered blade. Gently twist the cutter as you push it through the clay to make a circular hole.

7 Potter's needles are used for cutting the rims of pots even when throwing and are also useful as a gauge for testing the depth of a pot's base.

8 Trimming tools made from looped wire, usually sharpened on one edge, are used for trimming pots on the wheel and for hollowing out handbuilt shapes.

FORMING TOOLS

Wood always make the best forming tools because wet clay does not stick so easily to the surface.

1 Rolling pins should be good quality and about 2 in. (5 cm) in diameter.

2 Roller guides, made from wooden laths of identical thickness, will ensure that you roll slabs of even thickness.

3 Paddling tools can be purchased from suppliers or you can buy wooden spoons and spatulas from kitchenware stores—they are just as good. Try making your own from blocks of wood. Many potters carve designs into their paddles to make interesting patterns as they form and refine their work. This technique is popular in the orient, especially with the Ongii potters of Korea.

4 Modeling tools are available from all pottery suppliers in a vast array of shapes or you could make your own from scraps of wood. Plastic ones are cheaper but not as pleasant to use.

5 Throwing ribs made from wood, bamboo, or plastic can be obtained from suppliers. The profile can always be cut and altered if desired.

DECORATING TOOLS

This is the one area where potters are most likely to collect their own personal mark-making tools. Always be on the lookout for interesting shapes and tools you may use.

1 Brushes are the most essential of all the decorating tools. Wide, soft hake brushes are ideal for smooth, even applications of slip. Oriental brushes give a variety of expressive marks. Even toothbrushes are useful for spattering slip and joining edges of clay. Always buy the best you can afford—they are better quality and will last longer.

2 Slip trailers have a variety of uses and come in a range of sizes, some with interchangeable nozzles.

3 Sponges are a vital part of any potter's tool kit. Small natural sponges are best for smoothing clay, while artificial foam is ideal for cutting sponge stamps for decorating.

4 Stamps can be made from almost anything. You can buy sets of wooden stamps from suppliers or make your own by carving or scoring designs into small blocks of plaster or bisque-fired clay.

5 Wooden pastry roulettes can be used to make interesting marks in clay.

Studio Equipment

Studio equipment is obviously more expensive than hand tools but there are a number of items that are essential. All potters need a kiln, and those who wish to throw pottery will need a wheel. Whether you need the other studio equipment described here will largely depend on the amount of work you intend to produce.

Gas-fired kiln

Kilns are the most essential piece of equipment in a pottery studio. Electric kilns are obtainable in a whole range of sizes, from small main-operated hobby kilns to large commercial ones requiring a nondomestic power supply. Gas kilns are also available if you wish to fire reduction stoneware. Front-loading kilns are generally easier to pack but top loaders are usually cheaper.

Throwing wheels are available in three basic types: kickwheels, momentum wheels, and electric wheels. The type you choose will be a personal decision, balancing the aspects of production, the ease

of working, and the finished quality you wish to achieve. Kickwheels may be made of wood or metal and are usually propeled by a pedal or crank shaft operated by the potter's foot spinning a flywheel. Momentum wheels usually have a large, heavy flywheel powered directly by the feet or rotated with a stick placed in a notch on the wheelhead. Electric wheels come in a variety of sizes. Some are large with integrated seats and others small and more adjustable in height, with remote foot pedals. These types are especially useful for throwing large pots.

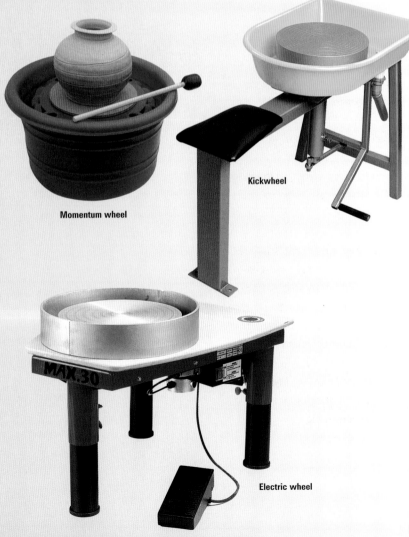

Momentum wheel

Kickwheel

Electric wheel

Banding wheels are used when coiling, handbuilding, and decorating. They come in different sizes and weights.

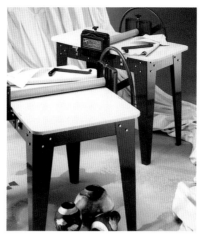

Slab rollers will produce large, even slabs of clay and are ideal for making large tile panels when many sheets of clay may be required. The clay is sandwiched between layers of canvas and squeezed through adjustable rollers.

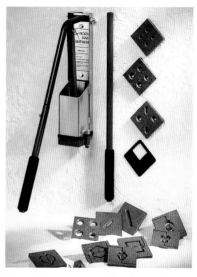

Extruders squeeze clay through cut metal dies to make coils, handle shapes, or even entire sides of pots. They can be table or wall mounted, depending on their size.

Pugmills use a series of rotating blades inside a metal casing to cut, mix, and extrude the clay. Modern de-airing pugs remove the need for wedging and are ideal for high-volume clay production.

Ball mills are used to grind down raw materials into fine powders and to mix glaze materials together. A ball mill is only necessary if you are digging your own materials.

Spraying equipment is needed if you intend to spray glazes or colors. A good-quality spray gun and compressor will be essential. Compressors come in various types, some with air reservoirs and some with only a direct feed to the gun. A spray booth with adequate extraction facilities is also recommended.

Pugmill

Ball mill

Spray gun and compressor

Spray booth

Health and Safety

A number of health and safety problems are clearly identifiable when working with ceramics, all of which need to be approached sensibly and with an awareness of local legislation. Potters and ceramicists are constantly exposed to raw materials, varying in toxicity from mildly irritant to poisonous. A well-developed common sense and good working practice are the best defense. Health and safety are factors you will constantly have to consider. All potters have to use some hazardous materials and equipment, so it is best to learn to be careful. There is no reason you cannot reduce the effects of these hazards to a minimum while still retaining your creativity and expression.

DUST

Dust is an ever-present problem. Unfired clay dust contains free silica, a dangerous substance when inhaled. The small particle size can severely damage your lungs over a period of time. While you can never totally rid your working space of dust, you can keep it to a minimum. Always wipe surfaces with damp cloths; never brush up dust because it will release particles into the air. Always wash tools after use and regularly wash your working clothes and towels. Disposable dust masks are relatively cheap and easily obtainable and should be worn when mixing clay, glaze, or sweeping up. Adequate ventilation is the best precaution and open windows are always best.

TOXIC MATERIALS

Many of the raw materials in the studio can be toxic to varying degrees and general precautions should be taken at all times. You should wear a dust mask when mixing glazes and wear surgical gloves if you have a cut or skin problem. Washing clay or glaze off your hands before eating or drinking will ensure that you never ingest glaze materials. Excessive inhalation of quartz dust may result in chronic lung damage.

CLEANING UP

• Keep working surfaces and shelves clean by wiping them with a wet sponge. Rinse out the sponge frequently and wipe the area twice.
• Clean up any spills of materials or liquids immediately whenever they happen.
• Floors must be washed or mopped to control dust circulating in the atmosphere. DO NOT sweep the floor with a broom.
• Try working on newspapers or paper towels so that it is easier to clean up afterward and dispose of the dust or materials.
• Keep dust under control.
• Clean off the rims of jars and lids of buckets before you close them to prevent a build-up of dried product materials.
• Always store materials in closed containers.

PERSONAL HYGIENE

• DO NOT smoke, eat, or drink when working in the studio.
• Wearing contact lenses is not recommended when working in dusty environments because particles may become trapped between the lens and the eye, scratching the eye's surface.
• Always wash your hands thoroughly when you are finished working.
• Make sure you clean up and store materials safely, especially if there are small children in the house.

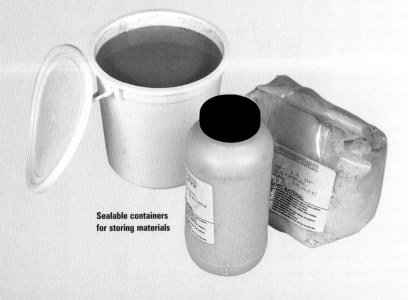

Sealable containers for storing materials

Respirator mask

Safety goggles

• DO NOT use any utensils that are also used in the kitchen.

• If there is an accidental inhalation or ingestion of toxic ceramic material, seek medical advice as soon as possible.

• Ceramic materials should not be handled when you have any cuts or open wounds. Wear surgical gloves if necessary to prevent materials from entering the bloodstream.

• Wear gloves and a dust mask or respirator mask when handling oxides and toxic materials.

KILNS

• Kilns should ideally be in a separate room because fumes will be given off during firing. Adequate ventilation should be ensured, and if necessary, extraction hoods and fans installed. Some fumes can be harmful, especially from low-fire lusters and enamels when the medium burns off. The plastic coating on printed transfers will create noxious fumes, especially in the early stages of firing.

• Make sure there are no combustible materials near the kiln that may catch fire.

• When looking at cones in the kiln, always wear shielded goggles (shade number 1.73.0), such as those used by welders. Normal sunglasses are inadequate.

• Wear heavy-duty gloves when opening kiln spyholes because they will be extremely hot. NEVER touch the outside of a kiln (other than the control panel) when it is switched on because the kiln surface can be very hot.

• DO NOT allow children near the kiln.

• Electric kilns should be installed in accordance with local electrical and fire safety codes and in accordance with manufacturer's suggested installation instructions.

• When unpacking the kiln, be careful of stilt marks or glaze drips because they can be sharp. Smooth them as soon as possible with a grinding stone.

• Wear safety goggles when using grinding wheels.

ELECTRICAL MACHINERY

• All moving parts should be suitably enclosed to prevent loose clothing, hair, or hands from getting caught. Special care should be taken with equipment such as pugmills and blungers.

• Be sure to turn off the electrical supply at the main outlet before adjusting or dismantling electrical machinery.

• Make sure that stop and start switches are always within reach of the operator.

SPRAYING GLAZES OR SLIPS

• If you are spraying glaze, it should ideally be done in an enclosed booth with an extractor fan or, at the very least, outdoors. Go outside periodically for fresh air, especially if you work in a small, airless workshop.

• Try to avoid spraying materials that contain certain potentially hazardous materials, such as lead or silica.

• Sprays and solvents should be adequately ventilated when used.

Heavy-duty gloves

Glossary

Airbrush A device operated with an air compressor used for spraying on colors, either in overall coverage or decorative form.

Antiquing A method of applying color and wiping it back to accentuate the detailed surface.

Banding wheel A turntable operated by hand, used for decorating purposes.

Bat A plaster or wooden disk for throwing pots on, moving pots without handling, or for drying clay.

Bat wash Another term for kiln wash.

Beating Another term for paddling.

Bisque (biscuit) Clay ware after the first firing, usually around 1830°F (1000°C).

Bisque firing The first firing of pottery to mature the clay, rendering it permanent. In a bisque firing, pots may be stacked on or inside each other because there is no glaze to stick them together.

Blunger High-speed mechanical mixer for slip, usually casting slip.

Body The term used to describe a particular mixture of clay, such as stoneware body and porcelain body.

Bone china A clay body with a quantity of bone ash in the recipe.

Calcine A form of purifying by heating oxides or compounds to drive out carbon gases or water and to reduce plasticity in powdered clays.

Casting Making pots by pouring slip into a porous mold to build up a layer of clay.

Casting slip A liquid clay used in the process of forming objects with molds. Also referred to simply as slip.

Cavity (of a mold) The inside section of a mold where the casting is formed.

Ceramic Any clay form that is fired in a kiln.

China A term associated with vitreous white wares and porcelain.

Chuck A hollow form made in clay or plaster that holds a pot securely during trimming.

Coiling Making pots using coils or ropes of clay.

Collaring The action of squeezing around a pot in order to draw the shape inward.

Cones See *Pyrometric cones.*

Crank Refractory support for tiles, plates, etc. Crank also refers to a type of heavily grogged clay body.

Crawling Movement of glaze over the clay body during the glaze firing, due to dust or grease on the surface.

Crazing The development of fine cracks caused by contraction of a glaze.

Decal Pictures or text printed onto special transfer paper and used to decorate pottery.

Deflocculation The dispersion of clay slip or glaze by the addition of an electrolyte—e.g., sodium silicate or soda ash—thereby increasing fluidity and decreasing thixotropy.

Dipping Applying a glaze by immersion.

Earthenware Pottery fired to a relatively low temperature. The body remains porous and usually requires a glaze if it is to be used for containing water or food.

Elements The metal heating coils in an electric kiln.

Enamels Low-temperature colors containing fluxes, usually applied on top of a fired glaze. Enamels require a further firing to render them permanent. Also known as on-glaze colors or china paints.

Engobe A white or colored slip applied to pottery before glazing. Usually the slip contains an amount of flux to fire it onto the bisque pot.

Fettling The process of cleaning up slip-cast pottery with a knife or sponge, especially when removing seams left by a mold.

Finger-sand The gentle rubbing of a glazed surface with the fingers to remove ridges.

Firing The process by which ceramic ware is heated in a kiln to bring glaze or clay to maturity.

Firing chamber The interior of the kiln in which pottery is fired.

Firing cycle The gradual raising and lowering of the temperature of a kiln to fire pottery.

Flange The rim on the inside of a lid and the ledge around the inside of a pot's opening that are used to locate the lid and hold it securely in place. The ledge on which the lid sits is sometimes called a gallery.

Flocculation The aggregation of suspended particles by the addition of electrolytes—e.g., calcium chloride to give a proper consistency for dipping, casting, etc. Flocculation decreases fluidity and increases thixotropy.

Flux An ingredient in a glaze or clay that causes it to melt readily, helping silica to form glaze or glass.

Food-safe Pottery or glaze that has been tested and determined to be safe for use with food or drink.

Foot The base of a piece of pottery on which it rests.

Footring The circle of clay at the base of a pot that raises the form from the surface it is standing on.

Frit Glaze ingredients that have been fused to give a more stable substance and to render harmless any dangerous material. Most lead compounds have been fritted to prevent the release of lead into food or drink.

Gallery See *Flange*.

Glaze A thin, glassy layer on the surface of pottery.

Glaze fit How well a fired glaze adheres to the clay body. Ideally, the glaze should have a slightly lower thermal expansion than the body, so that on contraction the body puts the glaze into compression. This avoids glaze crazing due to stresses.

Glaze stain Commercial color added to a glaze.

Glost Alternative word for glazed, more commonly used in industry.

Greenware Unfired clay ware.

Grog A ceramic material, usually clay, that has been heated to a high temperature before use. Usually added to clay to lessen warping and increase its resistance to thermal shock.

Hardening on Heating decorated bisque pottery to a temperature of approximately 1200–1290°F (650°C–700°C) in order to burn out the organic media of the decoration and to fix the color prior to glazing.

Heat work Energy input during firing, normally represented in terms of temperature and time.

Hot spot A section of a kiln that fires to a hotter temperature than the rest of the kiln.

Incise The process of carving a design into a raw clay surface.

Kidneys See *Ribs* and *Scrapers*.

Kiln The device in which pottery is fired. Kilns can be fueled with wood, oil, gas, or electricity.

Kiln furniture Refractory pieces used to separate and support kiln shelves and pottery during firing.

Kiln setting The way in which a kiln is packed for firing.

Kiln wash A coating of refractory material applied to kiln furniture to prevent it from sticking during firing.

Kneading A method of de-airing and dispersing moisture uniformly through a piece of clay to prepare it for use. Sometimes referred to as wedging.

Lead release The amount of lead that can be dissolved from the surface of a glaze that has been in contact with acidic solutions.

Leather-hard Clay that is stiff but still damp. It is hard enough to be handled without distorting but can still be joined.

Majolica Decorated tin-glazed earthenware with the color decoration being applied on top of the raw glaze surface.

Matte A soft finish with little or no shine.

Maturing temperature The temperature at which a clay body develops the desirable hardness, or glaze ingredients fuse into the clay body.

Mini bars Pyrometric bars used to measure the firing temperature of a kiln. They are usually used in a kiln sitter, a mechanical device that shuts off power to the kiln when the bar has bent enough to release a weighted switch.

Mold A plaster former in which clay can be pressed or slip cast to create forms. Molds can be made up of only one section or multiple pieces.

Mold strap (mold band) A band made of cloth or, more commonly, rubber used to secure parts of a mold together during the pouring process.

Nesting Stacking pottery in a kiln for bisque firing. Pots can safely be placed inside one another.

On-glaze color See *Enamels*.

Opaque Glazes that do not allow other colors to show through, as opposed to transparent glazes.

Oxidation Firing pottery in a kiln with sufficient supplies of oxygen.

Paddling Tapping a wooden tool against a piece to clay to alter its shape.

Peeling A defect in glazed pottery where the engobe or glaze separates from the body in flakes, usually due to high compression stresses in the layer.

Pinholes A glaze or body fault caused by trapped air erupting through the body or glaze during firing.

Plastic clay Clay that can be manipulated but still retains its shape.

Pour hole The opening of the mold used for pouring the slip into the mold cavity.

Prop A refractory clay pillar used for supporting kiln shelves during firing. Also known as posts.

Pugging Mixing and extruding clay from a pugmill.

Pyrometer An instrument for measuring the temperature inside a kiln chamber. Works in conjunction with a probe (thermocouple) placed through a hole drilled through the top or side of the kiln wall.

Pyrometric cones Small pyramids made of ceramic materials that are designed to soften and bend when a particular ratio of temperature and time is reached during firing.

Raku A firing technique in which pots are placed directly into a hot kiln and removed when red-hot.

Raw glazing See *Single fired*.

Reducing atmosphere Deficiency of free oxygen in a kiln atmosphere that causes the reduction of compounds rich in oxygen, which affects the glaze and clay color.

Refractory Ceramic materials that are resistant to high temperatures.

Resist A decorative medium, such as wax, latex, or paper, used to prevent slip or glaze from sticking to the surface of pottery.

Ribs Wooden or plastic ribs are tools used to lift the walls of thrown pots, while rubber ribs are used for compacting and smoothing clay surfaces. Some ribs are kidney shaped and may be referred to as kidneys.

Saggar A box made from fire clay used for holding glazed pots in a fuel-burning kiln to protect the pots from direct contact with the flames and gases.

Scrapers Thin metal and plastic tools used to refine clay surfaces. They may be either straight or kidney shaped, and are sometimes referred to as ribs or kidneys respectively.

Seam lines Small lines on pottery produced where two sections of a mold join or where sides come together in slab construction.

Semi-matte A satin-like surface that has a slight sheen to it.

Semi-opaque Colors that generally allow only dark colors to show through.

Semi-transparent Slightly colored and/or speckled colors that allow most colors to show through with only slight distortions.

Sgraffito The cutting or scratching through an outer coating of slip, glaze, or engobe to expose the different colored body beneath. From the Italian word *graffito*, meaning to scratch.

Single fired The making, glazing, and firing of pottery in a single operation. Also known as raw glazing.

Slab building Making pottery from slabs of clay.

Slip Liquid clay.

Slip trailing Decorating with colored slips squeezed through a nozzle.

Soak Keeping a predetermined temperature at the end of the firing cycle to maintain the level of heat in the kiln to enhance many glaze finishes.

Spare The section of a model that will form the pouring hole when casting a plaster mold.

Sponging Cleaning the surface of pottery before firing or a decorative method of applying slip or glaze.

Spyholes (vent holes) Small holes in the door or side of a kiln used for viewing cones and ventilating the kiln during firing.

Stains Unfired colors used for decorating pottery or a ceramic pigment used to add color to glazes and bodies.

Stilts Small shapes of bisque clay, sometimes with metal or wire spurs, used for supporting glazed pottery during firing.

Stoneware Vitrified clay, usually fired above 2190°F (1200°C). Any glaze matures at the same time as the body, forming an integral layer.

Terra-cotta An iron-bearing earthenware clay that matures at a low temperature and fires to an earth-red color.

Terra sigillata A very fine slip used as a surface coating for burnishing or other decorative treatments.

Thermal expansion The expansion that occurs in glazes and clays during firing.

Thermal shock Sudden expansion or contraction that occurs in a clay or glaze and causes damage, usually through sudden heating or cooling.

Thermocouple The temperature probe in a kiln that transmits information to the pyrometer.

Thixotropy The ability of clay suspensions to thicken up on standing. See also *Deflocculation* and *Flocculation*.

T material Highly grogged white plastic clay.

Toxic Any ceramic material, raw, gaseous, or liquid, that is injurious to health.

Transparent Clear base colors that are free from cloudiness and distortion.

Trimming (turning) Trimming thrown pots in the leather-hard state to refine their shape and, most commonly, to create footrings.

Underfiring Not firing hot enough or long enough, or both.

Underglaze A color that is usually applied to either greenware or bisque-fired pottery and in most cases is covered with a glaze. A medium, such as gum arabic, is usually used to adhere the color to bisque but needs to be fired on before glazing.

Vitrification point The point at which clay particles fuse together.

Vitrified Usually refers to porcelain and stoneware that are fired at a high temperature. The clay begins to become glass-like.

Wedging A method of preparing plastic clay by distributing clay particles and additives such as grog evenly throughout the clay mass.

Index

Credits

CERAMICISTS

Quarto would like to thank and acknowledge all of the ceramicists who kindly allowed us to reproduce examples of their work in this book. All of their names appear in the captions accompanying the relevant pieces of work except in the following instances:

p1 Elizabeth Raeburn, courtesy of Galerie Besson; p4 Martin Everson-Davis; p5 center left & below left Meri Wells; p5 top right Linda John; p5 right-hand column, third down Martin Mindermann; p55 top left courtesy of the International Ceramic Studio, Kecskemét, Hungary; p57 below right Jim Robison; p60 above left courtesy of the International Ceramic Studio, Kecskemét, Hungary; p63 below left courtesy of the International Ceramic Studio, Kecskemét, Hungary; p145 above right Craig Bragdy Design Limited; p153 below right Meri Wells; p154 below center & below right Craig Bragdy Design Limited; p155 below center David Binns; p155 below right Martin Mindermann; p159 below right Morgen Hall; p167 steps 1–3 Maria Geszler-Garzuly; pp206–207 steps 1–6 Nina Hole

PHOTOGRAPHERS

We would also like to acknowledge the following photographers. The numbers specified refer to the circled numerals on the relevant pages, not the step-by-step numbers.

pp1 & 54 no 1 Michael Harvey; p5 center left & below left Steve Mattison; p5 right-hand column, third down Jürgen Nagai; p7 no 3 Norbert Gerdes; p16 nos 1 & 2 David Binns; p17 no 4 Victor France; p17 no 5 Geza Molnar; p19 Steve Mattison; p22 no 1 Stephen Brayne; p23 no 4 Mark Somerville; p26 no 2 Steve Mattison; p27 nos 1 & 2 Steve Mattison; p28 Stephen Brayne; pp30–31 nos 1 & 2 Victor France; p31 no 3 Steve Mattison; p37 no 5 Alan Sidney; p40 no 1 Billy Adams; p41 no 2 Joanna Howells; p43 nos 1 & 3 Steve Mattison; p43 no 2 Beverley Bell-Hughes; p45 no 3 Len Grant; p47 no 2 Jerry Hardman-Jones; p48 no 1 Steve Mattison; p49 no 3 Doug Sandberg; p49 no 4 Motoi Nakatani; p49 no 5 Jerry Hardman-Jones; pp50–51 no 1 Steve Odgen; p51 no 2 Leo Marrero; p52 no 1 Victor France; pp54–55 nos 2 & 3 Steve Mattison; p56 below center Steve Mattison; p57 below center Steve Mattison; p58 step 1 Steve Mattison; p59 above left Steve Mattison; p60 no 1 Steve Mattison; p60 no 2 Edita Rydhag; p61 no 3 Gwyn Williams; p61 no 4 Susan Einstein, Los Angeles; p61 no 5 Philip Cornelius; pp62–63 nos 1, 3, & 4 Steve Mattison; p62 no 2 Hans Vuylsteke; p67 no 2 John Sinal; p68 no 1 Michael Harvey; p69 no 2 Joanna Howells; p73 no 2 Steve Mattison; p75 no 2 John Glick; p76 above right Steve Mattison; p79 no 2 Phil Martin; p81 no 1 John Sinal; p82 above James Robson; p85 above left Bruno Flament; p87 no 3 Jürgen Nagai; p88 no 1 Steve Mattison; p91 no 6 James Austin; p91 no 7 Steve Mattison; p92 no 1 Steve Mattison; p93 no 2 Patricia Aithie; p94 no 1 James Austin; p95 no 3 Michael Harvey; p95 no 6 Mark Somerville; p96 no 1 Stephen Brayne; p96 no 2 Yoshi Omori; p97 no 3 David Binns; p103 no 1 Aigars Jukna; p103 no 2 Czestaw Chwiszczuk; p108 no 1 Linda Caswell; p109 no 2 Stephen Brayne; p110 above left Linda Caswell; p112 no 2 Steve Mattison; p113 no 4 Walter Peter; p113 no 5 Geza Molnar; p113 no 6 Stephen Brayne; pp114–115 nos 2, 3, & 4 Steve Mattison; p116 no 1 Steve Mattison; p121 no 4 T. Hatakeyama; p121 no 5 Yoshi Omori; p121 no 6 Czestaw Chwiszczuk; p124 left & right Steve Mattison; p125 below right Steve Mattison; pp126–127 Steve Mattison; p128 no 2 Steve Mattison; p129 no 1 Steve Ogden; p129 no 2 Steve Mattison; pp130–131 nos 1 & 2 Steve Mattison; p132 no 1 John Meredith; p137 no 2 Bruno Flament; p139 above Steve Mattison; p145 below left Steve Mattison; p146 above right Meri Wells; p153 below right Steve Mattison; p155 above right Steve Mattison; p156 no 3 Peter Lane; p157 no 5 Willie Carter; p157 no 6 Steve Mattison; p163 no 1 David Gilroy; p166 above right Steve Mattison; p168 no 3 Steve Mattison; p169 no 4 David Gilroy; p169 no 5 Máris Kundzins ; p181 no 3 Phil Rogers; p185 no 3 Len Grant; p187 no 3 Geza Molnar; p188 Steve Mattison; p190 nos 1 & 2 Steve Mattison; p192 step 2 Steve Mattison; p195 Steve Mattison; pp196–197 Steve Mattison; p198 no 1 Steve Mattison; p199 Steve Mattison; p200 left & above right Steve Mattison; p200 no 1 Jerry Hardman-Jones; p201 no 2 Martin Everson-Davis; p201 nos 3 & 4 Jürgen Nagai; p202–203 nos 1 & 2 Steve Mattison; p204 above right Steve Mattison; p205 no 1 Ashraf Hanna; p206 steps 1 & 2 Steve Mattison; pp206–207 steps 3, 4, & 5 Claus Domine Hansen; p207 step 6 Nina Hole; p208 Steve Mattison

EQUIPMENT

Quarto would like to thank the following manufacturers for allowing photographs of their equipment to be reproduced in this book.

p191 Potclays; p212 top left & top right Potclays; p212 center Stow Potters Wheels; p213 below Roderveld; p213 all images except center Potclays; p213 center right Gladstone Engineering

AUTHOR'S ACKNOWLEDGMENTS

My thanks to the demonstrators David Frith, Margaret Frith, and Meri Wells and to all the artists who submitted images of their work for this book. Special thanks to Meri Wells, Morgen Hall, and Wendy Lawrence.

While every effort has been made to credit contributors, Quarto would like to apologize should there have been any omissions or errors.